STUDIES IN IMPERIALISM

...lished in the belief that imperialism as a cultural
phenomenon had as significant an effect on the dominant
as on the subordinate societies, Studies in Imperialism
seeks to develop the new socio-cultural approach which
has emerged through cross-disciplinary work on popular
culture, media studies, art history, the study of education
and religion, sports history and children's literature.
The cultural emphasis embraces studies of migration and
race, while the older political and constitutional,
economic and military concerns are never far away.
It incorporates comparative work on European and
American empire-building, with the chronological focus
primarily, though not exclusively, on the nineteenth and
twentieth centuries, when these cultural exchanges were
most powerfully at work.

*British culture and the
end of empire*

MANCHESTER
UNIVERSITY PRESS

AVAILABLE IN THE SERIES

British culture
and the end of empire

edited by Stuart Ward

MANCHESTER
UNIVERSITY PRESS
Manchester and New York

distributed exclusively in the USA by
PALGRAVE

Published by **MANCHESTER UNIVERSITY PRESS**
OXFORD ROAD, MANCHESTER M13 9NR, UK
and ROOM 400, 175 FIFTH AVENUE, NEW YORK, NY 10010, USA
http://www.manchesteruniversitypress.co.uk

Distributed exclusively in the USA by
PALGRAVE, 175 FIFTH AVENUE, NEW YORK, NY 10010, USA

Distributed exclusively in Canada by
UBC PRESS, UNIVERSITY OF BRITISH COLUMBIA,
2029 WEST MALL, VANCOUVER, BC, CANADA V6T 1Z2

British Library Cataloguing-in-Publication Data
A catalogue record for this book is available from the British Library

Library of Congress Cataloging-in-Publication Data applied for

ISBN 0 7190 6047 8 *hardback*
ISBN 0 7190 6048 6 *paperback*

First published 2001

10 09 08 07 06 05 04 03 02 01   10 9 8 7 6 5 4 3 2 1

Printed in Great Britain
by Bookcraft (Bath) Ltd, Midsomer Norton

CONTENTS

GENERAL EDITOR'S INTRODUCTION

Although there are now more than forty volumes in the Studies in Imperialism series, none of them – as Stuart Ward points out in his Introduction – have taken much note of the post-1945 period in British cultural imperialism. This collection of essays goes some way to remedying this omission, even if the essays are closer to being first rather than last words on the subject. At the very least, the research here justifies this field as a legitimate subject for study. It would, after all, seem highly unlikely that a state could divest itself of 'the largest empire the world has ever known' without there being some influence upon metropolitan culture. These essays demonstrate just how great that impact was, particularly when they reveal that cultural movements which were formerly seen as radical were often deeply embedded in the imperial experience.

The range of cultural expressions illustrated here, although wide, is far from exhaustive. This book contains excellent examples of analyses of elites and their pressure groups, of the theatre, satire, sports, films, children's popular literature, travel, 'reverse migration' and the experiences of people of Commonwealth origin in Britain. Yet much remains to be explored. The effects of the end of formal empire are surely also to be found in literature, art, architecture, music, museology, the development of the press and other media, and in shifts in educational practices and fashions. The fact of the matter is that the built environment and 'sites of memory', rather like the walls and structures of the Roman Empire, are going to be with us for a very long time. In that sense, the memory of empire and its cultural effects can never be wholly sloughed off.

It may be that those who hurry down Whitehall seldom reflect on the extraordinary imperial façade of the Foreign Office with its busts of heroes; that passers-by in Kensington Gore scarcely notice the statues of Livingstone and Shackleton that project from the walls of the Royal Geographical Society; and that visitors to the Victoria and Albert Museum are only dimly aware of the imperial origins of some of its collections. Moreover, even if familiar and overlooked, statues and war memorials everywhere speak of an imperial past. The very landscape of Britain has empire inscribed upon it. Grand towers to commemorate imperial heroes dominate the skylines of Dingwall and Glen Prosen in Scotland, while even the small northern Perthshire town of Alyth, where I now live, has its Boer War memorial in its central square.

Such examples of buildings, monuments and statuary, together with the dim memories and sometimes vague unease that go with them, can be replicated throughout the United Kingdom and Ireland. Not the least of such 'sites of memory' are the street names which bespeak of propagandist and celebratory naming practices of the past. London possesses no fewer than seven Livingstone roads or streets. The Indian 'Mutiny' heroes Henry Havelock and Colin Campbell have twelve and eight respectively, while Napier has as many as thirteen. The territories and geographical features of the former empire are also well represented.

Jamaica has three and Rhodes and Rhodesia four. The Nile has three (no doubt named for Nelson's victory, the Admiral himself having twenty-one!) and the Indus one, while many well-known and more obscure places in the Indian subcontinent are similarly remembered. Moreover, the naming of streets can act as a narration of the trading connections of Glasgow and other port cities.

Yet such sites of memory can also become sites of contest. Travelling once in the Orkney Islands, I discovered the great tower which commemorates the death of Lord Kitchener in the sinking of HMS *Hampshire* in 1916. Remotely situated though it is, someone had spray-painted 'Imperialist Scum' on its base. More formal controversies break out from time to time. Recently, the Mayor of London (ironically called Livingstone) proposed that the statues of unknown (to him and the general populace) generals like Havelock and Napier should be removed from Trafalgar Square. The tenor of the subsequent widespread and often choleric debate was highly instructive.

Such sites are inevitably going to stimulate an intriguing mix of controversy and indifference, protective and destructive urges for many years to come. Such reactions constitute another post-imperial fever chart, as do so many of the cultural forms represented in this book. Stuart Ward is to be congratulated for organising the 'Implosion of Empire' conference at the University of Southern Denmark in 1999 and for so creatively bringing these essays together.

John M. MacKenzie

NOTES ON CONTRIBUTORS

Antoinette Burton is Professor of History at the University of Illinois, specialising in the relationship between empire and the 'home front' in Victorian culture and society. In addition to her many scholarly articles, she has published *Burdens of History: British Feminists, Indian Women, and Imperial Culture, 1865–1915* (University of North Carolina Press, 1994); *At the Heart of the Empire: Indians and the Colonial Encounter in Late-Victorian Britain* (University of California Press, 1998); and, as editor, *Gender, Sexuality and Colonial Modernities* (Routledge, 1999).

Kathryn Castle is a principal lecturer in History at the University of North London. She is the author of *Britannia's Children: Reading Colonialism Through Children's Books and Magazines* (Manchester University Press, 1996), a study of children's literature and empire, 1890–1940. She has also authored numerous articles on issues of race and empire in British society. She is currently researching a book on 'nigger minstrelsy' in Britain.

Mike Cronin is a senior research fellow in History at the International Centre for Sports History and Culture at De Montfort University, Leicester, and the author of *Sport and Nationalism in Ireland: Gaelic Games, Soccer and Irish Identity Since 1884* (Four Courts Press, 1999). He is the joint editor, with David Mayall, of *Sporting Nationalisms: Identity, Ethnicity, Immigration and Assimilation* (Frank Cass, 1998), and has published widely on aspects of twentieth-century Irish political and sporting history.

Peter H. Hansen is Associate Professor of History at Worcester Polytechnic Institute, Massachusetts. He has published on mountaineering, imperialism, film and post-colonialism, and he is working on a book on the cultural history of mountains and mountaineering since the eighteenth century.

Richard Holt is Research Professor in History at the International Centre for Sports History and Culture at De Montfort University, Leicester. He is the author of a wide range of books and articles on the history of sport including *Sport and the British* (Clarendon, 1989). He is also the joint author, with Tony Mason, of *Sport in Britain, 1945–2000* (Blackwell, 2000).

Shompa Lahiri is a research fellow at the Centre for the Study of Migration, Queen Mary and Westfield College, University of London. She is author of *Indians in Britain: Anglo-Indian Encounters, Race and Identity 1880–1930* (Frank Cass, 1999). She has also published several articles on various aspects of the colonial Indian diaspora experience. Her current research focuses on constructions of the racial 'other' in colonial and post-colonial Britain.

John M. MacKenzie is Professor of Imperial History at Lancaster University. His research has encompassed the social, cultural and environmental history of the British Empire, as well as post-colonial critical theory. His publications include *Propaganda and Empire* (1984); *The Empire of Nature* (1988); *Orientalism: History, Theory and the Arts* (1995); and, as editor, *Imperialism and Popular Culture* (1986); *Imperialism and the Natural World* (1990); and *Popular Imperialism and the Military* (1992), all published by Manchester University Press. He is general editor of the Manchester University Press series Studies in Imperialism.

Alex May is a research editor for the twentieth century with the New Dictionary of National Biography, University of Oxford. He is the author of *Britain and Europe Since 1945* (Longman, 1999), and editor of *The Round Table, the Empire/ Commonwealth and British Foreign Policy* (Lothian Foundation Press, 1997) and *Britain, the Commonwealth and Europe: The Commonwealth and Britain's Applications to Join the European Communities* (Palgrave, 2001). He has been Secretary/Treasurer of the Round Table since 1997.

Kathleen Paul is Associate Professor of History at the University of South Florida. Her most recent book is *Whitewashing Britain: Race and Citizenship in the Post-war Era* (Cornell University Press, 1997), for which she was awarded the 1999 Morris D. Forkosch Prize for British History by the American Historical Association. She is currently working on a project on child migration from Britain in the post-war era.

Dan Rebellato is a playwright and lecturer in the Department of Theatre and Drama at Royal Holloway and Bedford College, University of London. His primary research interests lie in European theatre of the modern period, with a particular interest in twentieth-century British drama. He has published editions of plays by Terence Rattigan, and his most recent work is a major reinterpretation of post-war British theatre entitled *1956 and All That* (Routledge, 1999).

Jeffrey Richards is Professor of Cultural History at Lancaster University, specialising in cinema and society in Great Britain. He has published *Best of British* (Blackwell, 1983), *The Age of the Dream Palace* (Routledge, 1984); *Britain Can Take It* (Blackwell, 1986); *Films and British National Identity* (Manchester University Press, 1997); and, as editor, *Imperialism and Juvenile Literature* (Manchester University Press, 1989). He is general editor of the Manchester University Press series Studies in Popular Culture, and his book on imperialism and music will be published in autumn 2001.

Hsu-Ming Teo is a post-doctoral research fellow at Macquarie University, Sydney, specialising in popular literature and genre studies. She is also a writer of fiction, and her recent novel *Love and Vertigo* (Allen & Unwin, 2000) was awarded the Australian Vogel award for young writers. Her current research project is a comparative history of colonialism and race in British, American and Australian women's romance writing in the twentieth century.

NOTES ON CONTRIBUTORS

Stuart Ward is a lecturer in History at the Menzies Centre for Australian Studies, King's College London. He also holds a lectureship at the University of Southern Denmark. His research has focused on the political, economic and cultural history of Britain and the Commonwealth in the post-Second World War era. He has published *Australia and the British Embrace: The Demise of the Imperial Ideal* (Melbourne University Press, 2001), and, as editor (with R. T. Griffiths), *Courting the Common Market: The First Attempt to Enlarge the European Communities* (Lothian Foundation Press, 1996).

ACKNOWLEDGEMENTS

The idea for this volume had its origins at a conference in February 1999 at the University of Southern Denmark. My thanks are due to the British Council in Copenhagen for their financial assistance in organising that meeting, as well as to all of my colleagues in Denmark who lent their support, particularly Nils Arne Sørensen, Joyce Senders Pedersen and Flemming Andersen. The task of assembling a full complement of contributors was eased considerably by the generous assistance of John MacKenzie and Jeffrey Richards. John MacKenzie deserves a special thanks in his role as series editor. His encouragement and enthusiasm were instrumental in getting the project off the ground, and he has remained a source of ready advice throughout. The staff at Manchester University Press have also been highly constructive and supportive, and through their anonymous readers have proposed changes which served to broaden the scope of the book considerably. Finally, my thanks go to all of the contributors in the volume for their co-operation, enthusiasm and commitment. In particular, Hsu-Ming Teo has been an invaluable sounding-board from the outset, offering ideas and criticism far exceeding the usual demands on a contributor.

Introduction
Stuart Ward

The demise of British imperial power in the three decades following the Second World War is a familiar theme in the study of post-war British politics, economics and foreign relations. Yet there has been virtually no attention to the question of how these dramatic changes in Britain's relationships with the wider world were reflected in British culture. This is surprising, given the vast body of literature that has emerged in recent years dealing with the metropolitan dimensions of British imperialism. Since the early 1980s, historians have progressively shifted their focus away from the political and constitutional framework of the British Empire, and towards the impact of imperial ideologies and practices on British culture and society. While the new cultural history of imperialism has explored a wide array of social and cultural themes, from propaganda to children's literature, education, sport, cinema and other popular entertainments, a common thread has been the progressive dismantling of the traditional distinction between 'empire' and the 'home front' in British historiography.[1] These works have cumulatively built up a picture of the multifarious ways in which, to use Mary Louise Pratt's phrase, the 'periphery determined the metropolis'.[2] While there remains considerable room for debate about the extent to which the imperial experience shaped, or was shaped by, the evolution of political and cultural institutions in Britain, there is nonetheless broad agreement that empire can no longer be understood 'as some influence extraneous to the course of British history; something imposed on the British people as a transient late Victorian "age of Empire"'.[3] But despite the impressive range of this body of work, it is a field that has been largely confined to Victorian and Edwardian Britain, with occasional concessions to the inter-war years. As far as the post-1945 era is concerned, the rigid conceptual barriers between metropole and periphery are still very much intact. There remains a firmly entrenched assumption that the broad cultural impact of decolonisation was confined to the colonial periphery, with little relevance to post-war British culture and society. No attempt has been made to examine the cultural manifestations of the demise of imperialism as a social and political ideology in post war Britain. Indeed, as far as empire and metropolitan culture are concerned, it is as though the end of empire has signalled the end of the subject.[4]

It has been left to political and economic historians – working primarily on the official record in the Public Record Office – to survey the metropolitan dimension of imperial decline. This has produced a steady stream of extremely useful studies, exploring the reasons behind British disengagement from the Empire and Commonwealth, and investigating the attitudes of key politicians, political parties, lobby groups and business interests.[5] These works are an essential starting point for understanding the immediate political response to the dramatic changes in Britain's global fortunes in the post-war world, but they provide little sense of the wider social or cultural impact of the end of empire in Britain. To the extent that the loss of empire is said to have reverberated at all on the home front, this seems to have been largely confined to the corridors of Westminster and Whitehall. Beyond the realm of parliamentary pressure groups, Whitehall briefing papers and Cabinet deliberations, the prevailing orthodoxy holds that 'ordinary Britons' had grown indifferent to, or even positively hostile towards, the imperial ideal from the 1940s onwards (if not earlier). Comparisons are routinely drawn with the national upheavals in France during the Algerian crisis in order to indicate the relative passivity of the British people towards the changes wrought by the post-war years. Apart from an old guard of imperially minded public figures such as Lord Salisbury and Lord Beaverbrook, and the disgruntled remnants of the progressively disbanded colonial service, the demise of the British Empire is assumed to have left barely a trace on the broad fabric of British civic culture.

This view has manifested itself in a variety of ways, but a common starting point is the idea that decolonisation was a relatively benign issue in post-war political culture. John Darwin has made the perfectly valid observation that the end of empire was 'surprisingly undisruptive in British politics', prompting few electoral repercussions, and provoking no major constitutional upheaval.[6] Even the public outcry over Suez in 1956 was largely forgotten by the time of the 1959 election. Philip Murphy has made a similar point in relation to the Conservative Party, enquiring into the reasons 'why there were relatively few significant clashes' within the party ranks over decolonisation in Africa.[7] These questions have been well worth pursuing, but they have been widely understood to imply that the end of empire had scarcely any impact at all on post-war British society. All kinds of sweeping statements have been based on a narrow reading of the post-war political scene. Kenneth Morgan, for example, contends that:

the end of empire did not generate the kind of overwhelming strains in Great Britain visible in France in the retreat from Indo-China or Algeria – nor, indeed, apparent in somewhat more subtle ways in the United States after failure in Vietnam ... The civilised way in which the world-wide empire was dissolved relatively peaceably between 1945 and 1979 provoked national satisfaction and international congratulation.[8]

David Cannadine has made a similar blanket assertion: 'The British Empire may (or may not) have been won in a fit of "absence of mind", but as far as the majority of the population was concerned it was given away in a fit of collective indifference'.[9] And Bernard Porter concludes his discussion of post-war decolonisation with the verdict: 'The mass of people, as they had all along, cared very little'.[10]

Various explanations have been put forward for the allegedly striking absence of any wider social or cultural response to imperial decline. Bernard Porter argues that it was 'part of the style of British imperialism that it kept its distance from its subjects', and as a consequence British society was largely unaffected by the ebb and flow of Britain's fortunes abroad.[11] In a slightly different vein, Lord Beloff argued that the British had never been 'imperially minded' in the first place, and that the Labour Party in particular was 'on the whole indifferent to most of the Empire'. That being so, the muted civic response to the end of empire should hardly come as a surprise given the elitist nature of the whole imperial enterprise.[12] A more common explanation looks at the rise of welfarism, which prompted a shift in middle-class aspirations and a demand for a redirection of national resources towards the home front. In this climate, it is suggested, public opinion simply lost interest in the expensive task of defending Britain's overseas territories. As A. J. P. Taylor commented in 1965, by the end of the Second World War:

Imperial greatness was on the way out, the welfare state was on the way in The British Empire declined; the condition of the people improved. Few now sang 'Land of Hope and Glory'. Few even sang 'England Arise'. England had arisen all the same.[13]

More recently, D. George Boyce concluded that Britain underwent 're markably few traumas' as a result of the end of empire because 'grand ideas of imperial federation, a new moral order, and the like made little headway against the English tradition of resolving political issues in a way that enabled the old order to give way to the new, and that combined the benefits of practical thinking with the language of constitutional development'. Like other proponents of this view, Boyce favourably compared this British pragmatism against the more rigid, doctrinaire French, who paid a high price in terms of political and social dislocation for their failure to adapt to the changing determinants of the post-imperial world.[14]

[3]

The 'minimal impact' thesis has been broadly shared by British cultural historians dealing with the post-1945 era, who have tended to interpret their subject through the multifaceted prism of the Cold War, the post-war consensus, austerity and affluence, the rise of welfarism, the demise of deference, 'youth culture', and angry young men who never had it so good as they swung into the sixties. In this spiralling array of predominantly domestic themes, the end of the British Empire barely rates a mention. For example, Robert Hewison's three-volume study of post-war British culture, spanning the 1940s through to the 1980s, is all but silent on the question of imperial decline.[15] Another leading post-war cultural historian, Arthur Marwick, is slightly more attentive to the imperial dimension, but ultimately dismisses the idea that the loss of empire had any real impact on 'the British psyche'. For Marwick, 'the most notable consequences were felt by members of the upper and upper-middle classes who no longer had the raj as a territory in which to exploit their natural gifts of leadership'.[16]

In support of this view, much has been made of a survey commissioned by the Colonial Office in the late 1940s which revealed the widespread public ignorance of the geographical scope and constitutional makeup of the British Empire.[17] The fact that many Britons were barely able to identify a single colony by name, and often provided ludicrous answers to the survey questions, has been taken as indisputable evidence that the Empire was remote from the day-to-day concerns of ordinary Britons. But can we assume that popular ignorance of the precise extent and nature of Britain's imperial holdings was indicative of widespread public indifference to the idea of Britain as an imperial power? It is surely possible that while many people never bothered getting to know the particulars of empire, there was nonetheless a broad consensus about a preordained role in the world beyond Britain's shores. Or as John MacKenzie has argued, it is a 'generalised imperial vision rather than any sophisticated concept of Empire' that reveals the scope and social relevance of popular imperialism.[18]

As the vast body of work on empire and metropolitan culture has collectively shown, an imperial outlook had been an integral feature of British public life for several generations. Historians are generally in agreement that 'empire was a major component in British people's sense of their own identity, that it helped to integrate the United Kingdom, and to distinguish it in the eyes of its own citizens from other European countries'.[19] An apparently thriving empire promoted the idea of a world-wide British identity – the myth of a greater Britain – that resonated at all levels of metropolitan culture.[20] Although it was once assumed that popular imperialism barely survived the First World War, more recent work has shown that 'if anything the inter-war years witnessed a deeper cultural penetration of imperial ideals'.[21] It therefore seems hardly likely that the imperial mindset could have evaporated so quickly, particularly in the triumphal wake of the Second World War, even if the precise details of the colonial empire did not always enter into popular consciousness.

In other words, the rather thin film of evidence that is habitually stretched over the minimal impact thesis is hardly a conclusive means of establishing the wider metropolitan significance of the demise of the British Empire. On the contrary, not only are these factors open to alternative interpretations, they are by no means exhaustive as far as the available body of evidence is concerned. Time and again, the minimal impact thesis appears as a blunt assertion, implying a broad consensus that British culture and society in the post-war era were insulated against the periodic shocks that occasioned the demise of British power and prestige abroad. Thus, when the likes of Bernard Porter, David Cannadine, Kenneth Morgan, Arthur Marwick, A. J. P. Taylor, George Boyce and Lord Beloff articulate broad agreement (albeit for a variety of different reasons) on such a wide-ranging question, it is surely fair to say that we are in the grip of historiographical orthodoxy.

There are, however, signs that the minimal impact thesis is beginning to attract a degree of critical scrutiny. Ironically, two of its more prominent proponents, Bernard Porter and David Cannadine, have been among recent advocates of an 'alternative view'.[22] In a 1996 article in *History Today*, Porter surveyed the orthodox view that 'Britain relinquished her empire relatively smoothly, in a way that left few obvious scars' and reached the conclusion that something was surely amiss with this comfortable consensus. 'There must', he insisted, 'be more to it than that. Nations do not suddenly lose Empires without their leaving a mark.' Porter sketched out 'three great possible repercussions of decolonisation': the end of welfare socialism, the waning appeal of the monarchy, and the devolution of the British state. While his article was intended more as an opinion piece than a fully documented argument, he nonetheless underlined the idea that decolonisation 'was to have as big an impact on Britain's self-image as on the colonies granted independence'.[23] In a similar vein, David Cannadine has argued that 'the British did not see themselves – indeed, could not see themselves – in the same way without an empire as they had done when they possessed one'. In particular, he claims that 'perceptions of British society as a divinely ordained and successfully functioning hierarchy were very much diminished, ... in part because the hierarchical empire was unravelling'. As in the case of Bernard Porter, Cannadine's views have more the quality of *obiter dicta*, but his general line of thinking is clear – far from affirming the minimal impact thesis, he sees the end of empire reverberating at the very core of the traditional structure of British society.[24] It is not clear to what extent Porter and Cannadine have revised their earlier views, or whether they regard the idea of widespread public indifference as fully compatible with their more recent assertions about the profound political and social ramifications of the collapse of the imperial super-structure. On face of it, radical changes in the 'national self-image' would seem difficult to reconcile with a climate of mass apathy. But whatever the case, we have only heard the initial rumblings of a more general paradigmatic shift. As Cannadine has suggested in relation to the hierarchy theme, the wider social impact of imperial decline is a subject 'that still awaits its historian'.[25]

The basic premise of this volume is that the stresses and strains of imperial decline were not safely contained within the realm of high politics. We need only look at the official archival record to see how the broad spectrum of public opinion remained constantly at the forefront of government deliberations on imperial and Commonwealth affairs from the 1940s right through to the late 1960s. The Attlee Government's approach to Indian independence, for example, was hampered by the fear that a British withdrawal 'might be regarded as the beginning of the liquidation of the British Empire'. The Cabinet was acutely anxious that Labour would 'lose and lose irrevocably' in electoral terms should the public perceive the situation in India as an ignominious scuttle.[26] Similarly, Susan Carruthers has documented official anxieties about the potential volatility of public opinion on such issues as the Malayan Emergency, Palestine, Cyprus, and the Mau Mau insurgency, and the measures that were taken to ensure that public attitudes remained in step with colonial strategy.[27] Governments feared two alternative extremes of opinion, both of which had their roots in the imperial experience. On the one hand, any sign of a lack of British fortitude in the face of colonial insurgency – particularly when the lives and interests of fellow Britons abroad were at stake – would risk a backlash against the perception of a British surrender abroad. But on the other hand, as John Darwin has pointed out: 'If evidence appeared that colonial control depended too heavily on coercion, police brutality or too rough a justice, then the humanitarian instincts on which the champions of empire had played so artfully for so long ... might be roused successfully against the continuation of empire, in its classical form'.[28] Thus, British governments had to steer a delicate course between a firm display of British authority and control, without laying too heavy a hand on the scale.[29]

This delicate balancing act remained a constant theme of colonial policy into the late 1950s and early 1960s. On the occasion of Malayan independence in 1957, for example, Harold Macmillan declined to make any formal public broadcast out of concern for the possible electoral repercussions should such a gesture be interpreted as a sign of capitulation. Similarly, Macmillan agonised over the release and political rehabilitation of Jomo Kenyatta in the early 1960s, having been advised of the deleterious impact such a course of action would have on the Conservative Party and public opinion. For Macmillan and his Colonial Secretary, Iain Macleod, the problems of colonial Africa remained 'perhaps our most difficult problem as far as our relationship with the vital middle voters is concerned'.[30] Macmillan was equally wary of popular enthusiasm for the Empire and Commonwealth throughout his ill-fated European Economic Community (EEC) membership application in 1961–63. The Government went to enormous lengths to convince the British public that EEC membership would not entail an abandonment of the Commonwealth, and in so doing placed the British negotiators in an impossible bind in working out a Commonwealth package deal in Brussels. The Macmillan Government's enthusiasm for the Commonwealth ideal had been undeniably shaken by the recurring atmosphere of controversy and discord at Commonwealth prime ministers' meetings, particularly the acrimonious 1961 gathering which culminated in the expulsion of South Africa. But it was still widely assumed that public opinion was several steps behind the Government in assessing the relative merits of the Commonwealth association and EEC membership. As Macmillan's Commonwealth Secretary, Duncan Sandys, warned in September 1962, 'no British government could survive' that attempted to take Britain into the EEC without securing the interests of Commonwealth countries, particularly the 'old Dominions'.[31]

While official perceptions of public opinion obviously need to be treated with caution, at the very least this ongoing preoccupation with popular attitudes towards imperial and Commonwealth affairs hardly reinforces the idea of mass indifference to the whole imperial enterprise in the postwar era. Even in the aftermath of the 'wind of change' in Africa, the new Labour Government under Harold Wilson persevered with the idea that Britain's frontiers were in the Himalayas. The insistence on Britain's 'world role' remained an absolute orthodoxy of British political culture right down to the late 1960s. This 'anaesthetizing rhetoric', as John Darwin has termed it, relied heavily on the idea of the Commonwealth as a means of reassuring the British public that the steady demise of empire would in no way detract from Britain's prestige and influence on the world stage.[32] In the hands of someone like Harold Macmillan, it could even be rendered as the culmination of the imperial achievement, drawing on an intellectual tradition of imperial 'trusteeship' that stretched back to Macaulay.[33] This ready-made rationalisation of imperial decline was enthusiastically deployed by the Chairman of the Royal Empire Society, Lord De La Warr, upon substituting the word 'Commonwealth' for 'Empire' on the Society's masthead in May 1958:

> Our Empire has grown into a Commonwealth of free nations, because of Britain's deliberate policy towards her Imperial responsibilities. What has

happened today, therefore, is not a retreat but a direct fulfilment of the noble work done by our fathers and grandfathers in taking our traditions of liberal law and material progress to every quarter of the globe.[34]

There is every reason to believe that the Commonwealth idea, although ultimately a disappointment to its adherents, was a success from the point of view of keeping colonial issues out of electoral politics throughout the post-war era. But far from indicating public apathy towards the idea of Britain as an imperial nation, the relatively minor role of empire in post-war election campaigns was indicative of a broad consensus that the Empire was not really in decline, but merely in a state of transition.[35] The perceived need for an 'anaesthetizing rhetoric' only makes sense in the context of a British electorate steeped in an idea of British grandeur that had deep roots in the imperial past.

But this is not to say that the British public was lulled into a self-deluding slumber for more than twenty years, only to wake up happily in the mid-1960s without an empire. If we move beyond the narrow realm of British politics and look at the intellectual climate of post-war Britain, for example, there are signs of a more gradual and ambivalent awareness of British impotence in the world. The American sociologist Edward Shils commented in 1955 on the 'extraordinary state of collective self-satisfaction' that characterised British intellectual opinion at that time, and wondered why 'scarcely anyone in Great Britain seems any longer to feel that there is anything fundamentally wrong'.[36] But this climate was soon to change. The Suez crisis of 1956 prompted the first signs that the anaesthetic was beginning to wear thin. The Eden Government was subjected to the most damning criticism for its handling of the Suez affair, which culminated in Eden's demise as Prime Minister. The deep public divisions over Suez marked the first major rupture in the post-war consensus, allowing more general grievances to air themselves. This most famously took the form of discontent with the state of national culture as articulated by the so-called 'Angry Young Men' (and women) who contributed to Tom Maschler's *Declaration* volume in 1957. Other critics saw the whole 'anger' trend as part of the problem, arguing that Britain needed social regeneration rather than self-indulgent introspection. As David Marquand saw the situation: 'If ossification and lack of imagination are the marks of decadent civilization then for decadence this country must rival ancient Byzantium'.[37]

While the Suez crisis does not seem to have provoked spontaneous demands that the Empire be wound up, it nonetheless marks the point when the very idea of the 'end of empire' began to emerge more fully into the public arena. Although the idea had been touted by earlier generations by way of prophecy or warning, it took on a more literal sense as the changing external realities started to sink into the national consciousness. A. P. Thornton wrote in the aftermath of Suez, for example: 'the great question, What became of the British Empire? is one which, in 1957–58, it seems proper and timely to ask'.[38] The fact that Thornton felt obliged to broach the propriety of such a question is indicative that the idea was only beginning to gain currency. But by the turn of the decade it was articulated as indisputable fact in the title of John Strachey's unequivocal *The End of Empire*.[39]

As the idea of imperial decline became more commonplace, the question of Britain's post-imperial role in the world came under far greater scrutiny, and a more palpable sense of dissatisfaction with the state of the nation among public intellectuals emerged. From the late 1950s, a spate of articles, books and journal issues appeared in response to what seemed the all-important question: 'What's wrong with Britain?' Anthony Sampson's *Anatomy of Britain* (1961) was particularly prominent in popularising the idea of a chronic national ailment, but he was merely one of a broad assembly of journalists, economists, academics and public commentators who voiced grave concerns along similar lines. Historians have generally interpreted this trend in terms of the impatient aspirations of an affluent generation, and the relatively slow growth rates of the British economy. But the wider imperial context in these writings is unmistakable. As Sampson typically saw the situation at the time:

> A loss of dynamic and purpose, and a general bewilderment, are felt by many people, both at the top and the bottom in Britain today ... It is hardly surprising that, in twenty years since the war, Britain should have felt confused about her purpose – with those acres of red on the map dwindling, the mission of the war dissolving, and the whole imperial mythology of battleships, governors and generals gone for ever.[40]

The wave of 'state of Britain' writing in these years was essentially a reflection of shifting popular perceptions of the British ruling elite. The term 'the establishment' had been coined by Henry Fairlie in 1955 to describe 'the whole matrix of official and social relations within which power is exercised'.[41] The term acquired increasingly pejorative connotations as the sense of national disorientation deepened. For writers in the 'what's wrong with Britain' mould, the 'establishment' conjured up the shortcomings of a complacent, outdated ruling aristocracy, who had failed to respond adequately to the great national challenges of the post-war era. As Hugh Thomas commented: 'The Establishment is the present-day institutional museum of Britain's past greatness', sustained by a public school system which had been designed 'to provide a continuous stream of socially gifted and athletic amateurs to act as proconsuls in ... an empire that no longer exists in 1959'.[42]

It is precisely the imperial context that underpinned contemporary perceptions of national degeneration. Arguably, there was nothing particularly wrong with Britain at all in an era of sustained economic growth and a consumption boom, where only a few years earlier the Conservatives had won an election on the catchphrase 'you've never had it so good'. But it was in relation to the changing world outside that the prevailing sense of national malaise seemed so self-evident. Britain's declining share of world trade, the mounting international pressures on sterling, the humiliation at Suez combined with the steadily blowing 'wind of change' in colonial Africa cast serious doubts upon the age-old certainties about Britain's premier place in the world. It was against a deeply ingrained expectation of British primacy – an expectation rooted in the imperial experience – that the perception of national despair drew sustenance and credibility. Michael Shanks articulated precisely this backward-looking projection of present-day dilemmas in his widely discussed 1961 book, *The Stagnant Society*:

> What sort of an island do we want to be? ... A lotus island of easy, tolerant ways, bathed in the golden glow of an imperial sunset, shielded from discontent by a threadbare welfare state and an acceptance of genteel poverty? Or the tough, dynamic race we have been in the past, striving always to better ourselves, seeking new worlds to conquer in place of those we have lost, ready to accept growing pains as the price for growth?[43]

Shanks's prescription clearly shows how the widespread calls for national regeneration were imbued with imperial discourse. Almost without exception, these commentators directly linked Britain's perceived malaise to the loss of power and influence abroad. It was precisely the gradual, almost imperceptible course of imperial decline that was seen as the source of Britain's social, cultural and economic woes. The fact that no single, decisive blow to the imperial idea had ever been struck had worked to forestall any initiatives towards national renewal. As John Mander wrote in *Great Britain or Little England?* (1963):

> Europe had to learn by violence certain lessons which, however unpleasant at the time, were to prove salutary in the long run ... By violence, Europeans learned what it means to lose an Empire ... They learnt not only that loss of Empire is an irreversible and agonising process, but that it necessitates a total national reorientation. Nostalgia for Empire, powerful in Britain, has almost vanished from the continent of Europe. In the end, the loss of Empire has hurt us more.[44]

A more subtle argument was put forward by Anthony Hartley in *A State of England* (1963), where he argued that the post-Suez preoccupation among British intellectuals with 'our present discontents' was, in itself, symptomatic of a traumatic adaptation to the stark decline in Britain's global fortunes. As Hartley viewed the situation in 1963, the material and political consequences of imperial decline had 'caused a narrowing of horizons and a sense of frustration in English society'. The cruel irony was that while intellectuals generally applauded the liberal approach to colonial independence, 'nevertheless, the dissolution of the empire and the dwindling of Britain's world power aroused in them not altogether surprising regrets and misgiving'. He compared the situation with that of intellectuals at the time of the Spanish Civil War, who 'did not have to cope with the dismaying possibility that Britain might not be able to affect the issue one way or the other'. Thus, the torrent of disaffected writing on the state of the nation could not solve the inner dilemma of the English intellectual: 'How to give his own position its necessary universality from within a society which was no longer the centre of the world picture'. He warned of the consequences of failure to redefine a sense of national purpose in the wake of imperial decline:

> In the past, loss of power in the world has often been accompanied by a period of national decadence, by a decline affecting not only the external relations of a society, but also its own intrinsic quality ... shall we, too, be added to the ranks of these countries on whom the loss of empire, the loss of purpose, have had a crippling effect? Or shall we manage to escape the descent into limbo?[45]

Time and again in these writings, a potent blend of trauma, nostalgia, and resentment towards the ruling establishment converged around a deep sense of loss at the core of British civic culture. Hartley's comments are particularly illuminating, because he demonstrates how the psychological impact of imperial decline need not necessarily have taken the form of a consciously articulated complaint about the pace of decolonisation. Even those who were inclined to welcome the rapid transfer of power to nationalist movements in Asia and Africa could not escape the profound revision of national assumptions and aspirations that this process entailed. In this sense, the preoccupation of historians with the absence of any broad-based public protest has tended to overlook the fundamental ambivalence of the end of empire as a theme in post-war British culture. It may well be that a far deeper anxiety derived from the fact that, for a variety of reasons, the rhetorical space within which any opposition or resistance might have been articulated had been delegitimised.

The chapters in this volume, therefore, have been assembled with the broad object of exploring the wide-ranging impact of imperial decline in British culture and society. But in positing an alternative to the 'minimal impact' orthodoxy, it is not intended to suggest the diametric opposite: that the end of empire struck a deep note of inconsolable grief in the hearts of each and every Briton, sparking a spontaneous mass soul-searching that continues to paralyse the nation. The reality is infinitely more subtle. Just as the Empire itself 'could encompass a great range of British interests, ambitions and sympathies', from militarists to humanitarians, feminists, missionaries, capitalists, scientists and migrants,[46] so too the meanings of imperial decline were neither uniform nor universal. Rather than setting out to quantify the number of Britons who 'cared' about the end of empire, the broad approach of this volume is to examine popular understandings of imperial decline as articulated through a wide variety of cultural channels and institutions.

The chapters cumulatively demonstrate that it is in the very variety of cultural responses that the underlying tensions of imperial decline become evident. Making sense of Britain's fall from imperial grace was not a simple process of easy adaptation to new external realities. On the contrary, the demise of empire posed a formidable challenge, not only to the idea of Britain as a world power, but also to the legitimacy and credibility of key ideas, assumptions and values that had become implicated in the imperial experience. This point is particularly relevant to the debate about Britain's present-day imperial legacy. P. J. Marshall has put forward the intriguing idea that the imperial experience did not have any formative influence on British institutions and social structures. Rather, he contends, it was the other way around – the Empire could serve as a useful legitimating field that 'reflected and reinforced certain trends in British history, but rarely seems to have pushed it in radically new directions'.[47] But even if this were so (and the debate is still wide open), the very association of particular interests and ideologies with the imperial mission served to render these ideas dependent on the vitality of the Empire for their social and political legitimacy. It is in the end of empire, therefore, that the imperial legacy of contemporary Britain emerges clearly into view.

Ideas about British 'character', for example, became difficult to sustain as the external prop of the imperial world was progressively weakened. Notions of duty, service, loyalty, deference, stoic endurance, self-restraint and gentlemanly conduct were insidiously undermined by the steady erosion of the imperial edifice. Liberal assumptions about the humanitarian benefits of British 'civilisation' were equally subject to critical attention whenever coercion was needed to stem the tide of imperial decline. In the immediate aftermath of Suez, for example, the Duke of Edinburgh made a television appearance for British children, where he assured his audience that 'this great family of nations of ours ... sticks together not by force, but because we like each other'. The mere mention of 'force' was indicative of an era when, as the *Daily Mail* complained, 'so much that is untrustworthy and untrue is being spread about on the subject of British imperialism'.[48] Perhaps the greatest conceptual challenge of all was posed to popular notions of the extent and nature of British national community.

The link between empire and the idea of a 'greater Britain' was one of the formative influences on the evolution of a transnational 'British' identity in the late eighteenth and nineteenth centuries.[49] What Enoch Powell termed 'the illusion that there is a world elsewhere'[50] was one of the most difficult notions to reconcile with post-imperial realities, because it struck at the very heart of the idea of Britishness as a focus of civic identification.

The chapters in this volume map out these challenges to the traditional values and assumptions of empire, and offer a broad-based analysis of the many and varied cultural responses to imperial decline. The opening chapter offers an overview of the persistence of imperialism in popular culture in the post-1945 era. John MacKenzie's name has become virtually synonymous with the study of empire and metropolitan culture, and his reflections on the post-war era draw on his wide-ranging experience in the field, as well as his own personal reminiscences of growing up in the end of empire era. He takes up the question of popular indifference to the end of empire, discussing the ways in which popular imperialism proliferated throughout the 1950s, from literature to festivals, youth annuals, transport and migration. The popular cultural record, he suggests, raises questions about whether the end of empire was as widely foreseen in the 1940s and 1950s as has been assumed with the benefit of hindsight. Popular cultural markers continued to underpin an imperial view of Britain's place in the world, even as that world was undergoing profound changes. It was not until the end of the 1950s that a more sober view of Britain's declining fortunes in the world began to resonate more widely.

In Chapter 2, Alex May takes up these issues as they unfolded in the eyes of the Round Table – a group that was quite unambiguously preoccupied by the challenges of the post-imperial era. Although an elitist and unashamedly 'establishment' grouping, the Round Table had always been actively engaged in the wider dissemination of an imperial outlook. The conventional view that imperially minded elites responded uniformly to the end of empire in the most hide-bound, reactionary fashion is shown to be an oversimplification. While this was certainly true of marginal groupings such as the League of Empire Loyalists, the Round Table, by contrast, was highly influential in adapting the ideological foundations of empire to the needs of a changing world. This process was neither straightforward nor without its contradictions. It is argued that the broad cultural impact of imperial decline can only be fully comprehended by understanding the massive revision of assumptions that this process forced upon those sections of society most directly concerned with the imperial and Commonwealth ideal.

The Commonwealth anaesthetic was at its most effective at the time of Queen Elizabeth's coronation in June 1953, where the celebration of Britain's world-wide Commonwealth family was coupled with the confident heralding of a 'second Elizabethan age'. Chapter 3 examines the remarkable coincidence of the coronation and the conquest of Everest – an event that became heavily imbued with late imperial hubris. Peter Hansen argues that while the precise moment that produced the conjuncture of coronation and conquest was highly fortuitous, 'the power of the images produced by these events was not'. On the contrary, the imperial rhetoric surrounding the occasion had deep historical roots, combining the older images of imperial conquest with the new Commonwealth ideal of multi-racial partnership. But these alternative visions of empire were in many ways contradictory, producing a tension between the celebration of yet another 'British' triumph in the world, and a broader emphasis on a new spirit of international co-operation. The ambivalent meanings associated with Everest were thus indicative of the awkward adjustments inherent in the transition from Empire to Commonwealth.

In 'Look back at empire', Dan Rebellato shifts the focus to the post-war drama scene, interrogating the conventional view of John Osborne's *Look Back in Anger* as a dividing line between a pre- and post-imperial British theatre. He presents a more complex picture of a British theatre torn ambivalently between alternative political readings of the meaning of imperial decline. Earlier playwrights like Coward, Priestly and Rattigan were alive to the moral ambiguities inherent in the ideal of imperial trusteeship, while the 'anger' of the New Wave was by no means a straightforward rejection of the outmoded imperial values of the previous generation. A similar reading of the post-war cultural scene appears in my own contribution to the volume, where I argue that the 'satire boom' of the early 1960s derived largely from an unspoken dismay at the demise in Britain's global fortunes. The anti-establishment sentiment that characterised the new brand of satirical comedy, as typified by the 1961 stage revue *Beyond the Fringe*, was rooted in a backward glance at a more resolute age. In mocking the shortcomings of Britain's ruling elites, the new breed of satirists implicitly judged the failings of the present against the more admirable achievements of their imperial predecessors.

Chapter 6 examines the ways in which Britain's steadily dwindling imperial power was mirrored by the demise of English cricket. Cricket was the archetypal 'imperial game', embodying the values and ethos of the British Empire abroad, which in turn reinforced a particular vision of England at home. But as Mike Cronin and Richard Holt maintain, as the imperial trappings of cricket were increasingly brought into disrepute, the game itself was stripped of its ideological force and legitimacy. A game that had once held a central place in English sporting and cultural life – commanding the loyalties and affections of every class and region of England – increasingly came to symbolise the innumerable shortcomings of an enervated imperial establishment.

The cinema had been one of the prime vehicles for the dissemination of an imperial outlook throughout the inter-war years. Jeffrey Richards reminds us of the ongoing vitality of the empire epic in the post-war era, surveying the extent and variety of the imperial films that were produced. With the advent of decolonisation, the British cinema-going public did not simply lose interest in the Empire. Rather, imperial themes were adapted in a variety of ways to take account of the shifting political and ideological climate of the post-war world. At its most critical, the cinema could espouse an ostensibly anti-colonial ethic. Qualities that were once considered typical of the classic imperial gentleman-hero – audacity, stoicism, unflappability, good manners, a sense of duty, and an ability to command – could be subtly reworked to denote arrogance, stubbornness, callousness, snobbery, blind folly and a will to domination. Alternatively, there are numerous instances of classic imperial heroes redrawn for a post-imperial age, either by emphasising the new Commonwealth myth of a 'multi-racial partnership of equals', or, as in the case of *Lawrence of Arabia*, by recasting the hero in the role of colonial freedom fighter. But despite this disavowal of imperialist ambition on the part of the protagonists, these films nonetheless indulged in the most striking forms of imperial nostalgia, evoking the thrill of imperial battle, the glamour of the masculine hero, and exotic far-flung locations. It is this very ambivalence – evoking fond memories of empire while denying or even denigrating the politics of imperialism – that underscores the awkward adaptation to the less stable political verities of the post-imperial world.

Kathryn Castle's chapter offers an entirely different perspective on the culture of imperial decline, namely that of popular children's literature. She explores the variety of ways in which imperial themes were adapted and transformed in the post-war era, underlining the anxiety of children's magazines to 'end the chapter of empire on a positive note'. As the official line on decolonisation sought increasingly to represent decolonisation as the culmination of the imperial enterprise, from the late 1950s children's literature chimed in with the recurring theme of 'mission accomplished'. Yet this rosy conclusion seemed difficult to reconcile with the pervasive sense that an ongoing British influence in the post-colonial world would be not only desirable but necessary.

Chapter 9 explores the nostalgic trail of post-imperial British travellers. Even as the course of decolonisation unfolded in the 1950s, former colonies were being opened up as commercial tourist sites. Hsu-Ming Teo argues that the dominant modes of post-imperial wandering were 'refracted through the lens of nineteenth-century British travel'. Travel writers have persistently reiterated the themes of adventure, romance and the exotic, often seeking to relive the historical or literary world of empire in the most astonishingly self-conscious and deliberate fashion. One of the great

ironies of the post-war era was that in the very moment that the possibility of tourism opened up to a mass market, travel writers almost universally lamented the lost opportunity for 'real travel'. These sentiments, it is
argued, serve as a displaced longing for the imperial world, highlighting
the persisting imperial associations of the British travel experience.

The next two chapters look at one of the undisputed enduring legacies
of empire: the migration of British subjects to and from the British Isles.
Chapter 10 examines these issues from the perspective of policy-making
elites who were charged with the task of formally defining the outer community of 'Britishness' in the post-war era, while at the same time determining who should have rights of entry and settlement into the United
Kingdom. This involved an intractable conflict between the imperial imperative of endorsing the myth of a 'greater Britain', populated by British
subjects throughout the Empire and Commonwealth, and an instinctive
desire to delimit the flow of non-white British subjects into the imperial
motherland. Kathleen Paul shows how changes in migration and citizenship policy, from the all-inclusiveness of the 1948 Nationality Act to the
progressively restrictive Acts of 1962 and 1968, were predicated on changing official perceptions of the viability and credibility of the Empire/Com-
monwealth as a vehicle for British influence in the world. In other words,
she shows how the steady demise of empire was instrumental in
reconfiguring the multifarious meanings of Britishness in post-war civic
culture.

Shompa Lahiri looks at these issues from the other side of the immigration divide, focusing on the impact of imperial decline on South Asian
communities in the United Kingdom. The end of empire did not merely
challenge the outlook and assumptions of the dominant white British
community. Indian and Pakistani migrants were equally confronted by a
conceptual reordering of their world, which manifested itself in a variety of
often contradictory ways. While the cause of Indian independence received broad-based support among South Asian communities, this did not
necessarily lead to the wholesale rejection of many of the precepts and
practices of the colonial relationship. Britain remained the ambivalent
focus of 'attraction and alienation', particularly for a certain class of educated Indians torn between an imperial cultural fantasy and the 'rude
awakening' they experienced in confronting the realities of the post-
imperial metropole.

The final chapter looks at the theme of 'India in Britain' in a rather
different context. Antoinette Burton looks at the persistent hold of India
in the contemporary British imagination, taking Tom Stoppard's 1995
play *Indian Ink* as an example of the ongoing 'disaggregation of India from
the rest of Britain's colonial possessions and experiences'. The continual
restaging of the demise of the British Raj, she argues, offers an 'endless

opportunity to see empire one last time', underlining the ways in which empire and the home front continue to overlap imaginatively. She shows how the memory of the Raj lingers on in unexpected ways, such as the material presence of 'stranded objects' implicated in the imperial experience, which testify to the 'persistence, durability and commodification of empire in the contemporary present'. Stoppard's play is equally suggestive of the gendered determinants of imperial nostalgia, raising important questions about the ambivalent relationship between western feminism and colonial nationalism. The simultaneous depoliticisation and commodification of empire is shown to have wide-ranging implications for the memory of empire in metropolitan culture, in which a pervasive nostalgia is combined with 'just the appropriate tinge of regret and self-censure' about 'what we did over there'. This serves as a fitting conclusion to the volume, showing how the deep ambivalence that characterised metropolitan responses to the end of empire continues to resonate roundly in contemporary British culture.

The areas covered by these chapters are by no means exhaustive – on the contrary, the volume should be read as an initial foray into the field, rather than a comprehensive treatment of the topic. The end of empire in metropolitan culture lends itself to any number of thematic and institutional contexts, and it is to be hoped that this collection might act as a spur to others to investigate the theme more broadly. In any revisionist history, there is always the danger of overstating the case – of presenting a new interpretation in a way that can seem dismissive of previous approaches to the subject. It is therefore worth underlining that in emphasising the end of empire as a hitherto neglected paradigm in post-war cultural historiography, it is not suggested that this is the only relevant paradigm, impatiently brushing aside earlier preoccupations with the Cold War, the post-war consensus, the rise of consumerism and so on. Nevertheless, it has to be recognised that by incorporating the imperial context into metropolitan history, the overarching nationalist paradigm that sustained these earlier preoccupations is necessarily undermined. But at a time when devolutionary forces in the United Kingdom are rendering the idea of 'British nationalism' ever more problematic, it is perhaps all the more incumbent on historians to take an open ended approach to the study of 'British' history.

Notes

1   Key titles in this literature include: Edward Said, *Orientalism* (New York, Vintage, 1978); H. John Field, *Toward a Programme of Imperial Life: The British Empire at the Turn of the Century* (Westport, CT, Greenwood Press, 1982); John M. MacKenzie, *Propaganda and Empire: The Manipulation of British Public Opinion, 1880–1960*

(Manchester, Manchester University Press, 1984); John M. MacKenzie (ed.), *Imperialism and Popular Culture* (Manchester, Manchester University Press, 1986); J. A. Mangan, *The Games Ethic and Imperialism: Aspects of the Diffusion of an Ideal* (Harmondsworth, Viking, 1986); Kathryn Tidrick, *Empire and the English Character* (London, I. B. Tauris, 1990); Antoinette Burton, *Burdens of History: British Feminists, Indian Women, and Imperial Culture, 1865–1915* (Chapel Hill, University of North Carolina Press, 1994).

2   Mary Louise Pratt, *Imperial Eyes: Travel Writing and Transculturation* (London, Routledge, 1992), p. 6.

3   P. J. Marshall, 'No Fatal Impact? The Elusive History of Imperial Britain', *Times Literary Supplement*, 12 March 1993, p. 10; see also P. J. Marshall, 'Imperial Britain', *Journal of Imperial and Commonwealth History*, 23:3 (1995), p. 385; Andrew S. Thompson, *Imperial Britain: The Empire in British Politics, 1880–1932* (London, Longman, 2000).

4   John MacKenzie's Manchester University Press series Studies in Imperialism has been by far the most prolific source of historical works dealing with the social and cultural manifestations of imperialism in metropolitan Britain. Yet there is hardly a single essay in the series that takes the discussion beyond the early 1950s. This pattern is typical of the field more generally, and was recently duplicated in the five volume *Oxford History of the British Empire*, which features several excellent chapters on empire and metropolitan culture in the volume covering the nineteenth century, and somewhat fewer in the twentieth-century volume, but absolutely nothing relating to the post-1945 era.

5   John Darwin, *Britain and Decolonization: The Retreat from Empire in the Post-War World* (London, Macmillan, 1988); David Goldsworthy, *Colonial Issues in British Politics* (Oxford, Clarendon Press, 1971); Stephen Howe, *Anti-Colonialism in British Politics: The Left and the End of Empire* (Oxford, Clarendon Press, 1993); Philip Murphy, *Party Politics and Decolonization: The Conservative Party and British Colonial Policy in Tropical Africa, 1951–64* (Oxford, Clarendon Press, 1995).

6   John Darwin, *The End of the British Empire: The Debate* (Oxford, Blackwell, 1991), p. 1; see also Darwin, 'Fear of Falling: British Politics and Imperial Decline Since 1900', *Transactions of the Royal Historical Society*, XXXVI (1986), pp. 27–43.

7   Murphy, *Party Politics*, p. 2.

8   Kenneth O. Morgan, 'The Second World War and British Culture', in Brian Brivati and Harriet Jones (eds), *From Reconstruction to Integration: Britain and Europe since 1945* (London, Leicester University Press, 1993), pp. 40–1.

9   David Cannadine, 'Apocalypse When? British Politicians and British "Decline" in the Twentieth Century', in Peter Clarke and Clive Trebilcock (eds), *Understanding Decline: Perceptions and Realities of British Economic Performance* (Cambridge, Cambridge University Press, 1997), pp. 261–2.

10 Bernard Porter, *The Lion's Share: A Short History of British Imperialism, 1850–1995*, 3rd edn (Harlow, Longman, 1996), p. 347.

11 Ibid., pp. 356–7.

12 Max Beloff, *Imperial Sunset, Vol. 1: Britain's Liberal Empire, 1897–1921* (London, Methuen, 1969), p. 19; and *Imperial Sunset, Vol. 2: Dream of Commonwealth, 1921–42* (Basingstoke, Macmillan, 1989), p. 377.

13 A. J. P. Taylor, *English History, 1914–1945* (Oxford, Oxford University Press, 1965), p. 600.

14 D. George Boyce, *Decolonization and the British Empire, 1775–1997* (London, Macmillan, 1999), p. 270.

15 Robert Hewison, *In Anger: Culture in the Cold War, 1945–60* (London, Weidenfeld & Nicolson, 1981); *Too Much: Art and Society in the Sixties, 1960–75* (London, Methuen, 1986); *The Heritage Industry: Britain in a Climate of Decline* (London, Methuen, 1987). Hewison's trilogy contains only two throwaway references to the Empire in the index to the second volume. 'The cold war', by contrast, has a long list of entries throughout the series, and appears prominently in the subtitle of the first volume. The imperial blindspot is equally in evidence in James Obelkevich and Peter

Catterall's otherwise exhaustive volume, *Understanding Post-War British Society* (London, Routledge, 1994). Nor should one consult Dominic Striniati and Stephen Wagg (eds), *Come on Down? Popular Media Culture in Post-War Britain* (London, Routledge, 1992) for a discussion of the fate of popular imperialism in post-war Britain.

16 Arthur Marwick, *British Society Since 1945*, 3rd edn (London, Penguin, 1996), p. 103.
17 G. K. Evans, *Public Opinion on Colonial Affairs*, June 1948 (London, HMSO, 1948).
18 MacKenzie (ed.), *Imperialism and Popular Culture*, p. 9.
19 Marshall, 'Imperial Britain', p. 385.
20 See also Thompson, *Imperial Britain*, p. 10.
21 Ibid., p. 184. See also John MacKenzie's argument that 'imperial themes secured greater cultural penetration in the period following the First World War, and indeed prolonged their shelf-life until the 1950s', in *Propaganda and Empire*, p. 256. He makes a similar case in *Imperialism and Popular Culture*.
22 David Cannadine, *Class in Britain* (London, Penguin, 1999), p. 159.
23 Bernard Porter, 'The Empire Strikes Back', *History Today*, 46:9 (September 1996), pp. 11–13.
24 Cannadine, *Class in Britain*, pp. 159–60.
25 David Cannadine, *Ornamentalism: How the British Saw Their Empire* (Harmondsworth, Penguin, 2001), p. 172.
26 Quoted in Darwin, *Britain and Decolonization*, pp. 94–5. See also Nicholas Owen, 'Responsibility without Power: The Attlee Governments and the End of British Rule in India', in Nick Tiratsoo (ed.), *The Attlee Years* (London, Pinter, 1991).
27 Susan L. Carruthers, *Winning Hearts and Minds: British Governments, the Media and Colonial Counter-Insurgency, 1944–1960* (London, Leicester University Press, 1995).
28 Darwin, *The End of the British Empire*, p. 20.
29 See also David Goldsworthy, 'Keeping Change Within the Bounds: Aspects of Colonial Policy, 1951–57', *Journal of Imperial and Commonwealth History*, 18.1 (1990), pp. 81–108.
30 Michael David Kandiah, 'British Domestic Politics, the Conservative Party and Foreign Policy-Making', in Wolfram Kaiser and Gillian Staerck (eds), *British Foreign Policy, 1955 64: Contracting Options* (London, Macmillan, 2000), p. 70.
31 Public Record Office, Kew, CAB133/262, PMM(UK)(62)3, Memorandum by the Commonwealth Secretary, 4 September 1962. See Stuart Ward, 'A Matter of Preference: The EEC and the Erosion of the Old Commonwealth Relationship', in Alex May (ed.), *Britain, the Commonwealth and Europe: The Commonwealth and Britain's Applications to Join the European Communities* (London, Palgrave, 2001)
32 John Darwin, 'Decolonization and the End of Empire', in Robin W. Winks (ed.), *The Oxford History of the British Empire, Vol. V: Historiography* (Oxford, Oxford University Press, 1999), p. 547.
33 See the discussion of Macmillan's 'whig history large as life and twice as shameless' in John Darwin, 'British Decolonization since 1945: A Pattern or a Puzzle?', *Journal of Imperial and Commonwealth History*, 12:2 (1984), pp. 188–9.
34 Quoted in *Journal of the Royal Commonwealth Society*, 1:1 (May–June 1958), p. 1.
35 This idea is taken up in Nicholas Owen, 'Decolonisation and Post-War Consensus', in Harriet Jones and Michael Kandiah (eds), *The Myth of Consensus: New Views on British History, 1945–64* (London, Macmillan, 1996), pp. 157–81.
36 Edward Shils, 'The British Intellectuals', *Encounter*, 4:4 (April 1955), pp. 6–7.
37 Cited in John Osborne, 'They Call it Cricket', in Tom Maschler (ed.), *Declaration* (London, MacGibbon & Lee, 1957), p. 70.
38 A. P. Thornton, *The Imperial Idea and its Enemies: A Study in British Power*, 2nd edn (London, Macmillan, 1966), p. v. It is also significant that John Seeley's nineteenth-century classic, *The Expansion of England*, finally went out of print in the year of the Suez crisis.
39 John Strachey, *The End of Empire* (London, Victor Gollancz, 1959).
40 Anthony Sampson, *Anatomy of Britain* (London, Hodder & Stoughton, 1962), pp. xiii, 620.

41 Henry Fairlie, 'Political Commentary', *Spectator*, 23 September 1955, p. 380.
42 Hugh Thomas (ed.), *The Establishment: A Symposium* (London, Anthony Blond, 1959), p. 15.
43 Michael Shanks, *The Stagnant Society: A Warning* (Harmondsworth, Penguin, 1961), p. 232.
44 John Mander, *Great Britain or Little England?* (Harmondsworth, Penguin, 1963), p. 57.
45 Anthony Hartley, *A State of England* (London, Hutchinson, 1963), pp. 15–22, 67–77, 226.
46 See discussion in Marshall, 'Imperial Britain', pp. 385–9.
47 Marshall, 'No Fatal Impact?', p. 10.
48 *Daily Mail*, quoted in Osborne, 'They Call it Cricket', p. 66.
49 Linda Colley, *Britons: Forging the Nation* (New Haven, Yale University Press, 1992); C. A. Bayly, *Imperial Meridian: The British Empire and the World, 1780–1830* (London, Longman, 1989).
50 *The Times*, 'Patriotism Based on Reality not on Dreams', 2 April 1964.

CHAPTER ONE

The persistence of empire in metropolitan culture

John M. MacKenzie

The scholarly literature on the end of the British Empire is brimming with all kinds of evocative metaphors. To take just a small sample of this penchant for coining the all-encompassing phrase, we have leading titles such as *Imperial Sunset* (Max Beloff, 1969), *Eclipse of Empire* (D. A. Low, 1991), *Imperialism at Bay* (W. R. Louis, 1977), *Escape from Empire* (R. J. Moore, 1979), *Unscrambling an Empire* (W. P. Kirkman, 1966), *The Contraction of England* (D. A. Low, 1983), *The Retreat from Empire* (John Darwin, 1988) and *Britannia Overruled* (David Reynolds, 1991) – all of which, to some extent, convey the respective authors' particular view of imperial decline. More recently, decolonisation has been described as the 'Implosion of Empire', in order to convey a sense of the political upheavals on the colonial periphery reverberating inwards on metropolitan society.[1] Implosion is a dramatic word. It means 'bursting inwards'. It conjures up parts of the anatomy, like the appendix; or what happens to a vacuum flask when its skin is damaged. It is something which happens rapidly, dramatically, and indeed painfully. Perhaps there were some signs of implosion in the Dutch Empire in Indonesia or the French Empire in Indo-China and later Algeria, but the British Empire was so astonishingly vast that its decolonisation took place in stages from the inter-war years right down to the 1990s. If we leave aside the American seizure of independence in the 1770s and the handing back of the Ionian islands to Greece in 1864, decolonisation (at least in formal constitutional terms) began for the so-called white Dominions with the Statute of Westminster in 1931, and for other territories with the ending of the mandate in Iraq in 1932, and the treaty which permitted Egypt's entry into the League of Nations in 1936. Although imperial territories remain, the process can be seen as climaxing with the hand-over of Hong Kong to China in 1997.

If a sixty-year implosion sounds something like a contradiction in terms, perhaps we can think instead of a sequence of implosions, possibly ultimately detonating each other. Certainly, the years 1947–48 looked rather like an implosion with rapid decolonisations in India, Pakistan, Burma and Sri Lanka, the departure of Ireland from the Commonwealth, and the scuttle, implosion and explosion all at once in Palestine leading to the dramatic formation of the state of Israel. Then there was almost a decade's pause. Many have seen the Suez crisis as involving a sort of implosion of confidence, a moment of truth when the British realised that they could no longer discipline the 'awkward squad' at the periphery in the way that they had in the nineteenth century. Egypt is indeed a fascinating case, for the story starts with a colonel and it ends with a colonel. In 1882, the British had little difficulty in dealing with Colonel Urubi Pasha: they, alone, defeated him at Tel el Kebir; propped up their puppet the Khedive Tewfik; established their veiled Protectorate under one of the great proconsuls of the age (Sir Evelyn Baring, often known as 'Over-Baring'); and sent the Colonel into exile. In 1956, a mere seventy-four years later, they could do nothing with Colonel Nasser, who had overthrown King Farouk and nationalised the Canal Company with impunity. Even in league with France and Israel, it was now painfully apparent that the British could only flex imperial muscles with American support. Without them, Anthony Eden's fixation with Munich and the notion that 'dictators' should be dealt with firmly was as nought. Within months of Suez, though seemingly unrelated, the British were starting to decolonise in West Africa (Ghana) and South-East Asia (Malaya and Singapore). They were also agonising about their capacity to maintain any presence East of Suez. So perhaps we can identify implosion number two in 1956–57.[2]

The third implosion came in the massive wave of acts of decolonisation which took place throughout Africa in the years 1961–65, quickening particularly in 1963–65. The colonies of West and East Africa were cut adrift and the Central African Federation was broken up. By then the decolonising problems came not from blacks and browns, but from whites. Some 250,000 white settlers clung to a tenuous independence in Rhodesia/Zimbabwe for another fifteen years, until the Lancaster House agreements of 1980. South Africa seemed like an altogether different proposition. Paul Kennedy saw the Soviet Empire as being much longer-lasting and more intractable than the other declining great powers.[3] Yet both that Soviet Empire and the apartheid-ruled South Africa proceeded to implode in 1989–90.

The Falklands War of 1982 seemed very like a nineteenth-century imperial campaign, though the issues here were unquestionably more complex. The Thatcher Government had presented all the wrong signals; the aggressor was a dictator; and the inhabitants of the islands were quite clear that they wished to remain attached to a distant imperial mother. Here was certainly a distant explosion rather than an implosion. The hand-over of Hong Kong was decidedly not an implosion either and some would see it as the opposite of an act of decolonisation. Here was a carefully planned transmission of authority from one imperial power to another, which had been on the cards ever since the British had secured the 99-year lease to Kowloon and the New Territories in 1898, land without which their more permanent settlement on Victoria Island was entirely untenable. Though complicated by a democratically posturing and bullish final governor, this piece of the end of empire theatre is best symbolised by that astonishing display of synchronised hand-waving put on by sailors in the Chinese navy. It was intended as an act of friendship and encouragement, but it came over as a threatening instance of formidable collective action.

There was a similar paradox on the British side. The delivery of Hong Kong to the Chinese was presented as a piece of imperial theatre, taking its place with jubilees and coronations. The ceremonies, the troops, the hauling down of the flag, the images of Prince Charles and Governor Chris Patten on the beautiful royal yacht *Britannia*, significantly towards the end of a career which had started when the British still had imperial pretensions in the early 1950s, seemed to lead if anything to a swelling of national pride. Largely irrelevant to the lives of most people in Britain, this was the end of empire as a rather agreeable 'docu-soap', a television spectacle that had positive rather than negative resonances. Even in an act of departure and decline, the British could put on a 'good show'.

So a few islands are left, in the Caribbean, the Atlantic and the Pacific, together with the ever-anomalous Gibraltar. There are still imperial stamp issues, and the British find themselves complicit with off-shore tax havens, playgrounds for the rich, and maritime 'flags of convenience'. The mighty empire on which the sun never set is now a good deal smaller than that of Denmark in Greenland, although problems like the issue of the distribution of land in Zimbabwe still come back to haunt the British. So, given that we have a complicated mix of implosions, explosions, and small sputterings ranging from largish fireworks to happenings not much greater than Roman candles or hand-held sparklers, what cultural significance can be read into this sequence of events that runs over several decades?

Two points are worth making straight away. The first is that the notion that the British were indifferent to their Empire and accepted decolonisation with total equanimity constitutes an interesting piece of right-wing propaganda. It has been much put about by such figures as the late Lord Beloff, who argued into his eighties that an empire acquired in a fit of absence of mind could equally be lost by an indifferent oversight. Because the British had never developed a theory of empire, because they were fundamentally not an imperial people, they could view the loss of their imperial baubles with equanimity.[4] Not for them the reactions of the over-emotional French or Portuguese, who contemplated decolonisation with a series of domestic implosions, with revolutions, *coups d'état*, assassinations and new constitutions. Not for the British that gallic spectacle of overwrought French motorists driving round and round Paris beating out on their horns 'Al-gér-ie fran-çaise'. The English language does not have the beat; the British have not got the rhythm; and their cars probably do not have the horns.

Clearly, this notion of the utterly indifferent British is something of a self-justificatory and consolatory travesty. If it were true, then decolonisation would have had almost no cultural effects upon the British and the fundamental point of this book would be undermined. It also implies that decolonisation was foreseen in its entirety and that the British were able to prepare themselves psychologically and culturally for it. In fact it is hard to sustain such a proposition. In considering the long sequence of implosions and explosions that I have identified, we must be careful not to let the benefit of hindsight influence our assessment of the manner in which the British and others viewed the future of empire in the post-Second World War years. That the South Asian ring could not be held had been perfectly obvious to most intelligent observers since the 1930s. Even if Churchill huffed and puffed about the revolting spectacle of the half-naked fakir meeting the representative of the King-Emperor (that is, the encounters between M. K. Gandhi and viceroys of the inter-war years), or later declaimed that with the loss of India the British would immediately collapse to the status of a third-rate power, it was perfectly obvious to all perceptive observers that the Attlee Government had no alternative. The imperial fabric in India was thoroughly rotted through. To change the metaphor, a creeping decolonisation had been taking place for years, not only through constitutional change but also through personnel substitution. By the 1940s, it was Indians who were largely running the British Empire in India. As far back as the 1840s General Napier had said that the British ruled India by an astonishing act of bluff. With the end of the Second World War and the removal of the repressive military clamps, that bluff had become yet more transparent. Even if Mountbatten had his own reasons, it is not surprising that he speeded up the process of departure. The intriguing affair between Jawaharlal Nehru and Edwina Mountbatten somehow symbolised this dramatic reversal of fortunes. No wonder Mountbatten was eager to be off.

But when that Asian implosion was over and the British were desperately trying to warm themselves up after the horrendous winter of 1947–48, to what extent did they really think that the end of their Empire was on the cards, let alone that it was collapsing like a pack of cards? As they struggled to get coal and electricity supplies back, there were fresh horrors to come in Palestine and elsewhere.[5] But was this really the end?

There is a great deal of evidence to suggest that the British carefully subdivided their Empire and that this sectionalisation implied deep chronological differences. The Indian Empire was an old empire inherited in 1858 from a commercial company. Since the 1830s, the so-called Anglicist school, led by Lord Macaulay, had trumpeted that Indian independence, under the leadership of Indians who were English in tastes, in morals and in intellect, would be the greatest day in English history. Nehru, educated at Harrow and Cambridge, who heralded independence with a radio speech in the clipped and elegant expression of the Edwardian upper classes, seemed to symbolise the working out of that policy. Its western-educated elite had its origins in the early nineteenth century. British-style universities had been founded in the 1850s and graduates had been turned out by the countless thousand. However much an 'illusion of permanence' had developed for some in the later nineteenth century, the restoration of some form of independence remained within the logic of the British imperial system in India.[6]

But the rest of the Empire was not like that. It comprised either the white Dominions, vast territories inhabited by the kith and kin of the imperial race, or dependent territories – and notice the implication of that word dependent – where economic re-orientation to western forms, infrastructural development and elite formation seemed so much less advanced than in India. Although it has been argued that the presence of Arthur Creech Jones as Colonial Secretary in the Attlee Government and of a number of radical and far-sighted officials in the Colonial Office, like Sir Andrew Cohen, implied that full decolonisation was now recognised as a necessary policy option, I do not think that it seemed that way to the ordinary Briton on the streets.[7]

Many found that the end of the Second World War, as with the First, did not so much produce a land fit for heroes, as a period of depression and anxiety. Wartime rationing continued until the early 1950s. Although the post-war boom was to provide something of an illusion of full employment, British industry suffered from major under-investment and restructuring difficulties. Post-war Britain, as I know from my native Glasgow, looked not unlike that of the 1890s. There were extensive slums, grimy tenements coated in coal dust and smoke. Since coal remained the prime energy source, fogs and smogs were common. Many of the working class still struggled to make ends meet and retain respectability. The trams, those gondolas of the working classes, still trundled through the streets, many of them actually dating from before the First World War. When the sirens sounded, waves of workers still flooded out of the shipyards, docks, factories, iron foundries and steel works. In Glasgow, small ferries still plied back and forth across the river every hundred metres or so transporting (without charge) the workers from tenement homes to places of employment. The night sky was still ablaze with the flames of the foundries and noisy with the sirens, hooters and whistles of works, trains and ships. This was essentially a nineteenth-century world, not a brave new post-war dispensation. It is not surprising that in those conditions, the thoughts of the British should once again turn to empire as a solution to their social and economic problems.

As the great imperial shipping lines received their surviving ships back from troop transportation or built new tonnage, they still thought in terms of conveying emigrant hordes.[8] The mighty Cunard, Union-Castle and P&O lines again advertised their cabins for emigrants, often on assisted passages. P&O continued to operate in this trade right through the 1950s, although by now southern Europeans, often Italians or Greeks, were joining the British in heading for Australia. The *Daily Express* continued to try to persuade its readership to emigrate to South Africa throughout the 1950s. In Zimbabwean history, following the Cecil Rhodes example of 1890, we often joke about the 1947 pioneer column. My own father, fresh out of the wartime army and disillusioned with opportunities in Britain, joined that column and, as a result, part of my childhood was spent in Northern Rhodesia, now Zambia. When we arrived on the Union-Castle liner at Cape Town, we boarded a train for the four-day journey through Cape Province, Bechuanaland (Botswana) and Southern Rhodesia (Zimbabwe) to Northern Rhodesia. The British seemed in command of the region, at least outside Afrikaner nationalist South Africa. Everywhere, including Afrikaner-ruled South Africa, English was spoken and the currency was the pound. In the same period, other Scottish relatives were leaving for Canada and the United States.[9] Others, such as the family of another contributor to this book, Jeffrey Richards, considered emigration to New Zealand in the late 1940s, but decided against it.

Thus in the 1940s and 1950s, Britons were still convinced that the British Empire in the Dominions and in Africa would endure. The popular press certainly gave them this impression. So indeed did the policy-makers in Government. During my childhood in the town of Ndola, Northern Rhodesia was part of the Federation of Rhodesia and Nyasaland, the ill-fated Central African Federation which was dreamed up by the Labour Government and brought into being by the Conservatives in 1953. This federation was based on three premises: first, that the territories concerned could not achieve independence under black rule for a considerable period; second, that they constituted complementary economies which would work better if brought together under white rule; and third, that there was an opportunity to create a new white Dominion to stand over against the one that appeared to have been lost to the Afrikaners in South Africa. No one predicted that that Federation would encounter revolt and emergency as early as 1959 and that it would be broken up by 1964. It was camouflaged with propaganda about racial partnership, but the first federal Prime Minister, Sir Godfrey Huggins, later Lord Malvern, blew that particular cover by referring to it as the partnership of the rider and the horse.[10] I have a clear recollection of seeing a family displaying themselves as the Central African Federation in a fancy-dress parade on a Union-Castle liner: the father personified the white patriarchal Southern Rhodesia; he towed a trolley on which reclined his wife, clothed and painted in yellow to symbolise the copper riches of Northern Rhodesia, while his son, blacked up, walked alongside to represent the labour migrants of the poorer Nyasaland (Malawi). The gendering of the three territories was intriguing, for many saw the Federation as an opportunity for the Southern Rhodesian whites to exploit the riches of the North. Little did that family know how well they had represented it or how soon they would be split asunder.

Even in East Africa, where a policy of African paramountcy had been in place since the 1920s, there was little indication that black nationalist victory would soon be the rule rather than the exception. At the end of the Second World War, white authority seemed to be enhanced and Europeans in the Kenyan so-called white Highlands had been given full local self-government on a sort of county council basis. When Jomo Kenyatta returned to Kenya, he was advised by the Governor to involve himself in local government rather than nationalist politics. Throughout East and Central Africa, Africans continued to be denied the franchise since, as one authority has put it, the policy of 'multi-racialism' was 'too ingenious for electoral tests'.[11] Nationalists themselves, even Julius Nyerere in the former League mandate and UN trusteeship territory of Tanganyika, were to be taken by surprise by the speed of decolonisation from the late 1950s.

Pacific mandates arising from the defeat of Germany in the First World War were held by Australia and New Zealand, and their rule in those territories was if anything even more imperial and unthinking of the future than that of Britain itself.[12] For many observers of the world in the period, decolonisation in South and South-East Asia could seem like an exception rather than the norm. Certainly, the great majority of the British and the Dominions press gave little indication that the imperial game was up until at least 1959.

In Britain, the Conservative and Unionist Party continued to use imperial symbolism right through that decade. So too did such right-wing Dominion politicians as Sir Robert Menzies in Australia. Even the Americans were sending out confusing signals. If, after the Second World War, US policy-makers had been convinced that European imperialism presented an invitation to communist advance in Asia, in the Cold War conditions of the 1950s they were more inclined to think that some areas of surviving empire could act as a bulwark. Moreover, it is significant that when, in 1959, the Mau Mau campaign and the Hola Camp massacre, together with the emergency in Central Africa, convinced the radical Tory Iain Macleod that the British had to decolonise in Africa, the Prime Minister Harold Macmillan advised caution. It was not until after Macmillan had won a majority of over 100 seats in the British general election of 8 October 1959 that he put Macleod into the Colonial Office and unleashed 'the wind of change' with such a storm force that he enraged and alienated his own right wing. By that time, the British Government had significantly made the decision that Britain required a fully professional army. All those born after 1940 would no longer have to do national service. As campaigns raged in Kenya, Cyprus, Malaya, Borneo and later Aden, it was abundantly apparent that the British could no longer sustain a succession of colonial revolts.

It seems to me that it is this third implosion of empire, as I have characterised it, between 1959 and 1964, which is actually more important in cultural terms than the first one of the 1940s. It is true that in the 1940s there was good evidence that the British were exceptionally ignorant about their Empire. When the Colonial Office conducted polls in 1947 and 1948, they discovered that very few people could name a single colony. One man apparently suggested Lincolnshire. Given the intense rivalry between the adjacent counties, I think he must have been a Yorkshireman. Interestingly, 3 per cent of those polled thought that the United States was still in the Empire. And no one could define the difference between a dominion and a colony.[13]

Yet in that same decade the BBC was still projecting a confident image of imperial development. The Christmas Day flagship programmes on radio continued to tour the Empire, depicting a healthy and mutually beneficial economic imperialism, until as late as the 1950s. For example, the groundnut scheme in Tanganyika, shortly to be the graveyard of so many colonial developmental schemes, was heralded on these programmes as the great economic hope of the future. In 1947, it was described as 'offering solid ground for hope, hundreds of miles of jungle cleared by science and the bulldozer with a real promise of a better life for African and European'. In 1948, British groundnutters (unfortunate word) were celebrated as 'English families under canvas or in huts' to a background of African drumming and chanting. In 1951 the programme *The Gifts of Christmas* featured 'Zulu voices raised in thanksgiving', no doubt rejoicing at the development of the apartheid policies of the Afrikaner nationalists. There was also a section on the Gold Coast, including the commentary: 'once the white man's coming here meant terror and slavery; now he comes bringing gifts – gifts of learning – spelling the way to a fuller life'. And that very Gold Coast was only six years off full independence. Something of the importance of these programmes is conveyed by the fact that they were narrated by figures like Laurence Olivier, Robert Donat and John Gielgud, while composers of the eminence of William Alwyn, Benjamin Britten and Walter Goehr wrote the background music.[14]

Moreover, colonial exhibits, colonial months and trade fairs continued to tour the country until the early 1950s. A colonial week was held in Glasgow, a major imperial city, in 1951 and steam locomotives for the Empire and Commonwealth were exhibited in the city's central square. Other colonial exhibitions toured Britain as late as 1954 and 1955.[15] However, it is certainly significant that the major post-war exhibition, the Festival of Britain on London's South Bank in 1951, appeared to concentrate on metropolitan Britain. It has often been depicted as the first rather introspective exhibition, reflecting on a post-war Britain, possibly shorn of empire. The final great imperial exhibition in the sequence from the nineteenth century had been held in Glasgow in 1938. Although it had dominion and colonial avenues, with characteristic pavilions from all around the Empire, it is significant that the Indian Government had refused to participate in that one. The absence of 'the jewel in the imperial Crown' from such a major imperial show offered a hint of future break-up.

Yet in other aspects of ceremony and exhibition, the Empire and Commonwealth appeared to continue to be supremely important. In 1951, the Imperial Institute in South Kensington mounted an exhibition entitled 'Focus on Colonial Progress' as part of the Festival of Britain, although it received many fewer visitors than the main show. 'Queen and Commonwealth' exhibitions were held in association with the coronation in 1953.

There was a good reason for the need for these exhibitions to continue in their propagandist role. This was the renewed emergence of a strategy of colonial development and welfare after the war. This belated policy of government investment in imperial development had its origins in 1929, but it was only from 1945 that it became truly significant in both British and French efforts to regenerate their empires. As with the Tanganyika groundnut scheme, the policy was promoted with considerable optimism. Empire could at last be justified on the grounds of enlightened official notions of welfare, investment and development. The implication was that the Empire was now genuinely about trusteeship, partnership and state-sponsored investment. The ideals of the inter-war years had at last captured the high ground, some would think in pursuit of a self-interested containment. This same sense runs through Lord Hailey's monumental *African Survey*, first published in 1938 and revised in 1956 for publication in 1957.[16] Medicine, science, economics and education could now all be harnessed for the benefit of Africa and Africans. A renewed sense of the redemptive power of science had begun to emerge before the Second World War and it was thought that the post-war imperial world would be the setting for the enlightened activities of the 'expert'. Experts would transform agriculture, forestry, the environment, and the world of work.[17]

It has often been remarked that this same sense of optimism surrounded the coronation of Queen Elizabeth II in 1953. Symbolically, it was accompanied by that distinctive imperial event, the conquest of Everest.[18] That military metaphor reflects the extent to which the British and other imperial powers had seen the planting of the flag on the greatest mountain tops of the world as a vital ambition of the imperial spirit. Many times attempted in the twentieth century, it was now achieved by the perfect combination of the New Zealander Edmund Hillary and the Nepalese Tenzing Norgay. After all, Nepal had a special relationship with the British Empire through the recruitment of Gurkhas to the ranks of its army, where they remain to this day.

Many of these Gurkhas were indeed in London for the coronation, reflecting the manner in which this coronation was to be, presumably, the last of an imperial sequence. The words *Ind. Imp. (Indiae Imperatrix* or *Imperator)* had by now disappeared from the British coinage, and the Queen had indeed been demoted to a mere Queen, unlike her five predecessors. Yet the coronation was attended by troops, politicians, officials, young people, and other visitors from around the Empire/Commonwealth. The processions in London, as in Victorian times, offered exotic displays of imperial uniforms and costumes. (*Ind. Imp.* coins, incidentally, remained in circulation in Britain until decimalisation in the early 1970s.) After the coronation the Queen and the Duke of Edinburgh embarked on the most extensive tours of the Commonwealth and Empire that any British monarch had ever undertaken. The 15,900-ton vessel *Gothic* of the Shaw Savill line acted as the royal yacht for the extensive 1953–54 Commonwealth tour, *Britannia* being launched only in the latter year. These tours were prominently covered in the British press, in newsreels and radio and television. In the same period, the Edinburgh Festival military tattoo, together with the longer-standing Royal Tournament at Olympia in London, developed a tradition of displaying the drill, dancing and musical traditions of troops throughout the Empire/Commonwealth. Interestingly, this continues to this day, with armed forces from the Caribbean, South Asia, the Pacific, as well as the ex-Dominions, eager to attend and perform.

In publishing, imperial traditions also seemed to be alive and well. The works of G. A. Henty, Sir Henry Rider Haggard and R. M. Ballantyne, among many others, remained in print and still constituted some of the prime elements of the prize and present market for children.[19] A new tradition of youthful reading had yet to establish itself. Oral evidence suggests that many missionaries, settlers, politicians and soldiers continued to be influenced by such childhood reading experiences.[20] It was only from the early 1960s that a wholly new style of modern comics, concentrating on more futuristic themes like space travel, was to establish itself. Imperial hagiographical biographies continued to be read right through the 1950s. This is certainly true, for example, of the missionary-explorer David Livingstone. In Scotland, his national memorial at Blantyre remained a place of popular resort for schools and Sunday schools throughout that decade.[21] Only later did its visitor numbers begin to fall off. Indeed, it was not until 1973 that Livingstone received his first fully debunking biography, a very inadequate one by Tim Jeal.[22]

Moreover, it is possible to find an imperial tradition surviving in historical scholarship into the 1950s. Yet once more, it is to the 1960s that we look for the origins of a new history, pursuing more radical theorisation or searching for the hidden histories of indigenous peoples. Only then did resistance and revolt in Asia and Africa come to be interpreted in new and sympathetic ways. Even the supposedly radical Robinson and Gallagher continued to refer to colonial revolts as late as 1961 as romantic and backward-looking movements of peoples 'who would not be comforted'. By the end of the 1960s, such revolts were being formulated in very different ways.[23]

Another popular tradition, the *Empire Youth Annual*, also continued to be published throughout the 1950s, only adding Commonwealth to its title in the course of that decade. The annuals were filled with pictures, tales and yarns of Empire and Commonwealth, both fictional and non-fictional. In the same tradition, Saturday morning cinema shows offered up to their youthful audiences exciting serials of 'derring-do' in both the historic and contemporary Empire. Major Fred Ney's Empire Youth Movement, re-named Commonwealth Youth Movement soon after the accession of Elizabeth II, continued to organise youth exchanges and imperial events. Astonishingly, it used the language of imperial chivalry, quests, questors, vigils and so on, until the 1960s.[24]

In the realm of transportation, a sense of imperial excitement still prevailed. The locomotive works in Glasgow and Manchester were still producing both steam and, by now, diesel engines for the territories of the Empire and Commonwealth, although by this time they were facing fierce competition from the United States and more local producers. In Glasgow, those locomotives were hauled through the streets and loaded on to ships by a heavy-lift crane at Finnieston on the Clyde.[25] Tilbury, Southampton, Liverpool and Glasgow were filled with the ships of the old imperial shipping lines, still departing at regular intervals for the destinations of empire. P&O, Orient, British India, Royal Mail, Union-Castle, Ellerman, Anchor, Elder Dempster, Cunard, Canadian Pacific, among others, replaced their fleets after the war. Weekly passenger voyages for imperial and Commonwealth destinations continued to depart from the principal ports. For anyone living in or visiting those cities, with their prominent docksides, the Empire seemed alive and well. In the air, Short and

Sunderland flying boats had developed a new romance of long-distance travel, particularly to Africa and parts of Asia, but at such cost that they largely carried a privileged elite and failed to dent the passenger services of the shipping companies.[26] Although flying boat services were replaced by those of the new constellations and the first passenger jet, the Comet, it was not until the end of the 1950s that both of these distinctively British and imperial forms of transport began to feel the threat of the new Boeing 707.

In all of these ways it does seem to me that an illusion of imperial power, underpinned by popular cultural reflections, continued to be projected throughout the 1950s. Of course it was an illusion, in all sorts of ways. It was an illusion in military terms, as Suez and colonial revolts amply demonstrated. It was an illusion in economic terms, for the concept of a fully complementary empire, which really only flourished briefly after the 1932 Ottawa agreements, dissipated with great speed after the war. British indebtedness, including its major debts to its own Empire, ensured a continuing weakness when much of the rest of Europe was regenerating on Marshall Aid. The formerly mighty sterling area was now under considerable pressure. The pound was exceptionally weak in the face of the ever-strengthening dollar, as was again demonstrated in the Suez crisis. Imperial markets were no longer protected by culture and sentiment. Import substitution was rampant everywhere and the Treaty of Rome and new economic alliances in Europe soon indicated further writing on the wall for Britain.

But popular culture can have precisely this role of projecting illusion when a different form of reality has taken over. There comes a moment, however, when the illusion is exposed and its forms crumble. That moment came, not in the 1940s or the 1950s, but only in the early 1960s. It was only then that it became cruelly apparent that the British could no longer trade off (in both literal and metaphorical terms) a richly powerful imperial past. Thus it seems to me that both popular and intellectual culture only became fully aware of the underlying realities of power, of the extent to which empire was over in economic, political, military and conceptual terms, once the third implosion of the British Empire had occurred.

It was only after that third implosion that the stresses within the British state became truly apparent. It was only in the 1960s that domestic racial tensions became fully significant, taking up a central place in British political debate through the agency of Enoch Powell and the National Front. Those tensions produced legislation that restricted immigration, but also legislation that brought the weight of the law to bear against racial discrimination. The 'troubles' broke out in Northern Ireland in the last years of that decade, heralding a searing thirty-year struggle. Restless nationalisms in Scotland and Wales became more active, although I think that the relationship between Celtic nationalism and empire is often more complex and subtle than is sometimes suggested.[27] The British also realised that their preoccupation with empire had caused them to miss the European economic bus. The 1960s saw them desperately trying to run after it and jump on. Even the Thatcherite free market, monetarist experiment was in many ways a reaction to the loss of empire. However much she invoked the Tory icons of Disraeli and Churchill, she was of course, in economic terms, a Gladstonian.[28] Not for her the state controls and investment policies of empire. The fact is, for example, that most railway systems in the Empire were state-run in the nineteenth century. Nationalisation was a classic imperial policy. In Thatcher, imperial rhetoric and economic practice were totally at odds. Moreover, from at least the 1890s empire had been largely bi-partisan. Conservatives, Liberals and Labour had all been sucked into its seductive patriotisms. Empire was the forerunner of the so-called Butskellite (that is, left Tory and right Labour) consensus which Thatcher railed against. Whereas the possession of empire had tended towards a degree of class conciliation, Thatcher was prepared to raise the standard of economic and social civil war in intoning her cry of 'the enemy within'. It may also be the case that empire had preserved some of the rigidities of the British class system.[29]

To conclude, we can see imperial popular cultural forms as much as economic policies sailing serenely on through the first implosion of the late 1940s, one that was expected and was not regarded as heralding the rest. The second implosion of the mid to late 1950s began to check a dominant popular culture which had been in place since at least the 1890s. Only by the third implosion, of the 1960s, was British culture being channelled into wholly new grooves. Even then, as the excitements of the Falklands War of 1982 demonstrated, imperial pride was not wholly shattered. The 'heat and lust' school of internationally successful films and British television serials set in India continued to offer nostalgic images of an empire lost.

However, it is perhaps significant that a television series about Cecil Rhodes in 1996 was a good deal less successful, partly because the plotting was so complex that few viewers comprehended what was actually going on.[30] By then, as street 'vox pop' interviews revealed, no one in Britain seemed to have heard of Rhodes, the mighty Colossus of the late nineteenth century. The name had become inseparably associated with a television chef called Rhodes, with the distinctly unimperial first name of Gary. This culinary connection seems eminently appropriate. If the Empire never knew a Sir Gary as Governor or even as rampantly expansionist entrepreneur, Britain's imperial past had now come to be symbolised in that phenomenon known as 'the Empire strikes back'. From the late

1940s, with the arrival of that significantly named vessel from the West Indies, the *Empire Windrush*, the processes of migration had been dramatically reversed. Blacks and Asians from the West Indies, West and East Africa, South Asia, Hong Kong, and elsewhere colonised British cities, creating a new and lively multiculturalism. That ultimate joke of Europe, British cuisine, suddenly became cosmopolitan and exciting, even if adapted for British tastes. Ex-imperial peoples at last showed signs of bringing global civilisation to bear upon the ever-insular British.

Notes

1   This was the title of a conference at the University of Southern Denmark in February 1999, when this paper was originally given as an introductory lecture. Although this is a revised version, some of the informalities of that occasion have been retained, both as a matter of record and in the hope that some of the author's experiences constitute a form of historical source. *Implosion of Empire* is also the title of a forthcoming book by Lars Ole Sauerberg, to be published by Palgrave.

2   There is now a considerable literature on decolonisation, although this work is almost exclusively political and diplomatic in content. Little or nothing has been written about the cultural changes wrought by the end of the Empire and the transition to Commonwealth. See particularly John Darwin, *Britain and Decolonisation: The Retreat from Empire in the Post-War World* (London, Macmillan, 1988) and *The End of the British Empire: The Historical Debate* (Oxford, Blackwell, 1991); J. D. Hargreaves, *Decolonization in Africa* (London, Longman, 1988). For the Suez crisis, see W. R. Louis and Roger Owen (eds), *Suez 1956: The Crisis and its Consequences* (Oxford, Clarendon Press, 1989). Several chapters on aspects of decolonisation and the end of empire can be found in W. Roger Louis and Judith M. Brown (eds), *The Oxford History of the British Empire, Vol. IV: The Twentieth Century* (Oxford, Oxford University Press, 1999). Studies of the transition to the Commonwealth, again entirely political in content, include W. D. McIntyre, *Colonies into Commonwealth* (London, Blandford, 1966); David Adamson, *The Last Empire: Britain and the Commonwealth* (London, I. B. Tauris, 1989); Martin Kitchen, *The British Empire and Commonwealth: A Short History* (London, Macmillan, 1996); and W. David McIntyre, *The Significance of the Commonwealth, 1965–90* (Christchurch, Canterbury University Press, 1991).

3   Paul M. Kennedy, *The Rise and Fall of the Great Powers* (London, Unwin Hyman, 1988).

4   Max Beloff, *Imperial Sunset, Vol. 1: Britain's Liberal Empire, 1897–1921* (London, Methuen, 1969), p. 19 and many newspaper articles. Lord Beloff was very critical of the Oxford History of the British Empire project, which he saw as representing a modern and, to him, unsympathetic historiography. For a discussion of the significance of empire to British domestic history, see P. J. Marshall, 'Imperial Britain' (the Creighton Lecture, 1994), published in the *Journal of Imperial and Commonwealth History*, 23:3 (1995), pp. 379–94.

5   For the Palestine crisis, see W. R. Louis, *The British Empire in the Middle East, 1945–51* (Oxford, Clarendon Press, 1984) and W. R. Louis and Robert W. Stookey (eds), *The End of the Palestine Mandate* (London, I. B. Tauris, 1986). For the 1947 winter fuel crisis, see Alex J. Robertson, *The Bleak Midwinter* (Manchester, Manchester University Press, 1987).

6   Francis G. Hutchins, *The Illusion of Permanence: British Imperialism in India* (Princeton, Princeton University Press, 1967). See also Thomas R. Metcalf, *Ideologies of the Raj* (Cambridge, Cambridge University Press, 1995).

7   Robert D. Pearce, *The Turning Point in Africa: British Colonial Policy, 1938–48* (London, Frank Cass, 1982).

8   For post-war migrant patterns, including inward migration to the UK, see Stephen Constantine, 'Migrants and Settlers', in Louis and Brown (eds), *Oxford History of the British Empire*, pp. 163–187.

9   The background to these movements can be surveyed in Stephen Constantine (ed.), *Emigrants and Empire* (Manchester, Manchester University Press, 1990); see also Marjory Harper, *Emigration from Scotland Between the Wars* (Manchester, Manchester University Press, 1998).

10 For contemporary polemics relating to the Federation, see Sir Roy Welensky, *Welensky's 4000 Days: The Life and Death of the Federation of Rhodesia and Nyasaland* (London, Collins, 1964) and Patrick Keatley, *The Politics of Partnership* (Harmondsworth, Penguin, 1963).

11 John Lonsdale, 'East Africa', in Louis and Brown (eds), *Oxford History of the British Empire*, p. 541.

12 I. C. Campbell, *A History of the Pacific Islands* (Christchurch, Canterbury University Press, 1989), particularly Chapters 15 and 16; A. M. Healy, 'Colonial Law as Metropolitan Defence: The Curious Case of Australia in New Guinea', in Hermann J. Hiery and John M. MacKenzie (eds), *European Impact and Pacific Influence: British and German Colonial Policy in the Pacific Islands and the Indigenous Response* (London, I. B. Tauris, 1997), pp. 214–30.

13 David Goldsworthy, *Colonial Issues in British Politics, 1945–61* (Oxford, Clarendon Press, 1971), p. 399.

14 John M. MacKenzie, '"In Touch with the Infinite": The BBC and the Empire, 1923–53', in John M. MacKenzie (ed.), *Imperialism and Popular Culture* (Manchester, Manchester University Press, 1986), pp. 182–3.

15 John M. MacKenzie, *Propaganda and Empire: The Manipulation of British Public Opinion 1880–1960* (Manchester, Manchester University Press, 1984), pp. 117–18.

16 Lord Hailey, *An African Survey* (London, Oxford University Press, 1938 and 1957).

17 Something of the flavour of the expert's optimism can be derived from E. B. Worthington, *Science in Africa: A Review of Scientific Research Relating to Tropical and Southern Africa* (London, Oxford University Press, 1938). Worthington's book was compiled as part of Hailey's great survey project.

18 See the chapter by Peter Hansen in this volume. See also Gordon T. Stewart, 'Tenzing's Two Wrist Watches: The Everest Expedition and Late Imperial Culture in Britain 1921–1953', *Past and Present*, 149 (November 1995), pp. 170–97. For a general discussion of the significance of mountaineering in British imperialism, see Peter H. Hansen, 'Vertical Boundaries, National Identities: British Mountaineering on the Frontiers of Europe and the Empire, 1868–1914', *Journal of Imperial and Commonwealth History*, 24:1 (1996), pp. 48–71.

19 Jeffrey Richards (ed.), *Imperialism and Juvenile Literature* (Manchester, Manchester University Press, 1989).

20 See the compilations of Charles Allen, *Plain Tales from the Raj* (London, André Deutsch, 1975) and *Tales from the Dark Continent* (London, Deutsch for the BBC, 1979), and of Jeremy Weston for the University of Edinburgh (2000, private communication).

21 John M. MacKenzie, 'David Livingstone: The Construction of the Myth', in Graham Walker and Tom Gallagher (eds), *Sermons and Battle Hymns: Protestant Popular Culture in Modern Scotland* (Edinburgh, Edinburgh University Press, 1990), pp. 24–42.

22 Tim Jeal, *Livingstone* (London, Heinemann, 1973).

23 T. O. Ranger, *Revolt in Southern Rhodesia, 1896–97* (London, Heinemann, 1967).

24 The *Empire Youth Annual* was edited by Raymond Fawcett and published by P. R. Gawthorn, London. It adopted 'Commonwealth' (as *Empire and Commonwealth Youth Annual*) into its title only from 1953. Each year it carried a message from a Commonwealth prime minister. In 1952, the first non-white appeared when Don Senanayake of Ceylon assumed this role. On J. F. Ney see James Sturgis and Margaret Bird, *Canada's Imperial Past: The Life of F. J. Ney* (Edinburgh, University of Edinburgh

Centre of Canadian Studies, 2000).

25 John M. MacKenzie, 'The Second City of the Empire: Glasgow – Imperial Municipality', in Felix Driver and David Gilbert (eds), *Imperial Cities: Landscape, Display and Identity* (Manchester, Manchester University Press, 1999), pp. 215–37.

26 Graham Coster, *Corsairville* (London, Viking, 2000). See also Gordon H. Pirie, *Aviation and Empire* (Manchester, Manchester University Press, 2001).

27 Tom Nairn, *The Break-Up of Britain: Crisis and Neo-Nationalism* (London, Verso, 1981); John M. MacKenzie, 'On Scotland and the Empire', *International History Review*, 15:4 (1993), pp. 714–39.

28 For discussions of Margaret Thatcher and 'Victorian values', see Eric M. Sigsworth (ed.), *In Search of Victorian Values: Aspects of Nineteenth-Century Thought and Society* (Manchester, Manchester University Press, 1988) and Eric J. Evans, *Thatcher and Thatcherism* (London, Routledge, 1997).

29 David Cannadine, 'Empire and Social Hierarchy in Modern Britain', the Esmée Fairbairn lecture at the University of Lancaster, 4 November 1999, privately printed.

30 Antony Thomas, *Rhodes: The Race for Africa* (London, BBC, 1996) was the book of the series, which was also issued on video.

CHAPTER TWO

Empire loyalists and 'Commonwealth men': the Round Table and the end of empire

Alex May

Much of the scholarly debate about empire and metropolitan culture revolves around the thorny issue of 'popular imperialism'. To what extent did imperial culture 'penetrate' the broad realm of popular sentiment and collective identity? Or put more simply: did ordinary people really care about the Empire? But in tackling these difficult questions, it is surely relevant to examine those sections of the community who indisputably did care – namely, the interest groups and organisations that committed themselves to the advocacy of the imperial cause. In Britain, a wide array of empire-minded groups proliferated from the mid-nineteenth century, many of which have reconstituted themselves and continue to thrive today. The Royal Overseas League, for example, was founded in 1910 as the Overseas Club, 'a kind of "Grown-up Boy Scouts"' seeking to advance the idea of a 'united' empire.[1] The most venerable Commonwealth institution, the Royal Commonwealth Society, traces its history back to 1868, when it was founded (as the Colonial Society; it became the Royal Empire Society in 1928, and the Royal Commonwealth Society only in 1958) as a 'medium by which we may form our scattered colonies into a homogeneous whole'.[2] For those bodies which were set up to promote imperial 'unity' and the ideals of British imperialism, the end of Britain's imperial 'mission' presented particular moral, intellectual and political difficulties. The loss of empire inevitably led to a questioning of their *raisons d'être*; and their adjustment to the new, multi-polar and multi-racial Commonwealth which emerged from the dead husk of empire was neither automatic nor unproblematic.

This chapter will focus on one particular group, the Round Table. Founded in 1909 as an avowedly imperialist 'think tank', it published from 1910 a quarterly journal which rapidly established itself as a highly regarded and at times highly influential medium of opinion on imperial and Commonwealth matters.[3] The Round Table was in many respects unusual among Empire/Commonwealth bodies. Part dining club, part

[37]

editorial committee, part pressure group, part cabal, the London group was always small (15–20 members until the 1980s, 20–30 thereafter) and self-selecting, with members drawn from the worlds of academe, business, journalism, politics and public administration. Archetypically 'establishment', it met frequently in London clubs. Women were only invited to join in the 1970s. Until the 1980s, the most numerous group of its members might be described as left-wing or 'one nation' Conservatives, although it always contained a sprinkling of Liberal and Labour supporters, and a larger group of individuals who espoused no particular party political preference.

Through discussion, members of the Round Table attempted to arrive at a collective view on the most important issues of the day, which they then put forward through the journal, either by means of editorials written under collective guidance or by means of the selection and guidance of contributors, and sometimes the collective editing and amendment of contributed articles. Until 1966 all articles in the journal were anonymous. This was partly 'with the special object of being able to call on people … who really know the inner meaning of things, to contribute without embarrassment to them or their governments',[4] but partly also so that 'every article became in effect a leading article, carrying the authority of the journal and of its supposed influential and exceptionally well-informed governors'.[5] The London group controlled the bulk of the content of the *Round Table* journal, but until the late 1960s groups constituted on similar lines in Canada, Australia, New Zealand and South Africa (even after South Africa's departure from the Commonwealth in 1961) provided articles on or from their countries. In addition, the *Round Table* published quarterly articles from regular correspondents in India (from 1910), Pakistan (from 1948), and perhaps surprisingly the United States (from 1917 to 1967) and the Irish Free State/Eire (from 1922 to 1967). The journal had shorter-lived arrangements with correspondents in Ceylon (from 1948 to 1952), East Africa (from 1954 to 1958) and Rhodesia (from 1954 to 1967). Coverage of other parts of the Empire/Commonwealth was more fitful.

In organisation the Round Table was closer to the many, generally shorter-lived, 'ginger groups' which were such a marked feature of other areas of British political life in the early and mid-twentieth century, than to any of the other Empire/Commonwealth bodies which operated alongside it. Nevertheless its very distinctiveness makes it a particularly interesting prism through which to view the impact of the end of empire on the groups and lobbies which had once sustained it. The Round Table's members came from and were influential in many different parts of the 'establishment', and they were active in many of the other Empire and Commonwealth lobbies and associations of the time. Their deliberations and attempts to reach a collective view gave their opinions an emblematic quality. Moreover, the Round Table prided itself on its long-range planning and its willingness to confront the fundamental problems facing the Empire/Commonwealth. In the words of its principal founder, the Round Table's aim was 'not to consider what interests people, but rather to interest their minds in what really concerns them'.[6] The pages of the *Round Table* therefore contain a good deal of long-term speculation, which in the nature of things magnified the assumptions, prejudices, hopes and fears of its authors and promoters.

In some respects the Round Table had already declined from its own peak long before 1945. In the years immediately before the First World War it was able to employ two of its own members (Philip Kerr as editor, Lionel Curtis as organiser) and seven other full-time staff, with a suite of seven rooms at 175 Piccadilly. After 1945 the staff was reduced to a part-time editor and a part-time secretary, operating from a small office in the Royal Commonwealth Society building in Northumberland Avenue. The journal, which at one point had a circulation of 13,000, saw its circulation decline to some 2,500 by 1945, from where it declined steadily to about 1,500 in the 1960s. There were various reasons, among them increased competition from other quarterly journals and the general decline in the journals market caused by the more rapid availability of news and comment via newspapers, radio and television. Nevertheless, the *Round Table* retained a certain cachet as the foremost journal of opinion on the contemporary Empire and Commonwealth, and it continued to be quoted frequently in other parts of the press (a practice encouraged by the dispatch of relatively large numbers of free copies to journalists, and sometimes of a specially drafted resumé or press notice), and in Parliament. The circulation figures for the journal provide a poor indication of its actual readership, as a large and increasing proportion of copies was likely to have been read by a number of different readers; while the journal managed to retain a few individual subscribers, the bulk of its subscriptions in the post-war period came from university and public libraries, government departments, High Commissions and embassies, investment and trading houses, and newspaper offices. Its readership fitted closely with the Round Table's predominantly elitist conception of the political process. In 1920 Curtis stated that 'the *Round Table* is not intended so much for the average reader, as for those who write for the average reader'.[7]

For the first thirty years of its existence, the London Round Table group was dominated by the closely knit group of individuals who had founded it. Some of these survived into and remained active in the post-war period. Sir Reginald Coupland (Professor of Imperial History at Oxford) died in 1952; Lionel Curtis (Fellow of All Souls College, Oxford, and *éminence grise* of imperial politics), Lord Altrincham (Sir Edward Grigg, former Conservative MP for Altrincham, and editor of the *National Review*) and Sir Dougal Malcolm (President of the British South Africa Company) all died in 1955; while Lord Brand (Robert Brand, Director of Lazard Brothers and of the *Times*) died in 1963. The leading members of the post-war Round Table constituted a similar cross-section of the British 'establishment'. Politics and the civil service were represented by such figures as the Home Secretary of the early 1960s, Henry (Lord) Brooke, and those stalwarts of government committees and inquiries, Sir Oliver (Lord) Franks and Sir John (Lord Redcliffe-)Maud. Other members had returned from distinguished careers in the Indian Civil Service, such as Sir Malcolm (Lord) Hailey and Sir Olaf Caroe. Banking and financial interests were well represented, through such figures as Percy Horsfall, Managing Director of Lazard Brothers, and Sir Jeremy Morse, Chairman of Lloyds Bank. Finally, the press and academia provided key members, such as Harry Hodson (editor of the *Sunday Times* from 1950 to 1961) and Nicholas Mansergh (Smuts Professor at Cambridge from 1953 to 1970). The editor of the *Round Table* from 1945 to 1965 was Dermot Morrah, a journalist and leader-writer for the *Times*, then the *Daily Telegraph*. Author of numerous books on royalty, from 1953 he assumed the arcane post of Arundel Herald Extraordinary. There were times when Morrah's cultivated old-fashionedness had to be restrained by his Round Table employers, but these were not frequent. He saw himself not altogether inaccurately as merely 'the scribe who puts on paper the collective views' of the Round Table group.[8]

What drew these men towards membership of the Round Table was, essentially, a 'moral' view of empire. Among the older members, faith in the British Empire had an almost messianic flavour. Curtis – accurately described by Gerald Studdert-Kennedy as a 'pre-Butterfield Christian Whig'[9] – once posed the question, 'If Christ came back to earth, where, in the present day world, would he find that his precepts were best being practised?', to which he unhesitatingly provided the answer: 'The British Commonwealth'.[10] Curtis's profane enthusiasm sometimes embarrassed his colleagues. Nevertheless they fully shared his view that the British Empire was the greatest instrument the world had ever seen for preserving world peace and disseminating the values of liberal democracy. Not for them mere dominion over palm or pine; still less (despite the strong representation of financial interests within the group) the mere furtherance of Britain's economic interests. The moral earnestness with which such men viewed the Empire reflected an important strain in imperial ideology until the 1950s: the belief in Britain's 'civilising mission' so brilliantly reconstructed by A. P. Thornton, Kathryn Tidrick and others. Indeed, as Paul Rich has shown, Round Table members, both individually and collectively, played a crucial role both in formulating and in disseminating this ideology.[11] In doing so, they articulated assumptions which were widely held: that the British Empire, uniquely, stood for and promoted values of democracy, good governance, mutual tolerance, and respect for the individual; that 'Britishness' was not so much a matter of race or ethnicity as of cultural values, exported to the self-governing colonies through British settlers but also to the 'dependent' Empire through example and education; but that the dissemination of 'Britishness' was a long game, requiring decades and even centuries of imperial tutelage in order for alien cultures to be re-moulded in the image of Britain. These assumptions, it should be emphasised, were not the sole property of the Round Table: they were fundamental building-blocks of the imperial creed, as expounded by speakers at the Royal Empire Society and the Victoria League, by metropolitan politicians and colonial officials. They survived almost unchanged into the post-war period. Only then did they begin to dissolve, in parallel with the dissolution of the Empire for which they had provided such necessary and such powerful support.

The demise of 'imperial union'

The Round Table was founded, as an early fund-raising document put it, with the 'one and only purpose' of orchestrating a movement 'to bring about the closer union of the British Empire'.[12] By 'closer union', most, but not all, of the founders meant 'imperial federation' – a constitutional reconstruction of the Empire to produce a single parliament representative of the self-governing parts of the Empire as well of Britain, with control of foreign, imperial and defence policies. There were two main reasons why most Round Table members thought imperial federation a necessity. The first was that they believed 'that the principle of co-operation was insufficient as a means of holding together the Empire'.[13] The Dominions would eventually wish to have full control of their own affairs. They could do this in one of only two ways: through federation, or as 'independent republics'.[14] The second reason was 'that, if this country is to maintain herself in the years to come in the same rank with the US, Russia and Germany, the unit must be enlarged from the UK to the Empire'.[15] In other words, the Round Table was founded on a lively appreciation first of the inevitability of increasing self-government in at least the white settler colonies of the Empire (and, though only for some members of the group in 1910, in India and other parts of the Empire as well), and secondly of the acute vulnerability of British 'world' power.

The Round Table attracted considerable support in its early years, but also a good deal of opposition. Interestingly, the latter came not so much from the few advocates of outright independence for the self-governing Dominions as from defenders of the status quo, who believed that the Empire could happily survive by means of its existing policies and structures. The outbreak of the First World War curtailed the Round Table's activities, while demonstrating the effectiveness of imperial co-operation. After the war, the Round Table agreed that federation was not 'practical politics': even Curtis, its most ardent advocate, conceded that imperial federation would take 'the next few generations'.[16] Nevertheless, a majority agreed that *in the long run* co-operation would prove unworkable, and that the self-governing parts of the Empire faced a choice between federation and 'national independence in a world in which the British Empire has ceased to exist'.[17] The *Round Table* reiterated the group's commitment to imperial federation in 1935, and subsequently did so with greater stridency as global conflict once again loomed.

In 1942 Sir Patrick Duncan, Governor-General of South Africa and a founding member of the South African Round Table group, wrote gloomily that, even if the Allies won the Second World War, 'the British Empire will be gone beyond recovery'.[18] Such outright pessimism was rare. Nevertheless, there was a general recognition within the Round Table that the Second World War fundamentally changed the context within which the Empire would operate. Curtis continued to preach the federal gospel, but with the significant difference that only a union of the whole 'free world' (Western Europe as well as the British Empire/Commonwealth, and eventually the United States as well) could hope to prevent another world war. Countries such as Poland and Czechoslovakia 'should be invited to consider … the status of a British Dominion as it was before 1914'.[19] This proposal filled Horsfall with horror. 'What if the Dominions rejected the idea and the others jumped at it? We should find ourselves overnight a continental power and little else.'[20] For Brand, the most striking fact of the situation was that 'we are dependent on the United States'.[21] Canada, Australia and New Zealand would rely after the war far more on the US than on Britain for their defence, and 'I more than doubt if without the U.S., Canada, Australia, South Africa and New Zealand can be allied with the U.K. in an organic union'.[22] With the approach of peace the arguments within the Round Table became difficult to contain. In the absence of some of his fiercest critics, Curtis seized the opportunity to press through a re-statement of the Round Table's aims, with the result that in November 1945 the *Round Table* declared that 'the ultimate ideal remains the union of nations in an organic Commonwealth'.[23]

This was a remarkable affirmation of the Round Table's faith in its founding aims. As so often, hubris was swiftly followed by nemesis. The 'Dominion' groups reacted with bewilderment. The Toronto group was unable to produce a collective response, but when its secretary put the case for federalism at a meeting, 'the only person who gave me much support was the one member of the gathering who was tight'.[24] Within the London group itself, Curtis's critics increasingly chafed at the view put forward in the 1945 memorandum. Matters came to a head in 1947 when Altrincham threatened to resign. For him, federal union, which before he had seen as merely impracticable, was now 'wrong and very dangerous', given the profoundly altered context of international relations.[25] After an acrimonious debate the majority decided in October 1947 'that in future the statement should not be made that the Round Table was committed to the policy of organic union'.[26] The Round Table also decided, unprecedentedly, to open the pages of the journal to a debate, with articles still anonymous but explicitly disowned by the Round Table group as a whole. Interestingly, the debate petered out with contributions by David Maxwell-Fyfe and Max Beloff for and against closer integration with Western Europe.[27]

The abandonment of its belief in the possibility of an 'organic union' of the Empire was in many respects a traumatic event for the Round Table. Not only did it entail the loss of what had in effect been its guiding idea since 1910, it also reflected something far more fundamental, a loss of faith in the capacity of the Empire/Commonwealth to continue to act as a single 'unit' in international affairs. This was confirmed by the Round Table's reaction to subsequent developments in the late 1940s and early 1950s: the group accepted, not just with equanimity but with relief, the creation of the North Atlantic Treaty Organization (NATO) and the ANZUS pact between Australia, New Zealand and the US, even though they marked the end of the illusion that Britain and its Empire could form a power bloc on their own. Thus in 1950 the *Round Table* noted that 'no special apparatus for achieving a united Commonwealth policy either existed or was demanded by member governments'.[28]

The question naturally arises, whether the Round Table's crisis of the late 1940s reflected a more widespread loss of faith among imperialist lobbies and pressure groups, and among the British 'establishment' more generally. The Round Table's belief that some form of constitutional reconstruction was needed in order to ensure the continuation of the Empire was relatively unique. Its emphasis on Empire/Commonwealth 'unity' in foreign policy and its belief that the Empire/Commonwealth could serve to bolster Britain's role as a 'world' power were not. Nevertheless the reader of *United Empire* (the journal of the Royal Empire Society) would be hard pressed to find evidence of a belief that the international context within which the Empire operated had profoundly changed, just as the reader of contemporary Foreign Office minutes or of Ernest Bevin's speeches would be hard pressed to find evidence of a belief that Britain was no longer a 'world' power. The Round Table's early recognition of this sea-change was perhaps one reason why it adapted relatively easily to subsequent developments. Nevertheless the Round Table was slow in following through the wider ramifications of this change.

Decolonisation

While the Round Table recognised that the Empire as a whole was now unlikely to substitute itself for Britain as a 'world' power, it was by no means clear that the imperial game was up. Brand – one of the most realistic of Round Table members in assessing the consequences for the Empire of the new international dispensation – wrote in 1949 that 'we have got to have much better management than we now have of our public affairs, and a good deal of luck, to hold our place in the world'.[29] But it is clear that he thought that Britain *could* still hold its 'place in the world'.

In this respect, that other great event of the late 1940s, the independence of the Indian subcontinent, had less effect than either hindsight or the previous importance of India in the imperial system would suggest. Members of the Round Table had long realised that India would eventually have to be given self-government comparable to that enjoyed by the white Dominions. Before the war Hodson noted that 'in the long run, undoubtedly, the better course is to give India full self-government, since to prevent her from securing it might be [a] serious additional defence burden'.[30] Observing from close quarters the failure of the Cripps mission in 1942, Coupland could not see 'why Winston [Churchill] and Amery worry overmuch' about the Congress demand for a quasi-cabinet: 'We are going to abdicate in a few years … What does it matter if the Indian leaders are in virtual control of domestic government?'[31] When it did eventually come, in 1947, Indian independence affected some former imperialists profoundly. Enoch Powell (who entered politics with hopes of becoming Viceroy) spent 'the whole of one night walking the streets of London'; 'occasionally I sat down in a doorway, my head in my hands'.[32] That Powell's sense of loss was more widely shared is evidenced by the sustained applause which greeted the delegate to the 1947 Conservative Party conference who expressed anger that the 'finest jewel in the British Crown' had been 'cast like pearls before swine'.[33] Members of the Round Table reacted very differently. The *Round Table* hailed Indian independence as the 'logical' outcome of British rule.[34] Far as it was from reflecting the reality of British rule in India, this formulation was nevertheless consistent with Round Table views as they had evolved over the previous thirty or forty years.

Was Indian independence unique – or did it open the floodgates to decolonisation throughout the British Empire? Certainly, there were respects in which India was seen as setting precedents for the rest of the Empire. Hailey – one of the most influential voices in colonial policy – was clearly drawing on his own Indian experience when he declared that 'to judge at what stage ... a colonial power is to consider it justifiable to hand over authority' there was 'no other way than to apply the purely pragmatic test that when people really want it they will be able to show it so strongly that it is better to give it to them'.[35] Nevertheless he and other Round Table members had long been accustomed to think of the British Empire as a sort of hierarchy; or, as Hailey put it, a 'procession', with 'great distances separat[ing] the van from the rear'.[36] In the late 1940s, it was inconceivable that the example of India would be followed by other colonial territories as swiftly as it was.

Writing in the *Round Table* as late as 1961, Lord Howick (Sir Evelyn Baring) declared that the British Government's aim should not be to gain 'a perhaps transitory popularity with the more impatient and vocal ... Nationalists', but to give 'as good a chance as ... possible ... to a new and independent government to succeed'.[37] Round Table members and writers in the journal adduced numerous conditions which would have to be met before the British Government could satisfy itself that this was the case. One of the major differences between India and other parts of the colonial Empire (with the partial exception of Malaya and the Gold Coast) was that its administrative and political structures had been undergoing a process of 'indigenisation' long before independence was talked of as a realistic possibility. Round Table members assumed that a similar, protracted process would be necessary elsewhere. Moreover, the example of India provided reason to delay further the transfer of power elsewhere: the ethnic and religious violence accompanying the partition of India had to be avoided at all costs. Thus Elspeth Huxley asserted that 'fitness for self-government presupposes a political unit which is, so to speak, self-governable'; the 'cartographer-countries' of Africa would have to be re-designed before they could possibly be made into 'viable political units'.[38] The *Round Table* argued that in some cases – notably the Caribbean, east Africa, and central Africa – some form of regional amalgamation or federation would be necessary before independence could be considered a realistic possibility. In east and central Africa a further brake was imposed by the presence of significant numbers of white settlers; there the Round Table came only slowly to realise that self-government necessarily meant majority rule. Finally, the British Government's new-found concern for the economic development of colonial territories – a concern which Hailey in particular did much to foster – was another factor suggesting that the process of decolonisation would have to be a slow one. As Hailey argued, 'political advance will be an illusion, and may be a danger, unless it rests on a firmer foundation of economic and social achievement'.[39]

Throughout the 1950s those directing and associated with the *Round Table* journal believed that decolonisation would be a protracted process. They consequently found themselves repeatedly wrong-footed by government policy. In 1953 the *Round Table* asserted that Malaya could not be independent for 'at least a generation'.[40] It became independent in 1957. Similar examples abound. It was only in the 1960s, following the spurt of rapid decolonisation initiated by Iain Macleod and signalled by Macmillan's 'wind of change' speech, that the Round Table came to a more realistic assessment of the prospects for the continuation of Britain's colonial Empire. Then, the transformation was so swift and so complete that, as Hailey remarked, it left those who had devoted so much of their lives to the Empire feeling distinctly 'prehistoric'.[41]

The Round Table's experience was shared by other establishment-minded empire groups. The pages of *United Empire* are full of reports of former or serving colonial officials applauding steady progress in their particular colonies, while insisting that they were still far from ready for full independence; and of pious assertions only *ex post facto* that Britain had in fact made them ready. Nevertheless, it is difficult to see how this could have been otherwise. Successive governments made similar assertions, and wrong-footed *themselves* by the speed of their policy changes.

Attempts to halt or reverse the process of decolonisation were the preserve of 'fringe' groups such as the League of Empire Loyalists, which – after giving the Government a minor fright at the 1957 Lewisham North by-election – quickly found its natural home as one of the founding groups of the extremist National Front.[42] That bodies such as the Round Table and the Royal Commonwealth Society were not tempted to follow the same path had, of course, much to do with a pragmatic realisation of the military, political and economic costs of doing so. But another key factor was the availability of an existing ideological framework, which allowed these groups to portray decolonisation as the culmination and fulfilment of British rule – despite the illogicality of the argument, and the fact that 'fitness' for self-government was only ever discovered after the event. Nevertheless, the process of adaptation was contentious. The dissolution of the Empire and its replacement by a Commonwealth of equals entailed the challenging and questioning of fundamental assumptions about 'Britishness' and Britain's place in the world.

Commonwealths old and new

The Round Table could claim – and has often been given – credit, if not for inventing, then certainly for popularising the term 'Commonwealth'.[43] As early as 1919, the subtitle 'A Quarterly Review of the Politics of the British

Commonwealth' was substituted for 'of the British Empire'. In part, this reflected the Round Table's preoccupation with the white, self-governing 'Dominions': it was only in the 1930s that the journal published its first articles on either West Africa or the Caribbean, and throughout the 1940s and 1950s the former Dominions received a disproportionate amount of coverage in the journal. Nevertheless, the Round Table used the term 'Commonwealth' to describe the whole of the Empire, and not just the self-governing parts (as was the common usage). For the Round Table's founders, the term 'Commonwealth' implied a community of peoples moving at different stages and different speeds towards self-government, while remaining a single 'unit' in international affairs.[44]

The Round Table's commitment to imperial *union* dissolved rapidly in the 1940s, as a result primarily of the changes in the international system wrought by the Second World War and the onset of the Cold War. Hopes for intimate Commonwealth consultation and co-operation in foreign policy lingered longer, and dissolved more slowly. In 1947 Brand – while opposing formal machinery – still believed that it was 'urgently necessary to attempt to bring the Dominions to act more closely with us'.[45] The Commonwealth prime ministers' meetings of the early 1950s were watched anxiously for signs of agreement on the major foreign policy issues. The notion of Commonwealth consultation and co-operation in foreign policy was eroded, however, by India's policy of non-alignment, subsequently adopted by other newly independent Commonwealth states. It was dealt a fatal blow by the Suez crisis of 1956, when the reality of disparate actions and interests finally appears to have sunk in. Then, as the *Round Table* noted, the 'senior' member of the Commonwealth acted 'outside previously declared policies, in a way that intimately concerned [other Commonwealth members'] interests, and might have provoked war'; there could not be a clearer example of a Commonwealth member 'unwilling to fulfil the responsibilities of "belonging together"'.[46] Before Suez, the journal spoke of Commonwealth governments 'modifying [their] own several views'; after, it spoke only of governments 'know[ing] one another's minds'.[47]

In other respects, too, the Round Table adjusted only slowly to the realities of the new Commonwealth. India's adoption of a republican constitution in 1948 struck at the heart of the old Commonwealth relationship, since a shared monarchy was the only constitutional bond uniting the Empire/Commonwealth after 1932. Some members of the group preferred 'consolidating our system in its present form' to 'exploring the *terra incognita* of a Crownless Commonwealth'.[48] Others acknowledged that 'the existing recognised symbolism may ... actually work against the cohesion of the Commonwealth'.[49] The group as a whole adopted the latter view. Nevertheless the Round Table was slow to abandon the idea that the monarchy could be used to help hold the Commonwealth together. In 1951 Altrincham, Morrah and others were involved in an attempt to engineer the appointment of Princess Elizabeth as Governor-General of Canada, Altrincham stressing 'the crucial importance of using the power of the monarchy to the utmost in Canada during the next three or four years'.[50] Following her succession to the throne, the Round Table published a series of articles arguing for a Commonwealth role in her coronation, an increased Commonwealth representation in her staff, and even a peripatetic monarchy with residences in each of the monarchical countries within the Commonwealth.[51] De-coupling the monarchy and the Commonwealth was, for the Round Table as for the Commonwealth at large, a slow process.

Despite some unevenness in realising the implications of the changes that had taken place, by the late 1950s there was an almost tangible sense in the Round Table that the cohesion of the Commonwealth was slipping away. 'Is there anything which the Commonwealth does that cannot as well be done without it? ... Has it still a meaning and is it still worthwhile?'[52] The approach of the Round Table's golden jubilee in September 1960 was an opportunity to provide answers to these questions. Significantly, the Round Table abandoned the attempt to formulate 'a common policy to which all members of the Round Table groups [i.e. those overseas as well as in London] might be expected to subscribe',[53] and published instead a series of 'views' of the Commonwealth from each of the groups. The London group's was in effect an obituary for imperial 'union':

> Today ... the Commonwealth has quite ceased to be a unit of power ... We still seek to preserve world peace by concentrations of unchallengeable force; but the Commonwealth is not one of them ... The dream of all imperialism, of which Alexander was the originator and organic union was the last expression, that somehow a larger patriotism ... might transcend national rivalries – that exalted vision has perished for our time.[54]

It is striking that, even at this late stage, the Round Table could refer to imperialism as an 'exalted vision'. Elsewhere, members of the group acknowledged that 'it will be some time before the vision of the old Imperialists will be widely respected'.[55] Nevertheless, what is most striking is the appreciation that the 'dream of imperialism' had 'perished'. Not only the original aim of the Round Table group, but the assumptions on which it had operated, had, within a short space of time, disappeared. The Commonwealth was not a unit of power. It was not even an international unit in any meaningful sense of the word. The 'larger patriotism' which imperialists believed underpinned and made possible their vision of the Empire had simply ceased to exist.

What, then, was left? In place of the 'exalted vision' of imperialists, the

Round Table offered a more modest vision of the Commonwealth as based first on 'shared' values and secondly on its role as a 'bridge' between countries in all parts of the world, at different stages of economic development, and with very different national interests and priorities. The Round Table's understanding of shared values was premised squarely on the belief that the legacy of British rule was a 'stock of possessions' which would continue 'to fortify the nations of the Commonwealth': the English language, common law, an independent judiciary, freedom of the press, a high standard of business ethics, and parliamentary government. Its understanding of 'the bridge concept' was a way of saying that the Commonwealth was now primarily a forum for the exchange of views, and not for formulating a common view. Nevertheless, the idea of the Commonwealth as a bridge had a political bite: 'the determining feature of the present Commonwealth and its principal point of contrast with the Commonwealth of the past, is its multi-racial character. It is important to look at this as a positive foundation for the development of the future Commonwealth, and not as a dilution of its more concentrated integrity when under white hegemony.'[56]

The Round Table's new justification for the Commonwealth was in some respects an extension of the ideas which it had put forward as part of its earlier apologia for empire. Nevertheless, in the absence of the latter's overriding framework – the Empire as a single unit, with a long imperial tutelage necessary before the 'dependent' colonies could become full partners – the justification was qualitatively different. Indeed, it had more in common with the ideas put forward by members of the Fabian Colonial Bureau – such as Rita Hinden, who in 1948 had described the Empire as 'a bridge across the gulf of colour, and an alternative to dividing the world on the basis of race'[57] – than with the ideas the Round Table had earlier made its own. Unsurprisingly, fringe groups such as the League of Empire Loyalists took very different views of the 'multi-racial' Commonwealth. The Royal Commonwealth Society, while eventually adopting a stance similar to the Round Table's, was slow in doing so. Even within the Round Table, it took some time for the new conception fully to take hold. In 1964 Hodson confessed that 'the new multi-racial Commonwealth ... when all is said and done, is not so inspiring a motive for patriotic sentiment'.[58]

The Commonwealth's – and the Round Table's – commitment both to shared liberal democratic values and to the multi-racialism implied by the bridge concept was tested most severely by the white settler societies of southern Africa. The rise of apartheid in South Africa caused enormous difficulties for the Round Table group. Some (particularly the older) members were inclined 'to argue for a more sympathetic understanding of the complicated situations [white South Africans] have to face'.[59] Others were more forthright in condemning apartheid. Hailey, on a visit to South

Africa, argued that 'the maintenance of White supremacy must inevitably involve a régime which makes it impossible to maintain civil liberties'; 'I do not find', he added, 'that this conclusion shocks the White population here ... as much as it should'.[60] South Africa's decision (following India's example) to adopt a republican constitution and then to seek continued membership of the Commonwealth at the March 1961 prime ministers' meeting crystallised opinions. The *Round Table* asserted that there was no place in the Commonwealth for a country which so blatantly disregarded the emerging core values of the association. 'If there is any doctrine which can be called fundamental to the Commonwealth idea it is that of racial equality': South Africa's departure was 'the removal of a cancer from the Commonwealth body politic'.[61] It was again only in the 1960s that the Round Table turned decisively against the white settler regime in (Southern) Rhodesia. In 1953 Altrincham reminded his readers that Rhodes would never have dreamt of 'surrendering [Rhodesia's] defence and guidance to its present-day black inhabitants'.[62] As late as 1960 Morrah praised the Central African Federation's 'middle way' of 'partnership' between the races.[63] Its break-up and the subsequent unilateral declaration of independence by the white Rhodesian regime in 1965 nevertheless produced a robust response from the *Round Table* (unmatched by the British Government). Britain should re-impose direct rule and introduce a new constitution, if necessary by 'overwhelming and decisive' force; otherwise the Commonwealth would break up, and it was 'difficult to imagine a more squalid end to so hopeful an experiment'.[64]

Britain's decision to apply for membership of the European Economic Community (EEC) in the early 1960s also forced a re-appraisal of the Commonwealth connection – though less in the Round Table than in the Commonwealth at large. The Round Table had never had much truck with the 'imperial preference' ideas of Joseph Chamberlain and his successors, and in a series of articles had demonstrated that the supposed benefits of the preferences introduced at Ottawa in 1932 were largely illusory. It is perhaps not surprising therefore that the Round Table was sanguine about the British application. More surprising was its acknowledgement that 'if we enter Europe we enter for good'; that 'we cannot be sure that the Europe we enter will remain immutably a confederation of sovereign states, and will never develop on organic lines'; and that 'we shall ... inevitably be relying on our European associates more and our Commonwealth associates less'.[65] Opinion in the overseas Round Table groups was more circumspect, although in each case the groups were significantly more favourable to the British application than their respective governments. Nevertheless, the sense that the application marked a turning-point, especially in the 'old Dominions', was almost palpable. As was reported from New Zealand, 'one must face the fact that the atmosphere with regard to the Commonwealth generally has changed considerably' as a result of the application.[66] In Britain, too, 'a good deal of harm was done ... by the juxtaposition of Commonwealth and Europe as simple alternatives'. The debate was dominated on the one side by those 'who ... saw in the Commonwealth an economic burden Britain had too long nobly borne for the benefit of others, a relic of British isolationism from the world (i.e. South-West-Central Europe), not only *passé* but *démodé* and *déclassé*'; and on the other not by advocates of the 'living Commonwealth but ... the imperial visions of Lord Beaverbrook'.[67] It is perhaps significant that while the Commonwealth was prominent in the literature of the Anti-Common Market League and other opponents of the British application, Commonwealth groups were (with the exception of interest groups such as the Commonwealth Industries Association) notable by their absence from the debate.

The Round Table sensed that the 1960s witnessed a sea-change in British attitudes to the Commonwealth.[68] Before then, criticism of the Commonwealth was relatively mute; in the 1960s the debate was flung wide open. Partly this was a result of the EEC application debate, which cast the Commonwealth in the role of an obstacle to a more realistic pursuit of British interests. Partly, also, it was the result of a belated appreciation of the transformation of the Commonwealth from a symbol and vehicle of white supremacism into a symbol and vehicle of multi-racialism. The increasing embarrassment of British governments in relation to southern Africa crystallised the misgivings of many of those who had previously been imperialists. Particularly influential was Enoch Powell's anonymous article in *The Times* of 2 April 1964, which described the Commonwealth as a 'gigantic farce'. The *Round Table* responded by publishing a series of articles setting forward a positive view of the Commonwealth. Nevertheless it was recognised that Powell articulated a common British view, 'that the Commonwealth was conjured up to save British self-esteem while the Empire dissolved and the country got used to being Little England'.[69] Part of the reason for this view, the *Round Table* believed, was that there was 'an important lag in the British appreciation of what has happened to the institution in the creation of which they have played the leading, but by no means the sole, part'. There was thus 'a sense in which Britain itself has never joined the Commonwealth'.[70] In other Commonwealth countries there had been a questioning of the terms of a continuing relationship. Britain was a member of the Commonwealth by default. For Britain even more than for other Commonwealth countries, there had never been a clean break between the old Commonwealth and the new. Moreover, successive British governments had continued to portray the Commonwealth as a vehicle for British influence – an extension of the Empire. That the new Commonwealth was a very different creature only slowly became apparent. When it did so, it came as a shock to the British psyche.

The cumulative effect of changes in the Commonwealth and in British attitudes towards it prompted the Round Table to embark in the mid-1960s on a far-reaching re-appraisal of its policies and aims. A new editor, Leonard Beaton, was appointed in 1965, and in 1966 the *Round Table* abandoned its longstanding tradition of anonymity, in order to enhance its ability 'to promote discussion and thought throughout the Commonwealth'.[71] Ironically, the abandonment of anonymity led to the rapid dissolution of the overseas Round Table groups, which lost the main reason for their existence. The 'new' *Round Table* (launched in the same year as the Commonwealth Secretariat, the symbol of the end of British-centredness) promised 'strong views on public issues' and to counteract 'the enemies of the Commonwealth [who] are the racists, the narrow regionalists and single-minded believers in sovereignty'. Nevertheless the *Round Table* was careful 'not [to] expect too much from the Commonwealth'.[72] As the editorial board put it in 1970, 'the problem has become one of preserving and enhancing the association which the Empire has made possible. This task is very different from developing the modalities of a political, military and economic order. Rather it involves the exploration and cultivation of relationships which are the more numerous and the more stable because of their very modesty.'[73]

The Round Table's attitudes towards the 'end of empire' and towards the transition from Empire to Commonwealth evolved by a series of fits and starts, or by a series of crises followed by slow adaptations. Two periods of rapid change stand out: the late 1940s, and the early 1960s. The first marked a significant transformation in Round Table attitudes towards the Empire/Commonwealth, which had previously been thought of as a potential 'world power'. No longer was it possible to think in terms of the 'union' of the Empire on a basis which would ensure its long-term viability. *Ipso facto*, no longer was it possible to think of the Empire as a thing of the future rather than of the past. This was in many respects a crucial turning-point, when the 'end of empire' impacted strongly on the Round Table's own aims and activities. Nevertheless, the Round Table's adaptation to these events was only partial, and imperial attitudes survived longer. It took the cumulative effects of events in the late 1950s and early 1960s – notably the acceleration of the pace of decolonisation, the crisis in southern Africa, and the cathartic effects of Britain's application to join the EEC – to induce a more profound alteration of attitudes, and a recognition that the days of empire had come to an end.

For the Round Table, the 'end of empire' was a traumatic experience. It involved the questioning and progressive dismantling of the most fundamental assumptions underlying it as a political project. Its transfer of loyalty from the Empire to the new Commonwealth was accomplished only slowly, and with some difficulty. Nevertheless, by the late 1960s it emerged with a reasonably coherent, positive and forward-looking commitment to the new Commonwealth, not as a replacement for empire but as an association *sui generis*. In some respects the Round Table adapted more successfully – or at least more quickly – than other Commonwealth lobbies. The Royal Commonwealth Society encountered financial difficulties, curtailed its research and publishing activities, and appeared to many visitors to have lapsed into a sort of post-imperial stupor. Lord Casey, a friendly critic, found in 1963 that 'many of its social and other activities – and of the addresses made under its auspices – represent nostalgic recollections of the glories of the past, not anxious constructive looking-forward into the future'.[74]

Part of the problem for the Round Table, for other Empire/Commonwealth groups, and for the British public at large, was the *expectation* of a seamless transition from Empire to Commonwealth. The process was expected to be gradual and firmly under British control; and post-imperial arrangements were expected to perpetuate many aspects of the old imperial relationship. Such expectations served the very useful purpose of smoothing the trauma of loss of 'world' power and of colonial rule. Nevertheless they allowed older assumptions concerning Britain's imperial enterprise to continue undisturbed long past the point at which they were relevant either to Britain's actual position in the world or to the actual nature of the Commonwealth. The Suez crisis, the spurt of rapid decolonisation from the late 1950s onwards, the crisis in southern Africa, and the debate over EEC membership induced the questioning of Britain's role which was long overdue. In each of these contexts, it became clear that the Commonwealth could no longer be primarily a vehicle for British interests or for its continuing greatness. For many in Britain, it appeared rather as a complicating, and in some respects a debilitating, factor. The result was widespread disillusionment, indifference and in some cases hostility towards the Commonwealth, which had so signally failed the expectations held of it. For the Round Table and other bodies which emerged from the end of empire committed to the new Commonwealth, it was a very different world from that in which they had been conceived.

Notes

1   Sir Evelyn Wrench, *Uphill* (London, Nicholson & Watson, 1934), p. 266.
2   Trevor R. Reese, *The History of the Royal Commonwealth Society, 1868–1968* (London, Oxford University Press, 1968), p. 15.
3   Much has been written on the early history of the Round Table. See, in particular, Walter Nimocks, *Milner's Young Men: The Kindergarten in Edwardian Imperial Affairs* (Durham, NC, Duke University Press, 1968); John Kendle, *The Round Table Movement and Imperial Union* (Toronto, Toronto University Press, 1975); H. V.

Hodson, 'The Round Table, 1910–1981', *Round Table*, 71:284 (October 1981), pp. 308–33; and Alex May, 'The Round Table, 1910–66', D.Phil. thesis, University of Oxford, 1995. Deborah Lavin's *From Empire to International Commonwealth* (Oxford, Clarendon Press, 1995) is an entertaining biography of its principal founder, Lionel Curtis. For an unremittingly hostile view, see Carroll Quigley, *The Anglo-American Establishment from Rhodes to Cliveden* (New York, Books in Focus, 1981).

4 Round Table office files (c/o Round Table editorial committee), 'Dormant', Sir Olaf Caroe to Krishna Menon, 15 December 1950.
5 Hodson, 'The Round Table', p. 332.
6 Lothian Papers, Scottish Record Office, Edinburgh, GD 40/17/252, fol. 629, L. Curtis to L. Hichens, G. Dawson, R. H. Brand and Lord Lothian, 6 August 1930.
7 Lionel Curtis, *Dyarchy* (Oxford, Clarendon Press, 1920), p. 74.
8 Curtis Papers, Bodleian Library, Oxford, 98, fol. 92, D. Morrah to L. Curtis, 16 January 1946.
9 Gerald Studdert-Kennedy, *Providence and the Raj* (New Delhi, Sage, 1998), p. 157.
10 Arnold Toynbee, *Acquaintances* (Oxford, Oxford University Press, 1967), p. 146.
11 Paul B. Rich, *Race and Empire in British Politics* (Cambridge, Cambridge University Press, 1986); A. P. Thornton, *The Imperial Idea and its Enemies* (London, Macmillan, 1959); Kathryn Tidrick, *Empire and the English Character* (London, I. B. Tauris, 1990).
12 Round Table Papers, Bodleian Library, Oxford, MS Eng hist c778, fols 195–208, 'Round Table Statement', 1913.
13 Lothian Papers, 11, fols 1–6, Minutes of Round Table Meeting, Plas Newydd, 4–6 September 1909.
14 Lionel Curtis, *The Problem of the Commonwealth* (London, Macmillan, 1916), preface.
15 Selborne Papers, Bodleian Library, Oxford, 73, fols 5–6, Lord Selborne to E. Prettyman, 9 September 1903.
16 Round Table Papers, c811, fols 10–11, L. Curtis to M. Wrong, 3 November 1920.
17 Lothian Papers, 17, fols 16–29, Circular to Dominion Groups, 22 December 1920.
18 Round Table Papers, c813, fol. 88, Sir Patrick Duncan to L. Curtis, 28 July 1942.
19 Round Table Papers, c784, fols 13–16, 'Personal View of Lionel Curtis on the Line to be Followed by the Round Table', 17 September 1940.
20 Round Table Papers, c784, fols 20–2, P. Horsfall, 'The Round Table', 26 September 1940.
21 Round Table Papers, c784, fols 18–19, R. H. Brand, 'Memorandum', circulated 3 October 1940.
22 Curtis Papers, 98, fols 57–62, R. H. Brand to L. Curtis, 13 August 1943.
23 Curtis Papers, 158, item 9, 'Memorandum on Round Table Aims and Policy', November 1945.
24 Round Table office files, Toronto group, H. W. Macdonnell to D. Morrah, 8 April 1948.
25 Round Table office files, minute book, Lord Altrincham to D. Morrah, 7 October 1947, stapled into minutes of 29 October 1947 meeting.
26 Round Table office files, minute book, Round Table minutes, 29 October 1947.
27 D. Maxwell-Fyfe, 'Next Steps for a "United Europe"', *Round Table*, 38:152 (September 1948), pp. 742–8; M. Beloff, 'Britain and European Federation', *Round Table*, 42:167 (June 1952), pp. 211–18. Previous articles were published from March 1948 onwards.
28 D. Morrah, 'The United Nations in Action', *Round Table*, 40:160 (September 1950), pp. 299–303.
29 Brand Papers, Bodleian Library, Oxford, box 17, Lord Brand to J. M. A. Ilott, 16 December 1949.
30 Brand Papers, box 153, H. V. Hodson, 'The Round Table', circulated 6 January 1939.
31 Coupland Papers, Rhodes House Library, Oxford, 5/2/69–99, R. Coupland, Indian Diary, 10 April 1942, p. 226.
32 Enoch Powell, *Reflections of a Statesman* (London, Bellew, 1991), p. 55; Peter Hennessy, *Never Again: Britain, 1945–51* (London, Jonathan Cape, 1992), p. 235.

33 David Goldsworthy, *Colonial Issues in British Politics* (Oxford, Clarendon Press, 1971), p. 180.
34 H. V. Hodson, 'Valediction to India', *Round Table*, 37:148 (September 1947), pp. 330–8.
35 Lord Hailey, 'Post-War Changes in Africa', *Journal of the Royal Society of Arts*, 103:4955 (8 July 1955), pp. 579–90.
36 Lord Hailey, 'The Future of the Colonies', *Round Table*, 33:129 (December 1942), p. 9.
37 Lord Howick, 'Transition in Kenya', *Round Table*, 51:203 (June 1961), pp. 272–7.
38 E. Huxley, 'African Independence and After', *Round Table*, 46:181 (December 1955), pp. 17–26.
39 Lord Hailey, *World Thought on the Colonial Question* (Johannesrand, Witwatersrand University Press, 1946), p. 8.
40 Sir Sydney Caine, 'Malaya After the Emergency', *Round Table*, 43:172 (September 1953), pp. 350–8.
41 Round Table Papers, c868, fol. 130, Lord Hailey to D. Morrah, 5 March 1964.
42 Neil Nugent and Roger King (eds), *The British Right* (Farnborough, Saxon House, 1977).
43 S. R. Mehrotra, 'On the Use of the Term "Commonwealth"', *Journal of Commonwealth Political Studies*, 2:1 (1963), pp. 1–16.
44 For the 'principle of the Commonwealth', see in particular Lavin, *Empire to International Commonwealth*.
45 Round Table Papers, c784, fol. 73, Lord Brand to D. Morrah, 20 December 1947.
46 H. V. Hodson, 'The Commonwealth and the Crisis', *Round Table*, 47:186 (March 1957), pp. 114–20.
47 H. V. Hodson, 'The Future of the Commonwealth', *Round Table*, 46:183 (June 1956), p. 220; D. Morrah, 'The Commonwealth, A United Kingdom View', *Round Table*, 50:200 (September 1960), p. 338.
48 Lord Altrincham, 'Episodes of the Month', *National Review*, 132 (January 1949), pp. 3–7.
49 H. V. Hodson, 'The British Subject', *Round Table*, 38:151 (June 1948), p. 656.
50 Round Table office files, Rhodesias file, Lord Altrincham to D. Morrah, 28 July 1951.
51 D. Morrah, 'The Coronation and the Commonwealth', *Round Table*, 42:168 (September 1952), pp. 297–304; 43:169 (December 1952), pp. 3–8; and 43:172 (September 1953), pp. 306–15.
52 Hodson, 'The Future of the Commonwealth', pp. 218–19.
53 Round Table office files, minute book, Round Table minutes, 4 March 1959.
54 Morrah, 'The Commonwealth, A United Kingdom View', pp. 333–4.
55 Round Table office files, Editor's file, L. Beaton, Report on Round Table Trip, May and June 1965.
56 Morrah, 'The Commonwealth, A United Kingdom View', pp. 339–40 and 336.
57 Rita Hinden, *Empire and After* (London, Essential Books, 1949), preface.
58 Round Table office files, New Zealand group, H. V. Hodson to D. Morrah, 6 April 1964.
59 Round Table office files, South Africa file, D. Morrah to H. Kidd, 29 April 1960.
60 Round Table office files, South Africa file, Lord Hailey to H. V. Hodson, 13 October 1959.
61 'A Commonwealth Year', *Round Table*, 52:206 (March 1962), p. 170.
62 Lord Altrincham, 'Rhodes and Rhodesia', *Round Table*, 43:170 (March 1953), pp. 103–17.
63 D. Morrah, 'A Republic of South Africa', *Round Table*, 51:201 (December 1960), pp. 3–6.
64 L. Beaton, 'A Policy for Rhodesia', *Round Table*, 56:222 (March 1966), pp. 107–11; Denis Austin, 'Why Not Surrender to Mr. Smith?', *Round Table*, 56:223 (July 1966), pp. 238–44.
65 D. Morrah, 'Britain in Europe', *Round Table*, 52:208 (September 1962), pp. 323–26.
66 Round Table office files, New Zealand group, J. M. A. Ilott to D. Morrah, 6 April 1964.

67 J. Holmes, 'Can the Commonwealth Survive?', *Round Table*, 54:213 (December 1963), pp. 13–14.
68 S. C. Leslie, 'British Attitudes to the Commonwealth', *Round Table*, 63:251 (July 1973), pp. 363–75.
69 T. Raison, 'Is the Commonwealth a Farce?', *Round Table*, 54:215 (June 1964), p. 216.
70 Holmes, 'Can the Commonwealth Survive?', pp. 15–16.
71 Round Table office files, 'Moot' file, 'Draft Statement of Aims', 3 March 1965.
72 T. Raison, 'The New Round Table', *Round Table*, 56:223 (July 1966), p. 214.
73 Editorial, 'Empire to Commonwealth and Beyond', *Round Table*, 60:240 (November 1970), p. 380.
74 Lord Casey, *The Future of the Commonwealth* (London, Frederick Muller, 1963), p. 38.

CHAPTER THREE

Coronation Everest: the Empire and Commonwealth in the 'second Elizabethan age'

Peter H. Hansen

On 2 June 1953, the coronation day of Queen Elizabeth II, *The Times* reported that a British expedition had reached the summit of Mount Everest. British newspapers hailed the 'conquest' of Everest as a 'Coronation gift for the Queen', the 'crowning glory', and 'a brilliant jewel in the Queen's diadem'. The ascent of Everest opened the 'new Elizabethan age' by demonstrating that 'the qualities displayed by Drake and Raleigh are triumphantly present in the Britain of today'.[1] BBC radio announced the ascent with great pride 'because British mountaineers have finished the job they began 32 years ago'. The announcer intoned that 'another "far horizon" has been achieved' and 'the conquest of Mount Everest by British climbers is a victory worthy to resound through history, for long centuries to come'.[2] To the men and women waiting in rain and sleet and hail for the coronation parade, news of the ascent of Everest gave 'a lovely warm feeling inside to think that we, the British, had got there first'.[3]

The coronation parade included the Queen's glittering carriage surrounded by a phalanx of horse guards, as well as sultans, prime ministers, heads of state, and military troops from throughout the Empire and Commonwealth. That evening, Prime Minister Winston Churchill introduced the Queen's coronation day speech on radio and television: 'Let it not be thought that the age of Chivalry belongs in the past. Here at the summit of our worldwide community is a lady', the Queen. The Queen's own remarks drew strength 'not only from the splendid traditions and annals of more than a thousand years, but the living strength and majesty of the Commonwealth and Empire'. These diverse societies, lands and 'races' possessed different histories but were 'by God's will united in spirit and in aim'. Thus, 'my Coronation is not the symbol of a power and a splendour that are gone but a declaration of our hopes for the future'. BBC television concluded its most successful broadcast day ever with newsreels, the Queen waving from the balcony at the Palace, a Mount Everest talk, and fireworks on the Thames.[4]

To a casual observer, the simultaneous celebration of the coronation and conquest of Everest might appear to be a coincidence. British climbers had tried to climb Everest since the 1920s, and plans for this attempt had begun before the Queen ascended to the throne in 1952. The British expedition that placed Edmund Hillary, a New Zealand beekeeper, and Tenzing Norgay, a Sherpa, on the summit of Everest on 29 May 1953 had been on the mountain for several months and was dependent on the vicissitudes of the weather. After Hillary and Tenzing returned from the summit, James Morris, *Times* correspondent with the team, rushed down the mountain to send a coded message by runner and telegraph to the British Embassy at Kathmandu, where it was decrypted and forwarded to London on 1 June. *The Times*, the Foreign Office and Buckingham Palace then held the news overnight, irrevocably linking the coronation and Everest in British memories of both events.[5] Morris succinctly captured the mutually reinforcing relationship of the two events in the title of his book about the ascent – *Coronation Everest*.[6]

If the coincidence of conquest and coronation required some luck, hard work and savvy public relations, the imperial rhetoric surrounding these events in Britain stemmed from deeper historical roots and wider contemporary contexts. British mountaineers in the Alps and Himalayas had described their climbing as a form of imperial conquest, exploration and adventure since the mid-nineteenth century.[7] Historians have identified two predominant visions of empire, the 'peace' empire of improvement and development and the 'heroic' empire of military conquest and manly character.[8] By the mid-twentieth century, British representations of mountaineering were compatible with both visions of empire, and the British reaction to the ascent of Everest included images of imperial conquest alongside those of international partnership. Indeed, the partnership of Hillary and Tenzing on Everest was represented in Britain in terms that oscillated between these two positions at the moment Britain was attempting to redefine the 'British Empire' as a 'Commonwealth of Nations'.

This chapter examines the representations of the Empire and Commonwealth in the conquest of Everest in British culture in the 1950s. The imperial connotations of the ascent of Everest were shaped in the interwar years, but altered by the Second World War and the independence of India. Although British mountaineers were initially unprepared for these changes, they benefited from new state support and recent scientific research as well as the expansive definition of 'Britishness' and the Commonwealth. After the ascent, British reactions to Everest took into account competing reactions in other parts of the world and shifted uncertainly between nationalist and internationalist interpretations.[9] The persistence and adaptation of the imperial theme in the conquest of Everest calls into question the assertion that the Empire had a 'minimal impact' on British culture in this period. In Britain, the conquest of Everest was widely seen as evidence that British prestige was undiminished, and that British leadership would enable her former colonies to become the multi-racial Commonwealth of Nations that the Queen hoped for on coronation day.

Mount Everest had possessed imperial connotations since the mid-nineteenth century, when the Survey of India identified the remote peak as the highest mountain in the world and named it after Sir George Everest, a former Surveyor-General of India. From the 1890s onwards, British mountaineers proposed the ascent of Mount Everest, often with the encouragement of Lord Curzon, the Viceroy of India, who believed the ascent would maintain British prestige on the boundaries of India. Nevertheless, proposals to climb Everest before the First World War foundered on the opposition of British diplomats who considered any plans to climb Everest in conflict with the geo-political strategy to exclude all outside interference from Nepal or Tibet.[10]

The aftermath of the Great War altered the earlier priorities of the Great Game, and continued British domination of India led to permission to climb Everest. In the early 1920s, British diplomats aided the Tibetans in a war against China by trading weapons with Tibet in exchange for permission to climb Everest. Nepal remained closed to foreigners. After a reconnaissance of Everest from Tibet in 1921, the British tried to climb the peak in 1922 and 1924, when George Mallory and Andrew Irvine disappeared high on the mountain. The deaths of Mallory and Irvine gave the British the sense that Everest was *their* mountain. In 1930, Frank Smythe told the British envoy in Kathmandu: 'What British mountaineers feel is that Everest has got to be climbed by a British party. British lives have been sacrificed there.' If British diplomats could squash German proposals to climb Everest, 'it would be regarded very favourably throughout the British Empire'.[11]

British mountaineers between the wars need not have worried about access. As long as the British ruled India, there was no chance that climbers from anywhere else would be granted permission. After Sir Percy Cox pleaded that Everest was 'a national ambition', the India Office stated publicly that the issue was up to the Tibetans, but decided privately that British climbers would be given preference: 'We should do nothing to facilitate the transmission of a foreign application until the time is propitious for making a British application'.[12] As a result, national expeditions tackled separate peaks, with the British on Everest, the Germans on Nanga Parbat, the Americans on K2, and so on. As the British repeatedly failed to climb Everest in the 1930s and several large German expeditions to Nanga Parbat ended in tragedy, some climbers entertained doubts about the large, military-style expeditions and experimented with smaller-scale efforts.[13] The outbreak of the Second World War postponed any further climbing plans, but British mountaineers expected that the earlier pattern would resume after the peace.

The end of empire and beginning of the Cold War in the early post-war period dramatically altered control over access to Everest. After Indian independence in 1947, Nepal began to open its borders to mountaineering parties. The Chinese invasion of Tibet in 1950 also closed the old route to Everest from the north. Independent India had replaced Britain as the dominant regional power, and thus when climbers wanted to ask Nepal for permission to climb Everest from the south, it was New Delhi (rather than London) that they sounded out before asking Kathmandu.[14] After the British received permission for an Everest expedition through Nepal in 1951, they continued to assume that they had the field to themselves: their plans for 1951 extended no further than a leisurely 'reconnaissance' led by Eric Shipton, a former tea planter in Kenya. The British presumed that they could mount a more serious attempt on the summit in later years, as they had done between the wars.

But the older imperial deference was gone. The Nepalese did not distinguish between a 'reconnaissance' and a 'real' attempt to climb the mountain, and in 1952 they granted access to Everest to the Swiss delegation in Delhi. After the British hastily made their own request for 1952, the Nepali Government asked if the two proposals could be combined for a joint Anglo-Swiss attempt. The Everest organisers in London still wanted an 'all-British' expedition, however, and were only prepared to consider a joint-expedition if Eric Shipton were the leader. The Swiss proposed joint-leadership of a joint-expedition but refused to accept sole British command. Although Shipton himself was amenable to joint-leadership, the British organising committee refused. The British Foreign Office, which had actively encouraged a joint-expedition, was very disappointed at their recalcitrance, which exhibited the assumptions of the earlier era of imperial dominance.[15]

In 1952, the Swiss twice tried to climb Everest, while the British settled for a training expedition led by Shipton to Cho Oyu, a peak in the same region. The Swiss team identified the best route to the summit of Everest and two climbers, Tenzing and Raymond Lambert, a Swiss guide, reached the highest elevation ever. In contrast, the British Cho Oyu team was unfocused and ineffectual, as Shipton preferred to explore new territory rather than organise a unified attempt to reach the summit. After receiving permission for an Everest expedition in 1953, the British organising committee chose to replace Shipton as leader with Col. John Hunt, a military officer, because of its 'responsibility to the nation and Commonwealth' in a matter of 'national importance'.[16] Hunt had limited climbing experience in the Himalayas but a reputation as a 'thruster' and good organiser.

Hunt's arrival is sometimes interpreted as the reassertion of an earlier imperial model. Shipton disliked the atmosphere of international competition, while Hunt was a serving military officer who recognised the urgency of the situation. Hunt put his background as a member of Field Marshall Montgomery's wartime planning staff to good use, and developed a systematic plan for co-ordinating the logistics of the summit 'assault'. Most Everest expeditions between the wars had been led by military officers, and one of the organisers told Col. Hunt that in choosing him they were looking for 'another General Bruce', the officer who spearheaded Everest plans from the 1890s to the 1920s.[17] Yet by the 1950s, the implications of a military leader could now be uncomfortable. The Royal Geographical Society (RGS) strongly advised British diplomats in Nepal and India to downplay Hunt's status as a serving military officer as the expedition approached.[18]

Indeed, there is evidence that the 1953 Everest expedition was 'a company of sahibs attended by their multitudinous servants', and, as Jan Morris aptly puts it, 'recognizably a formation of Empire'.[19] But the sahibs had to adjust to changes among the servants. The effect of the Swiss giving the Sherpas higher pay and more respect than previous British parties was, one British climber in India warned, 'rather similar to the effect of the Americans on the servant problem here during the war'.[20] As the expedition began, the British did not appreciate the Sherpas' greater expectations. In Kathmandu, the British climbers were lodged in rooms at the British Embassy, while the Sherpas were allocated a 'garage, formerly a stable' without any toilets. The next morning, some of the Sherpas 'showed their displeasure by using the road in front of the garage as a latrine'.[21] The rift was soon bridged by Tenzing, the leader of the Sherpas, and Major Charles Wylie, a Gurkha officer who spoke Himalayan languages. After the Sherpas were promised that they could keep their equipment, the rest of the expedition experienced remarkably little dissension between the Sherpas and the British.[22]

Hunt's military efficiency and meticulous planning were undoubtedly crucial, and the imperial style of the expedition was also clearly recognisable. However, these features have obscured the extent to which the British success on Everest was aided by recent developments of the early 1950s. The contribution of the British state to the ascent, for example, has been vastly underestimated. The public purse paid the salaries of most British team-members, including two army officers, two doctors, two scientists and a statistician. Of the other British climbers, a schoolmaster and travel agent were privately employed. Only a student and two New Zealanders scraped by without institutional support. Col. Hunt convinced the War Office to provide rations at cost, free transport to the Himalayas, as well as 'loans' of clothing, equipment and supplies that later became gifts.[23] Previous Everest expeditions had received only very limited support of a similar nature from the Government of British India, funded by Indian taxpayers. In contrast, the 1953 Everest expedition received so much official assistance that it should be considered a change from the earlier pattern of benign British neglect, and perhaps a transferral of responsibility from the imperial to the home government.

The Second World War had also provided a significant impetus for British research into high-altitude physiology and oxygen equipment for aircraft pilots. The adaptation of wartime research in these areas for use on Everest are 'small' examples of the influence of 'big science' in the early years of the Cold War.[24] The Medical Research Council's Human Physiology Division, founded after the outbreak of the Korean War, sent Griffith Pugh to do physiological research on the Cho Oyu expedition in 1952. Pugh joined the Everest team in 1953 and recommended changes in diet, hygiene, and the use of oxygen that contributed substantially to the successful ascent.[25] The Royal Aircraft Establishment tested most of the Everest equipment at Farnborough, and one of their rocket scientists, Tom Bourdillon, used an oxygen set on Everest that he had developed in his job.[26] *The Conquest of Everest* film paid tribute to these research efforts in scenes showing the testing of tents, boots, and oxygen equipment, and a climber losing consciousness in a pressure-chamber to simulate the effects of high altitude.

As the film soundtrack reaches a crescendo, the Everest preparations culminate in the packing of small British flags with the assault rations. Along with the nationalism of the Union Jack, Col. Hunt wrapped himself in the flag of the United Nations (UN), symbol of a new internationalism. Hunt brought the UN flag to recognise the efforts of the Swiss the previous year.[27] When Tenzing reached the summit of Everest, he waved from his ice-axe four flags representing Nepal, India, Britain and the United Nations. Indeed, these flags reflected the cosmopolitanism of this 'all-British' team. While the team included men from the British military, public schools and universities, Hunt expanded his talent search to include a Blackpool travel agent, two New Zealanders, and Sherpa Tenzing. The New Zealanders had been on Shipton's training expedition to Cho Oyu, and Tenzing was making his seventh Everest expedition. If Hunt had wanted to make the expedition narrowly 'all-British', he could have done so.[28] That Hunt chose Hillary and Tenzing for the summit party reflects not only a recognition of their abilities but also an inclusive definition of 'Britishness' consistent with the expansive definition of the Commonwealth articulated at the time of the coronation.

To summarise, the British expedition reached the summit of Everest as a result of three new factors in the early 1950s: military planning, scientific research sponsored by the British state, and an internationalism based on an expansive definition of 'Britishness'. The military planning and scientific research complemented one another. The application of Hunt's military planning and Pugh's research on physiology and oxygen to the problem of climbing Everest were both peace dividends – deferred compensation for investments by the British state in fighting the Second World War and the Korean War. The British expedition provided Hillary and Tenzing with the supplies of oxygen, food and fluid at their highest camp in 1953 that the Swiss expedition had notably failed to provide for Lambert and Tenzing in 1952. The climbers' abilities each year were comparable (even identical in Tenzing's case); yet the logistics and lessons learned about high-altitude physiology resulted in significant improvements in 1953. Equally important, the inclusive definition of 'Britishness' contributed to their success. The co-operation of the Sherpa porters was not a foregone conclusion. The Swiss had treated the Sherpas much better than previous British teams, and even the 1953 expedition got off to a rocky start in Kathmandu. If the expedition's *modus operandi* on the mountain outwardly resembled the pattern of sahibs with their servants, their successful co-operation also reflected the adjustment of earlier imperial assumptions to new post-war and post-colonial conditions.

To commemorate the event, Leslie Haworth wrote a ballad on the 'The Ascent of Mount Everest'. The British folk singer began by entreating 'all you loyal subjects of Queen Elizabeth' to listen to the daring deed of 'thy heroes of her Commonwealth and of one friendly state'. The lilting rhythms of the song ended with the bestowing of British honours on the climbers:

> It was upon the morning that our Queen was to be crowned,
> When through her wide dominions these tidings did resound.
> She called to her Sir Winston says this day is well begun,
> What honour should we give these men because of what they have done?
> Let Hillary and Hunt be Knights and Tenzing be G.M.
> That is the very least that we can do for such as them.
> For they've climbed 29,000 feet and then a couple more,
> And set their foot where mortal man has never stood before.[29]

Indeed, once they reached London, Tenzing and Hillary received several honours and were often depicted as members of the Commonwealth. Upon their arrival at the airport, Col. Hunt waved the Union Jack from his ice-axe and the team was greeted by the Secretary of State for War. 'The whole Commonwealth', said Brigadier Anthony Head, 'is moved, and is proud of your great achievement.'[30] In an airport interview, Hunt said he was delighted that Hillary and Tenzing 'representing, in a sense, members of the Commonwealth, had been successful in getting to the top. It was only right and proper.'[31] But interviews broadcast from the airport also carried the sounds of Hillary's antipodean accent and Tenzing speaking in a foreign language which suggested the ambivalence of their position in Britain.[32]

The ambiguous definition of the 'Commonwealth' rendered the question of honours for the Everest climbers more complicated than had seemed possible on coronation morning. The British Government conferred knighthoods on Hunt and Hillary within days of the coronation, and announced its intention to honour Tenzing: 'Since he is not a British subject, this requires consultation, and no immediate announcement can be made'.[33] Tenzing had no conception of national identity, and said he had been 'born in the womb of Nepal, and raised in the lap of India'.[34] Both Nepal and India claimed Tenzing as their citizen and showered him with awards.[35] Rumours that Tenzing would receive the George Medal, the highest civilian award for gallantry, prompted allegations of discrimination. When asked during Prime Minister's Question Time about the disappointment that Tenzing had not been given the same award as Hillary, Sir Winston Churchill replied: 'That does not entirely rest with Her Majesty's Government'.[36]

The different awards for Tenzing and Hillary reflected the convergence of multiple imperial pasts into a complex Commonwealth present. Tenzing was not given a British knighthood because the Prime Minister of India, Jawaharlal Nehru, refused to allow him to accept one of the honours that had been central to representing British authority in India under the Raj.[37] Nehru's rejection of a knighthood reasserted Indian independence and incorporated Tenzing into the traditions of Indian nationalism that had rejected British honours as symbols of British domination.[38] Hillary's position was paradoxically similar. Hillary was awarded a knighthood because the Prime Minister of New Zealand, Sidney Holland, had accepted it for him. Hillary learned about his knighthood while hiking back to Kathmandu. 'It should have been a great moment, but instead I was aghast. ... I had never really approved of titles and couldn't imagine myself possessing one.' Since the KBE had already been accepted, Hillary felt he had no choice and was 'miserable rather than pleased'.[39] Tenzing's knighthood was rejected to defy incorporation into an expansive definition of 'Britishness'; Hillary's knighthood was accepted to promote it. The claims on both Tenzing and Hillary exemplify the ambivalent positions of 'colonials' in Britain.[40] British representations of both climbers as members of the 'Commonwealth' responded to this ambivalence by attempting to incorporate them into 'greater Britain'.

Hunt seemed to occupy a less ambiguous position than either Tenzing or Hillary. However, John Hunt's triumphal return to his home on the Welsh/English border also complicated these images of a unitary Britain.

Hunt waved the British flag from his ice-axe as local farmers towed him in a cart up a steep hill to his house, and it soon became known that he had flown the Welsh flag at his camps on Everest.[41] After the Welsh nationalist party announced that Hunt had sent them a message, the War Office reminded Hunt of his pledge to remain non-partisan in the military. Hunt replied that he had merely expressed 'my sympathy with the preservation of the culture and traditions of Wales'.[42] To the British Government, however, such gestures of Welsh solidarity undermined the image of a unitary British nation.

The British monarchy had rejuvenated itself between the wars through the proliferation of the honours system throughout the British Empire, and the awards for the Everest climbers reflected that 'tradition' as well as the recent compromise making the monarch the symbol of the 'New Commonwealth'.[43] After a garden party at Buckingham Palace, the Queen knighted Hunt and Hillary, presented Tenzing with the George Medal, and gave other climbers special Coronation medals. In the evening, Prince Philip presided at a small state dinner that his office limited to 'men only'. Wives and other guests later joined the men for a state reception at Lancaster House. Access was tightly controlled since the press 'might photograph Ministers or other eminent persons in the act of drinking and these photographs might be used against them in later years'.[44] Stag parties and alcoholic indiscretions were but one dimension of the relationship between monarchy and masculinity that linked the conquest and coronation. As one woman wrote to the climbers on coronation day: 'It is fitting that your team should symbolise for us the vigour, vitality, and high endeavour of manhood, as the Queen symbolises the sweetness, grace and dutiful service of a woman'.[45]

The British press was deferential in its coverage of the state reception but had directly confronted the more controversial issues to emerge since the coronation. While the expedition had been in Nepal and India, questions concerning Tenzing's nationality and whether Hillary or Tenzing had reached the summit first were both hotly debated.[46] As a result of these debates after the ascent, British rhetoric about Everest shifted uncertainly between a triumph of 'Britain' or the 'Commonwealth' or the 'human spirit' more generally. The British reaction to Everest was thus a complex amalgam of images of military leadership and planning, science and technology, nationalism and internationalism, and partnership within the 'Commonwealth'.

The climbers themselves became the main emissaries of these images when they appeared on television and radio, and in public lectures. On BBC television, Hunt described the ascent with a scale model of Everest, and the interviewer asked Bourdillon about the oxygen, Wylie about the porters, Hillary about the summit, and Tenzing about himself.[47] Tenzing also demonstrated the oxygen mask and cylinders while Hunt described how they worked. After the ascent, scenes of Sherpas demonstrating the oxygen were repeated frequently, and represented visually an older ideology of European technological dominance that had formerly underpinned imperialism, but now bolstered images of British tutelage of the Commonwealth in the 1950s.[48] Afterwards, the BBC considered this programme 'suitable for emergency transmission during a period of national mourning'.[49] On BBC radio, the climbers themselves told the story of the ascent in a dramatic and well-paced narrative. The announcer depicted Everest not as a national mountaineering problem, but 'in the realm of human endeavour, ... a challenge to man'.[50] This programme received higher ratings for 'audience appreciation' than any other radio broadcast in 1953 apart from the coronation and an England cricket victory over Australia in a test match.[51]

The expedition organisers also struggled with the implications of a 'British conquest' in *The Conquest of Everest* film. A draft press release announced that a feature film was being made 'on the conquest of Everest, to show the world the full sequence of this great British achievement'. The RGS wondered: 'should we say "British" achievement when in our communiqué etc. we have mentioned Swiss efforts and in view of Tenzing disputes, etc'. After internal discussions, the RGS and *The Times* decided to 'leave "British" in'.[52] As the film went into production, Col. Hunt also asked if the word 'conquest' could be omitted from the film's title. Although the film retained the assertive 'conquest', Hunt gave his book the more neutral title, *The Ascent of Everest*.[53]

The Conquest of Everest film opened to a Royal Première and rave reviews in October 1953. Throughout the British Isles at smaller cinemas with local dignitaries, Army and Navy Cadets or Boy Scouts and Girl Guides in uniform, book displays and commercial tie-ins, the Everest film continued to juxtapose images of the coronation and Everest. In the film, the photograph of Tenzing on the summit is followed by the headlines announcing the conquest of Everest as the 'crowning glory' to throngs of flag-waving well-wishers, who line the route of the coronation procession. Images of the Queen's carriage in London are followed by scenes of Tenzing and other climbers riding in state in Kathmandu. By the end of the film, after the climbers' ascent and safe return, the overall theme is teamwork and partnership: 'Sherpas and British alike. All had their share in this.'[54]

The British promotional material for *The Conquest of Everest* film also attempted to accommodate the dual message of a 'conquest' that was both British and international. A sample letter from a cinema manager to local schools touted the conquest as a 'great British achievement', and suggested that since 'this film should be seen by every British child we are offering a special concession in prices'. At the same time, the press book recommended that each theatre festoon its front 'with the flags of the United Nations, together with ample bunting'.[55]

Overseas, the British Government sponsored the film and lecture tours by the climbers to promote British prestige. After the British ambassador to Ethiopia asked to show the film in Addis Ababa, 'not from a revenue producing or theatrical point of view, but purely as magnificent British propaganda', the film was circulated in the diplomatic pouch.[56] Indeed, the climbers themselves travelled on extensive lecture tours throughout Britain, Europe, America and the Commonwealth. After Hunt was promoted to Brigadier, he lectured in Paris and at the NATO headquarters where he had formerly served, as well as in Berlin and Moscow in Cold War showcases. The RGS considered the extensive Everest lecture series in Europe, 'from a prestige point of view, highly successful'.[57] James Morris reported that the American lecture tour had created much goodwill and 'did a great deal of good for Anglo-American relations and for mountaineering'.[58]

The Queen herself became an emissary for the combined image of conquest, coronation and Commonwealth. Shortly after the *Conquest of Everest* première, the Queen embarked on a post-coronation journey around the world that landed her in Auckland, New Zealand, at Christmas. To introduce her 1953 Christmas Day speech, British, Australian and New Zealand radio broadcasters produced *The Queen's Journey*, a programme conveying Christmas greetings and pledges of loyalty. After a Maori Haka dance and greetings from Sydney, the programme jumps 'to Britain, to the homeland, cradle of pioneers, discoverers and creators of the Commonwealth'. Tributes then pour in from Bermuda, Jamaica, Canada, Fiji, Tonga, New Guinea, Hong Kong, Sarawak, Singapore, Pakistan, India, Ceylon, South Africa, Central African Federation, Rhodesia, Nigeria, Uganda, Kenya, and research stations in Antarctica and North Greenland. The narrator finally announces:

> We have girdled the world, and flashed from pole to pole. (Music) We the people of the Commonwealth are gathered now. Waiting for the Queen to speak to us from New Zealand, from the green and white city of Auckland. (Music up) This great family circle, the Commonwealth, looks back on a year to remember with pride. The year of Coronation, the year when peace came to Korea, the year when Everest was conquered. (Music builds to climax)
>
> The Queen's journey is revealing and renewing the strength of the Commonwealth, the reality of shared responsibility and shared freedom under a young Queen. This is a great pyramid of unity, a mountain massive as Everest, a peak still clouded by the future challenges to all men of goodwill and courage. (Music builds to conclusion)[59]

Edmund Hillary, then at his sister's house in Norfolk, not far from Sandringham, a royal residence, sends the final greeting to the Queen, then in

Auckland, his hometown, before the British national anthem introduces her Christmas Day address.

The Queen's speech expressed her hopes for the Commonwealth and the 'Elizabethan age'. Though she did not feel like her Tudor forebear, she identified 'one very significant resemblance between her age and mine'. Her kingdom was 'great in spirit and well endowed with men who were ready to encompass the earth'. While her ancestors had founded an empire, in the Commonwealth 'the United Kingdom was an equal partner with many other proud and independent nations. And she is leading other still backward territories forward for the same goal. *All* these nations have helped to create our Commonwealth.' Unlike previous empires, the Commonwealth was built on 'the highest qualities of the spirit of man: friendship, loyalty, and the desire for freedom and peace. To that new conception of an equal partnership of nations and races I shall give myself heart and soul, every day of my life.'[60] The Queen did not directly mention the partnership of Hillary and Tenzing on Everest, but she didn't have to: *The Queen's Journey* had already hailed the Commonwealth as 'a great pyramid of unity, a mountain massive as Everest'.

By the late 1950s, the conquest of Everest continued to provide cause for optimism in the future of the Empire and Commonwealth. But more pessimistic signs were apparent. Following the example of the Everest team, a British expedition to cross Antarctica with motor-sledges during 1955–58 was organised by Vivian Fuchs as a 'Commonwealth' endeavour with a group of New Zealanders led by Sir Edmund Hillary. Hillary was asked to play the role of loyal subordinate by creating supply depots for the British party led by Fuchs across the continent. Left to his own devices, Hillary squirrelled away enough supplies to make his own dash to the South Pole, creating a widely publicised 'race' with Fuchs that Hillary won handily. The British press was furious, but the New Zealand Cabinet firmly backed Hillary's right to go on his own. Hillary later said he had gone to Everest as an honorary Britisher, but went to the South Pole as a New Zealander.[61] The transition from one to the other had been rapid. The 'British Commonwealth Trans-Antarctic Expedition' had departed as a happy family in 1956 but returned dysfunctional in 1958.

Events elsewhere during these years also suggested that the internationalism of 'Coronation Everest' might have been the product of a fleeting moment. The Queen's rhetoric of a multi-racial partnership at her coronation had appeared prophetic when news of the triumph of Hillary and Tenzing arrived with such impeccable timing. After the Suez crisis in 1956 and the 'wind of change' in colonial Africa, however, Britain's influence had diminished and signs of successful partnership were few. Looking back from the late 1960s, one historian of the Commonwealth wrote that the early 1950s had been the 'brief and, retrospectively, golden years of hope in a multi-racial Commonwealth'.[62]

Although the moment that produced this particular conjuncture of coronation and conquest and Commonwealth may have been fleeting, the power of the images produced by these events was not, and they left an enduring impression on post-war British culture. Images of 'Coronation Everest' persisted, long after the 'second Elizabethan age' had faded, because Everest helped to renegotiate and redefine the British Empire as something new – the Commonwealth of Nations. 'Coronation Everest' combined older images of imperial conquest with the new partnership of the Commonwealth. The rhetoric of the Commonwealth during these years has been called 'anaesthetising' in that it obscured fundamental changes in the international structures of power that had permanently reduced the scope of British influence.[63] Even after signs of imperial 'decline' became visible, the conquest of Everest remained a tangible re-minder that the 'Commonwealth idea' could inspire hopes for the future, and the 'Elizabethan age' might represent something more than glorious memories of a distant past. As Sir George Middleton, British envoy to India at the time of the ascent, recalled: 'empires die and go away but it doesn't happen overnight. There is a lot of confetti lying around still, and the confetti of empire was still very visible in 1953.'[64] To understand why the effects of the Commonwealth rhetoric were so powerful – why so many people in Britain believed in empire and Commonwealth for so long despite abundant evidence of British weakness – is not a question that finds an answer in the posturing of politicians at diplomatic summits. Rather, the popular appeal of the Commonwealth in the years after the coronation is to be found in the enduring but ambivalent images of Hillary and Tenzing standing together on the summit of Everest.

Notes

1   *Glasgow Herald*, 2 June 1953; See also *The Times, News Chronicle, Daily Mail, Yorkshire Post*, 2 June 1953; *Manchester Guardian*, 3 June 1953; *Birmingham Post*, 4 June 1953.
2   BBC Written Archives Centre, Caversham (hereafter WAC), Scripts, *The Conquest of Everest*, 2 June 1953; and British Library, National Sound Archives, London (hereafter NSA) recording 19226 (made 23 May, broadcast 2 June).
3   Royal Geographical Society Archives, London (hereafter RGS Archives), Everest Expe-dition Archives (hereafter EE) Box 89, J. Maltby to J. Hunt, 12 October 1953.
4   NSA, 1CD0126380, Queen's Coronation Day Speech. Some 1953 recordings are excerpted in NSA, H1595, 'Coronation Day: All this and Everest too' [1993]. For the broadcast schedule: http://www.bbctv-ap.freeserve.co.uk/coroneve.htm.
5   Public Record Office, Kew (hereafter PRO), FO371/106879, Alan Lascelles to William Strang, 1 June 1953.
6   James Morris, *Coronation Everest* (London, Faber, 1958).
7   Peter H. Hansen, 'Albert Smith, the Alpine Club, and the Invention of Mountaineer-ing in Mid-Victorian Britain', *Journal of British Studies*, 34:3 (1995), pp. 300–24. See

also Felix Driver, *Geography Militant: Cultures of Exploration and Empire* (Oxford, Blackwell, 2001).

8   See John M. MacKenzie (ed.), *Imperialism and Popular Culture* (Manchester, Manchester University Press, 1986); P. J. Marshall, 'Imperial Britain', *Journal of Imperial and Commonwealth History*, 23:3 (1995), pp. 379–94; Richard Drayton, *Nature's Government* (New Haven, Yale University Press, 2000).

9   See Peter H. Hansen, 'Confetti of Empire: The Conquest of Everest in Nepal, India, Britain and New Zealand', *Comparative Studies in Society and History*, 42:2 (2000), pp. 307–32; Gordon T. Stewart, 'Tenzing's Two Wrist Watches: The Conquest of Everest and Late Imperial Culture, 1921–1953', *Past and Present*, 149 (November 1995), pp. 170–97; and Peter H. Hansen, 'Debate: Tenzing's Two Wrist Watches: The Conquest of Everest and Late Imperial Culture, 1921–1953: Comment', *Past and Present*, 157 (November 1997), pp. 159–77.

10 See Peter H. Hansen, 'Vertical Boundaries, National Identities: British Mountaineering on the Frontiers of Europe and the Empire, 1868–1914', *Journal of Imperial and Commonwealth History*, 24:1 (1996), pp. 48–71; and see, generally, Walt Unsworth, *Everest* (London, Grafton, 1989).

11 PRO, FO766/14, Frank Smythe to Col. Daukes, 30 June 1930.

12 British Library, Oriental and India Office Collections, London, L/P&S/12/4242, J. C. Walton, minute, 7 June 1934, in response to P. J. Cox to Secretary of State for India, 25 May 1934.

13 See Peter H. Hansen, 'Modern Mountains: The Performative Consciousness of Modernity in Britain, 1870–1940', in Martin Daunton and Bernhard Rieger (eds), *Meanings of Modernity: Britain from the Late-Victorian Era to World War II* (Oxford, Berg, 2001), pp. 185–202.

14 PRO, FO371/92928, H. H. Phillips, minute, 19 June 1951.

15 See PRO, FO371/92928, Kathmandu to London, 23 November 1951; PRO, FO371/101162, R. H. Scott and H. H. Phillips, minutes, 7 January 1952.

16 RGS Archives, EE/90, draft minutes of Himalayan committee, 11 September 1952. See also the correspondence in RGS Archives, EE/66/1; and British Library, London, Add. Mss. 63120, fols 70–82; Add. Mss. 63122, fols 22–34.

17 RGS Archives, EE/68, B. Goodfellow to J. Hunt, 10 July 1952.

18 PRO, FO371/101163, London to India and Nepal, 7 October 1952.

19 Jan Morris, *Conundrum* (New York, Signet, 1974), p. 94; Jan Morris, 'Coronation Everest', http://www.salonmag.com/wlust/feature/1998/05/04feature2.html.

20 RGS Archives, EE/68/Himalayan Club file, C. Crawford to H. W. Tobin, 4 October 1952.

21 Tenzing Norgay, *Man of Everest* (London, Harrap, 1955), pp. 230–1; *Daily Express*, 2 July 1953. See also Sherry Ortner, *Life and Death on Mt. Everest* (Princeton, Princeton University Press, 1999).

22 See Tenzing, *Man of Everest*, p. 234; *Daily Express*, 2 July 1953. See also Peter H. Hansen, 'Partners: Guides and Sherpas in the Alps and Himalayas, 1850s-1950s', in Jas Elsner and Joan-Pau Rubiés (eds), *Voyages and Visions: Towards a Cultural History of Travel* (London, Reaktion, 1999), pp. 210–31.

23 See RGS Archives, EE/68. Another British soldier and five Gurkhas stationed in Malaya also donated their time to supervise the 'coolies' who carried the supplies.

24 See James H. Capshew and Karen A. Rader, 'Big Science: Price to the Present', *Osiris*, 2nd ser., 7 (1992), pp. 3–25; Robert Bud and Philip Gummett (eds), *Cold War, Hot Science: Applied Research in Britain's Defence Laboratories 1945–1990* (Amsterdam, Harwood, 1999).

25 See Michael Ward, 'The First Ascent of Mount Everest, 1953: Dr. Griffith Pugh's Solution of the Altitude Problem', in John R. Sutton, Charles S. Houston and Geoffrey Coates (eds), *Hypoxia and Molecular Medicine* (Burlington, VT, Queen City, 1993), pp. 184–9; John B. West, *High Life: A History of High-Altitude Physiology and Medicine* (New York, Oxford University Press, 1998).

26 See, for example, PRO, FD1/9042, and PRO, AVIA54/1476.

27 Hunt interview with the author (1996); see also *Statesman* (Calcutta), 27 June 1953.

28 The inclusion of two New Zealanders had been announced when Shipton was leader. All other foreign climbers were informed that the committee had decided 'the composition of the party should be entirely all-British'. See RGS Archives, EE/66/12, J. Hunt to D. Bertholet, 12 January 1953; EE/66/8, B. Goodfellow memo to J. Hunt, 18 September 1952; EE/90, C. Elliot to C. Wylie, 15 October 1952.

29 NSA, recording 21157, Leslie Haworth, 'The Ascent of Mount Everest'.

30 *Yorkshire Post* and *The Times*, 4 July 1953.

31 See RGS Archives, EE/89, for the transcript; and NSA, T19520, for the recording.

32 See British Pathé Archives, London, 53/50, *Everest Heroes Home*; and British Movietone Archives, London, 59344:Iss.1257, *Everest Victors Here*.

33 See *Observer*, *Sunday Times* and *Times of India*, 7 June 1953.

34 *Daily Express*, 2 July 1953; Tenzing, *Man of Everest*, p. 287.

35 For Tenzing's national identity, and the reception of the ascent in Nepal and India more generally, see Hansen, 'Confetti of Empire'.

36 See Parliamentary Debates (Commons), 5th ser., {1953}, vol. 516, col. 971 (oral answers). The George Medal was announced on 1 July 1953.

37 British officials told Hunt that Nehru vetoed Tenzing's knighthood (Hunt interview, 1996). British public records regarding Tenzing's award have been destroyed or remain closed. See, for example, PRO, FO371/106880.

38 Bernard S. Cohn, 'Representing Authority in Victorian India', in Eric Hobsbawm and Terrence Ranger (eds), *The Invention of Tradition* (Cambridge, Cambridge University Press, 1983), pp. 165–209; Bernard S. Cohn, *Colonialism and its Forms of Knowledge* (Princeton, Princeton University Press, 1996).

39 Edmund Hillary, *Nothing Venture, Nothing Win* (London, Hodder & Stoughton, 1975), pp. 163–4; Hillary interview with the author (1998).

40 See Angela Woollacott, '"All This Is Empire I Told Myself": Australian Women's Voyages "Home" and the Articulation of Colonial Whiteness', *American Historical Review*, 102:4 (1997), pp. 1003–29. See also Antoinette Burton, *At the Heart of the Empire: Indians and the Colonial Encounter in Late-Victorian Britain* (Berkeley, University of California Press, 1998).

41 Hunt interview (1996). On his arrival, see *News Chronicle*, *Birmingham Post* and *Daily Express*, 6 July 1953. On the Welsh flag, see *Statesman*, 27 June 1953, and RGS Archives, EE/69, Hunt to Barmouth Urban District Council, 22 July 1953.

42 RGS Archives, EE/89, Hunt to War Office, 22 October 1953.

43 See David Cannadine, 'The Context, Performance and Meaning of Ritual: The British Monarchy and the "Invention of Tradition", c. 1820–1977', in Hobsbawm and Ranger (eds), *The Invention of Tradition*, pp. 101–64; Tom Nairn, *The Enchanted Glass: Britain and its Monarchy* (London, Hutchinson, 1988); R. J. Moore, *Making the New Commonwealth* (Oxford, Clarendon, 1987).

44 PRO, CAB124/2924, Government Hospitality Minutes, 6 July 1953. See also PRO, PREM11/458 and FO371/106880.

45 RGS Archives, EE/69, J. Reynolds to J. Hunt, 2 June 1953.

46 See Hansen, 'Confetti of Empire'.

47 BBC Television, London, *The Conquest of Everest*, broadcast 14 July 1953. This television programme was different from the feature film of the same name. See also *Reputations: Hillary and Tenzing, Everest and After*, broadcast BBC2, 18 June 1997.

48 See Michael Adas, *Machines as the Measure of Men* (Ithaca, Cornell University Press, 1989); Gyan Prakash, *Another Reason* (Princeton, Princeton University Press, 2000).

49 WAC, T32/145, Paul Johnstone to T. O. Tel, 5 February 1954. See also RGS Archives, EE/83.

50 NSA, recordings 19207–19212, *Everest 1953: The Story Told by the Climbers Themselves*, broadcast 24 July 1953; WAC, Scripts, *Everest 1953*.

51 WAC, R9/6/13–24, 'Listening and Viewing Barometer' and 'Audience Research Reports' for 1953.

52 RGS Archives, EE/84, R. B. Williams-Thompson to L. P. Kirwan, 22 June 1953 and attached notes; RGS Archives, EE/66/11 for the communiqué.

53 RGS Archives, EE/84, L. P. Kirwan to J. Taylor, 29 July 1953, and correspondence

regarding the book in RGS Archives, EE/82.

54   National Film and Television Archive, British Film Institute, London, *The Conquest of Everest* (1953).
55   British Film Institute Library, London, press book for *The Conquest of Everest*.
56   RGS Archives, EA/84, D. Busk to L. Kirwan, 2 December 1953.
57   RGS Archives, EE/90 and EE/68, Everest Fourth Progress Report.
58   RGS Archives, EE/68, Everest Fifth Progress Report, 13 May 1954.
59   NSA, recording T27351, *Queen's Journey*; WAC, Scripts, *Queen's Journey*.
60   Tom Fleming (ed.), *Voices Out of the Air: The Royal Christmas Broadcasts, 1932–1981* (London, Heinemann, 1981), pp. 72–4. See also John M. MacKenzie, '"In Touch with the Infinite": The BBC and the Empire, 1923–53', in MacKenzie (ed.), *Imperialism and Popular Culture*, p. 181.
61   Hillary interview (1998); *A View From the Top: Hillary* (Television New Zealand, 1998), and Hillary, *View from the Summit* (London, Doubleday, 1999), pp. 124–89.
62   Nicholas Mansergh, *The Commonwealth Experience* (London, Weidenfeld and Nicolson, 1969), p. 337; W. David McIntyre, 'The Commonwealth', in Robin W. Winks (ed.), *The Oxford History of the British Empire, Vol. V: Historiography* (Oxford, Oxford University Press, 1999), pp. 560–1.
63   John Darwin, 'Decolonization and the End of Empire', in Winks (ed.), *The Oxford History of the British Empire, Vol. V: Historiography*, p. 547.
64   See Hansen, 'Confetti of Empire', p. 311.

CHAPTER FOUR

Look back at empire:
British theatre and imperial decline
Dan Rebellato

After the Second World War, for those who could afford to go, Paris provided welcome escape from the austerities of post-war British life. At a loose end one day in July 1946, Noël Coward wandered over to the British Embassy to drop in on his friends the Duff Coopers, who were there to assist with post-war reconstruction. Instead he found 'nobody about but Winston Churchill. He was very amiable and we talked for about forty minutes and I played him some of the operette tunes.'[1] The operette to which Coward refers was *Pacific 1860*, a musical comedy set in Samolo, a fictional British colony, populated by singing natives and colonial admin istrators with nothing more pressing than romance and etiquette to occupy their minds.

This cosy vignette of Churchill and Coward sitting around an embassy piano might reinforce the widespread belief that the major playwrights of the post-war West End had a sentimental affection for empire, if not a positively hawkish attachment to it. *Pacific 1860* opened five months later at the Theatre Royal, on 19 December 1946, the day before Winston Churchill would famously denounce the Labour Government's offer of independence to Burma as a 'scuttle'.[2] Later, Coward's views would line up very precisely with the die-hard Suez Group, who tirelessly denounced any hint of scuttle in British imperial policy, in 1956, as the crisis over Nasser's nationalisation of the Suez Canal mounted, Coward wrote in his diary: 'All this could, of course, have been avoided if we had not caved in and been just and fair and decent and foolish ... It is the same tedious old story, weak-kneed humanitarianism instead of dignified strength.'[3]

Coward prefaced the published text of *Pacific 1860* with an imitation gazetteer describing the history of Samolo, explaining that 'the islands became officially a British possession in 1855 during the reign of King Kefumalani II who wrote personally to Queen Victoria begging her to allow his land to have the privilege of belonging to the British Empire'.[4] This happy union of interests continues undaunted across the hundred years

[73]

that separate the settings of Coward's two 'Samolo' plays. While there are those in *South Sea Bubble* (Lyric Theatre, April 1956) agitating for self-rule, supported by a liberal-minded colonial governor, it is nothing that cannot be deflected with a little deviousness and a lot of suave implacability.

Only a week after *South Sea Bubble* opened, John Osborne's *Look Back in Anger* began previewing at the Royal Court. This play has become the marker that divides twentieth-century British theatre into before and after, a gateway between the star-ridden conservatism of the West End and the challenging progressiveness of the new subsidised popular art theatre, centred on the Royal Court. Its title helped to name the 'Angry Young Men', a loose grouping of playwrights, novelists, poets and film-makers who sought to loosen the grip of a conservative establishment on the throat of British culture. In *Declaration* (1957), the closest thing to a manifesto that they ever produced, the theatre critic Kenneth Tynan railed at the tired old West End plays which 'continue to be written on the assumption that there are still people who live in awe of the Crown, the Empire, the established Church, the public school and upper classes'.[5]

Scornful of such deference, the New Wave refused to treat the British Empire as an eternally benign feature of the world landscape. *Eleven Dead at Hola Camp* (Royal Court, July 1959) was a part-improvised performance, with music and masks, performed under club conditions, responding to reports of the atrocities committed by British troops against Mau Mau detainees in Kenya. Willis Hall's *The Long and the Short and the Tall* (Royal Court, January 1959) concentrated on a bickering and mutinous group of British soldiers in the Malayan jungle at the end of the Second World War. The Suez crisis in 1956 also provided an imperial target for the rage of the Angry Young Men. Kenneth Tynan recalled that 'those who were anti-Suez also tended to be supporters of *Look Back in Anger*. In the heat of the crisis, while smoke bombs were bursting in Downing Street and mounted police charged the crowds in Whitehall, Osborne conceived his second play, *The Entertainer.*'[6] In Michael Hastings's *Don't Destroy Me* (New Lindsey, August 1956), the angry young protagonist rails drunkenly at some dinner guests, 'Do you think, Rabbi – the Suez Canal will enter the next Olympics? ... I do.'[7] After so many plays which seemed unable to envisage the sun ever setting on the British Empire, even such oblique comments must have been exhilaratingly insolent.

Indeed critics have even claimed that by challenging the glittering, complacently imperialist West End, dominated as it was by the elegantly powerful producer 'Binkie' Beaumont, the New Wave was striking a blow for colonial freedom. When John Elsom writes of the Suez fiasco that 'in November 1956, Beaumont's empire suffered a particular blow', one is encouraged to see the West End and the British Empire as concentric forces, sharing profoundly in the same decline.[8]

Certainly, the tendency of the earlier generation to set their plays in fictional rather than real territories might suggest a wilful evasion of colonial realities. Coward wrote two plays and a novel, *Pomp and Circumstance* (1960), set on 'Samolo'.[9] His earlier play, *Point Valaine* (Ethel Barrymore Theatre, New York, January 1935), takes place on the West Indian island of its title. J. B. Priestley's *Home is Tomorrow* (Cambridge Theatre, October 1948) unfolds in Corabana, and Dorothy and Campbell Christie's *His Excellency* (Princes, May 1950) on Salva. T. S. Eliot's *The Cocktail Party* (Royal Lyceum, Edinburgh, August 1949) has one of its characters meet her death off-stage on the island of Kinkanja, about which we discover little but that its inhabitants are 'a band of half-crazed savages'.[10] Most of these plays dealt largely with the white colonialists, and often the 'natives' were marginal characters, usually played by white actors in blackface. Looking back at old theatre programmes, the juxtaposition of actors and characters can be seen as curiously bathetic, especially when we discover that the firebrand Samolan party leader, 'Hali Alani', was played by 'Ronald Lewis', or that the Prime Minister of Salva, 'Emil Zamario', was given by 'Owen Fellowes'.[11]

But this is history written by the winners and it unduly homogenises the work of the losers. There are differences of approach between these playwrights, and indeed differences within individual oeuvres. Noël Coward is a particularly interesting case; although by the 1950s his views had certainly drifted rightward, his dramaturgy displayed a more sceptical and questioning tone towards the adventures of empire. *Cavalcade* (Theatre Royal, October 1931), an episodic portrait of British social and political history since the turn of the century, is often cited as the beginning of Coward's drift towards the establishment. But there is much in the play itself which sharply challenges its sentimental reputation. Most interestingly for our purposes, the play begins with preparations for the Boer War. We see this conflict tersely ironised in a scene where two children play toy soldiers, British forces against the Boers, wreaking what we associatively understand to be petulant and cruel acts of bloodshed. In scene five we are part of a theatre audience watching a musical comedy, at the end of which the stage manager takes the stage to announce the relief of Mafeking to heartfelt cheers. Yet this is itself put in the uncomfortable context of the musical comedy which features a sextet of 'ample girls' in uniform singing a patriotic anti-Boer song. As such the scene suggests a critique of banal patriotic excess.

1935's *Point Valaine* does deal in colonial stereotypes. Yet while the Samolo of *Pacific 1860* and *South Sea Bubble* is little more than an exotic backdrop for the westerners to conduct affairs of state and the heart, there is an attempt in *Point Valaine* to present the terrain as an active participant in the lives of its characters. The play follows an assortment of individuals booked into an isolated hotel on an island in the British West Indies. A romantic triangle breaks apart and the abandoned lover takes his own life. Throughout the play a series of motifs reminds us of the dangers of the environment: the westerners try vainly to keep tropical rainstorms, mosquitoes, sharks and barracudas at bay with blinds, nets and ointments, and underwater fencing. This has its affinities with an imperialist vision of a dark continent, primitive and unruly. But when we see two passionate embraces underscored by intensifying tropical rainfall,[12] there is at least a suggestion that these forces are rising unbidden from the western unconscious, which troubles any easy division between the civilised West and barbarian other. Theatrically too it puts in question the comfortable convention of the setting. The faded chintz and french windows of the Point Valaine Hotel, which were a staple of West End décor right up to the 1950s, seem conspicuously inadequate in this harsh and forbidding environment. There is little sign of the colonial confidence of the later plays and instead we hear Martin declare, 'This place doesn't agree with me, really ... I think I'd be better at home.'[13] These people know that they do not belong.

A minor but telling inclusion in *Point Valaine* is the journalist and would-be dramatist Hilda James, who has written a play set on a colonial island. Her clichéd narrative, locked entirely into the conventions of romantic melodrama, contrasts ironically with the cruel and unsettling drama we are watching. Curiously, Hilda's play, as first described, resembles notes for Coward's musical comedy *Pacific 1860*, which follows a love affair between Elena Salvador and Kerry Stirling, grievously broken off and then re-established at curtain fall. The natural environment is far more placid now and the Samolans are represented largely through their happy singing. (When Elena points out, 'All the natives on this island sing, don't they?', Coward is perhaps coyly acknowledging his representational limitations.[14]) However he is not attempting to privilege the colonisers over the colonised in an imperialist sense. As Kerry hurries to catch his beloved before she boards the boat that will take her from the island, Coward sets up two groups of characters: on the right, 'a group of Samolans in full native regalia' singing a traditional song to mark the departures, and on the left 'a group of earnest missionaries with a harmonium ... singing, with a certain dogged determination, a fairly cheerless hymn'.[15] When Kerry realises that his sweetheart has already gone, he shouts at (presumably) both groups to stop singing, suggesting that the play's real interest is in offering love as a way of transcending colonial difference. Passion is not a product of the colonial setting as it is in *Point Valaine*, but a means of escaping it.

It is also important not to isolate these plays from the wider performance traditions, in particular the forms of empire propaganda, with which they coexisted. In the 1920s and 1930s theatrical events were frequent ingredients of the annual Empire Day celebrations. Short plays were made available to schools, with titles like *Britannia and her Daughters*, *Birth of the Union Jack* and *The British Lion*.[16] In the 1940s, for the three years spanning the end of the war, Festivals of Empire were held at the Royal Albert Hall organised by the Empire Day Movement. The 1945 Festival featured a performance entitled *The Visit* in which 'the Soul of the Empire, symbolised by a knight, dedicates itself anew to the service of God and Mankind and prepares for the Great Crusade against the forces of evil. As the knight kneels in prayer men and women gather behind him, offering themselves in service. The knight rises and, followed by the people, goes forth to the Great Adventure.'[17] Against such grimly mythical propaganda, Coward's decision in the same year to write a musical set on a colonial island looks positively subversive in its frivolity.

But while Coward did display a drift in his later plays towards a complacent empire-loyalism (no doubt an easier stance to maintain from the comfort of his Bermuda tax haven), other playwrights made very different kinds of intervention. When in *South Sea Bubble* a novelist is found reading a book called *Tomorrow is the End*, it may be a sly reference to J. B. Priestley's *Home is Tomorrow*, which could hardly be more different from Coward's play. Although, again, the setting is fictional, the details are far more realistically sketched in. It is set in a former Spanish colony, which is now under temporary administration by the United National Underdeveloped Territories Organisation (UNUTO). Like Coward in *Point Valaine*, Priestley is keen to stress the island as a dangerous, hostile place. Fortrose, the UNUTO administrator, declares that 'Out there – only a few hundred yards away – is darkness – primeval darkness – like the old Unconscious, full of vengeful gods, vampire goddesses, demons, ghosts. Here is a little lighted place, where consciousness exists, where – God help us – we try to see things clearly and for what they are.'[18] This seems plainly to equate the colonial other with primitive and unconscious forces, but Priestley gives this notion a twist. The play follows the machinations of Lerma, a South American businessman trying to remove UNUTO from the island and give it back to the indigenous peoples. But it becomes clear that his aim is to exploit the island's mineral rights without international interference. In this he is being supported by the American government, as part of a Cold War redefinition of territorial alliances. UNUTO's French economic adviser, Riberac, tells another member of the team, 'There used to be a vaudeville trick called Sawing a Woman in Half. Now it is no longer a trick, an illusion. You can hear the saw scraping the ribs of the world.'[19] Fortrose's dark forces are those of globalisation and the Cold War. At the pessimistic end of the play the rebel leader, Vezebar, confronts and shoots Fortrose, who collapses over his desk, thereby (and with fortuitous symbolism) sending a globe crashing to the floor.

In the two years before Priestley's play began its regional tour, independence had been achieved by Pakistan, India, Burma, Ceylon and Palestine. Also appearing in its wake was Terence Rattigan's *Adventure Story* (St James's Theatre, March 1949) following Alexander the Great's colonial expansion across the ruins of the Persian Empire. The play begins with Alexander on his death bed, his new Empire in an uncertain, precarious state; a voice-over lets us into his unspoken thoughts, as he asks, 'Where did it first go wrong?'[20] Christopher Innes has suggested that this 'echoes what must have been a common British response to the loss of global prestige – while the transience of Alexander's Empire, which disintegrated with his death, was all too apt'.[21] Is Innes right that this was a coded hymn of regret for the passing of the British Empire? The play certainly shows an empire being won and lost; we follow Alexander's military victories from beginning to end, and we see it in crisis and decline at the end of his life. That this historical story has contemporary relevance is emphasised by the dialogue which, despite its period details, is all in a firmly twentieth-century register.

But what we actually see is an idealism being soured by the very practice of empire building. Alexander begins with what appear to be strong ethical principles. When Cleitus brings him the captured Persian Royal Family and makes them kneel, Alexander is furious at the calculated insult to them, and insists that even though they are hostages they should be treated humanely.[22] His determination to act well is emphasised visually. When we first see Darius's tent, it is 'large and regally sumptuous ... the furnishings and objects that we now see are of an opulence and luxury that give the tent more the appearance of a throne-room in a palace than of a commander-in-chief's headquarters in the field'.[23] At a time of rationing in Britain, this would have been a particularly calculated signifier of extravagance. When Alexander defeats Darius he takes over use of the same tent: 'The furnishings, however, have been considerably changed. A long bare table replaces the sumptuous Persian one, and the gold and silver decorations have been removed.'[24] The title of the play recalls the children's comics of the time, most of which still focused on episodes of imperial heroism, and adds to the sense of conquest being carried out with a fine sense of moral purpose.[25]

Soon, however, Rattigan shows Alexander's firmly principled stand wavering. Fearing revolts, but without evidence, he orders the murder of one of his generals. In anger after an argument he kills his closest friend. And when we see him in Darius's tent, 'its original finery ... had now been largely restored'.[26] Alexander tells his Persian wife about his predicament: 'The Master of the World has many enemies, you know, Roxana. He doesn't want to have enemies. He wants everyone to love him. But he also wants to remain Master of the World.'[27] In this, Rattigan, like Priestley, was by no means mourning the loss of India, but rather engaging in a debate about the ethical basis of imperialism. What the play suggests is that the means are in conflict with the ends. In Alexander's final agonised question on his deathbed, 'where did it first go wrong?', it is not the loss of empire that is the 'wrong' but the means needed to retain it. Recalling his 'solution' of the Gordian Knot, Alexander ponders: 'I never did solve that puzzle, did I? How can one solve a puzzle with a sword?'[28]

Alexander's dilemma, with some suitable historical adjustment, begins to resemble the quandary with which the British Empire faced the post-war world. In the 1920s, as the first waves of widespread criticism of imperialism began to be felt, a new justification of empire was launched, in the form of Lugard's 'dual mandate' thesis. In 1943, the historian Keith Hancock enthusiastically defined it as

a trust. The trust has two aspects. First, the sovereign power must assure economic opportunity for all nations: it is 'trustee for the commerce of the world'. The second aspect is more important; it is fundamental. The governing power must respect the life and safeguard the opportunities of weaker races. It is trustee for those peoples who are unable as yet to stand on their own feet under the strenuous conditions of the modern world.[29]

This 'benevolent trustee thesis', as it has been dubbed, ran into difficulties during the Second World War. From the beginning of the war, colonial nationalists made much of the affinity between Nazism and the notion of 'weaker races' that seemed to underpin the strategy. The connection was reinforced by the 1942 Atlantic Charter which demanded that 'sovereign rights and self-government [be] restored to those who have been forcibly deprived of them', originally targeted at the Axis powers, but plainly applicable to the Allied empires. At home, a group of Fabian thinkers in the Labour Party Advisory Committee on Imperial Questions, nicknamed 'The Troublemakers' by A. J. P. Taylor, began to promote the notion of withdrawal.[30] The independent Common Wealth party stood on an anti-imperial platform and won three seats between 1943 and 1945.

The Empire began to seem much less secure, and a fairly swift change in perceptions is visible. In 1943 Eric Walker's *The British Empire* could confidently speculate that after the war the Empire might 'continue, changed indeed, but still recognisably the Empire'.[31] Ten years later, in the second edition, Walker feels compelled to make the subtle adjustment 'changed indeed but still recognisably "the Empire"'[32] – a pair of inverted commas that suggests a stepping back from the full-throated confidence of the war years. Another marker of the changed atmosphere came in February 1954, with the founding of the Movement for Colonial Freedom, bringing together various disparate campaigns and individuals, in an attempt to create a mass anti-colonial drive.

As opposition mounted in colonial territories, the notion of benevolent trusteeship was subtly transformed into benevolent decolonisation. Harold Macmillan explained the case in his memoirs, when he claimed that the British people 'did not conceive of themselves as having the right to govern in perpetuity. It was rather their duty to spread to other nations those advantages they had won for themselves.' These comments were broadly consistent with the 'dual mandate', until he added, 'the independence of India, therefore, was ... the culmination of a set purpose of nearly four generations'.[33] This entertaining stuff has been rightly scorned by historians for ignoring the bloody and tenacious attempts of British forces to hold on to power in places like Kenya, Nyasaland and Cyprus. It is, as John Darwin has put it, 'Whig history large as life and twice as shameless'.[34]

This attempt to pass off decolonisation as the very epiphany of empire did not go unremarked. In the autumn of 1954, the Suez Group was formed by disgruntled Tory MPs in protest at the agreement to plan the withdrawal of British troops from the canal zone. Their view of decolonisation is an important part of understanding the range of competing interpretations at play in the 1950s. Julian Amery, a leading member of the Group, hints at their position in his claim that their work might mark 'the beginning of a return to ... faith in Britain's imperial mission and destiny',[35] as if a change of heart was all that was needed to stem the decolonising tide. While some might stress the importance of colonial nationalists, coupled with the near-bankruptcy of Britain after the war, or pressure brought by global capitalists for whom the protectionism of the sterling area was an impediment to exploring new markets, the right-wing Suez Group's interpretation was simple: Britain had lost the will to rule.

Corelli Barnett defended and developed this view in his book *The Collapse of British Power*, in which he claims that the decline of empire was due to Romantic anti-materialism, etiolated public school classicism, and a middle-class do-gooding mentality. These combined to produce the view that 'moral principle and moral purpose rather than strategy or mere interest alone should be the inspiration of English policy'.[36] This led to a squeamishness at the harsh realities of colonial government, which led in turn to a loss of faith in the Empire, and thence to its disintegration. It is the same idea that lurks in Coward's opposition between 'weak-kneed humanitarianism' and 'dignified strength'.

If the right wing believed that the Empire had crumbled because of an enfeeblement in British culture, the left saw the opposite. The Movement for Colonial Freedom held the view that the Empire was corrupting to British society. As one historian remarks, 'there was even a Hobsonian echo in the claim of its treasurer, Anthony Wedgwood Benn, that ending imperialism was a prerequisite to extending democracy at home'.[37] Or as Stephen Howe notes, for the Movement for Colonial Freedom, 'colonialism was an evil for British society, as well as for the colonised, because it was morally corrupting, inimical to the better self of British, or English, national identity'.[38]

Establishing this spectrum of positions makes clear the differences between West End playwrights in the immediate post-war period. In *South Sea Bubble*, Sandra, the Governor's wife, flirts with the young Samolan nationalist Hali Alani, who tries drunkenly to rape her. She knocks him out with a bottle and leaves. The next morning, it seems as if the incident will be twisted to help the nationalist cause. Yet Sandra's *sang-froid* throughout is vindicated when Hali appears, begging forgiveness. The implication seems to be that keeping a level head can see off any attempt at nationalist resistance, and places Coward once again firmly in the ambit of the Suez Group. Priestley's *Home is Tomorrow*, however, leans more closely on a Marxist reading that capitalist expansion was driving the demolition of imperial protectionism. In places it overlaps with more recent historiography which stresses the tactical role played by American Cold War-gaming in supporting or undermining imperial policies.[39] And it is not difficult to imagine what Corelli Barnett might have thought of Rattigan's Alexander and his stricken moral conscience.

Dorothy and Campbell Christie's *His Excellency*, a major West End success in 1950, demonstrates the ambivalences and uncertainties of those caught between such positions. The play is set on the fictional Hispanic island of Salva. His Excellency is the new Governor of the island; appointed by the Labour Government, he is an ex-docker, thoroughly committed to breaking down the old patrician ways and helping the islanders to run things for themselves. As such he is a working-class version of *South Sea Bubble*'s Sir George Shotter, described as being 'a bit Leftish in his views ... in the nicest way possible of course'.[40] Unlike *South Sea Bubble*, however, *His Excellency* allows the Governor space seriously to express his progressive approach to colonial advancement. In particular, when a dockyard strike spreads into public disorder and his advisors urge him to call out the troops, he is eloquent and persuasive in his abhorrence of the plan. He recalls his own experience as a young corporal in India being asked to fire on a demonstration. But the Lieutenant Governor, one of the 'old boys' passed over for the top job, tells him 'You're not a corporal any longer – you're Governor of this Colony, and you must think like a Governor'. The Governor yields and calls out the troops. He turns out the lights and sits lamenting 'three months – and this is all I done for 'em', as offstage we hear a bugle and the shout of 'Fall in!'.[41] The moment is deeply ambivalent; there is a clearly presented clash between the Governor's idealism and the *realpolitik* of colonial government, but with which side of the contradiction the audience's sympathies are supposed to lie is left open. Barnett might consider opening fire on unarmed strikers admirably unsentimental but the moment could also imply a moral decay in the imperial project.

This ambivalence, within the available attitudes of the time, is preserved until the end. The strike has remained solid and threatens the whole of the Governor's socialist strategy. In a desperate eleventh-hour intervention, he goes to the dockyard and addresses the men himself. The reported key phrase that convinced them all to return to work is: 'You're no more fit to govern yourselves than a lot of black-faced baboons!'.[42] Contemptible though this is, it also represents the wretched anger of the trustee thesis in conflict with a restive empire in decay. In *South Sea Bubble*, Coward had given a native politician the incredible lines with which to decline the offer of liberation: 'Believe me, we are too young yet for such brave experiments. Too young and gay and irresponsible to be able to do without our old Nanny.'[43] *His Excellency* at least allows textual space for the audience to decide whether the Governor's collapse into patrician racism is his triumph or his tragedy.

Where does the New Wave fit into this range of positions? The broadly leftist reputation of Osborne and certain of the Angry Young Men might lead one to imagine that they would be firmly opposed to empire. But establishing this has proved surprisingly difficult. Of Jimmy Porter – the anti-hero of *Look Back in Anger* – some critics have argued that his mockery of imperial imagery is tied to a deeper indebtedness and affection for it.[44] And it is not only in hindsight that the Angry Young Men's position on empire appears confused. There is a telling entry in the diary of Tony Benn, recalling a conversation with his Oxford contemporary Kenneth Tynan. Benn wonders, 'How are we to adjust ourselves to this new world without becoming wildly frustrated and defeatist and bitter and apathetic? The problem of power contraction does threaten our political system. Someone said the Angry Young Men were a symptom of the shrinking pains of the British Empire.'[45] Anyone seeking contemporary testimony to the New Wave's anti-imperialism would find the word 'symptom' disturbingly ambiguous.

On the eve of *Look Back in Anger*, the *Spectator*'s drama critic, Anthony Hartley, bemoaned the impoverishment of a British stage shrouded in rituals and attitudes 'artificially maintained from before the First World War'.[46] But despite hoping to see a serious theatre, he admits a problem for any *engagé* playwright: 'at the minute there are no fundamental political problems in this country, so it is difficult to put politics on the stage'.[47] This complacency was oddly characteristic of the 1950s, and it was part of a habit of thought which Hartley would himself criticise seven years later in his book *A State of England* (1963).[48] Its author now promoted to Foreign Editor, the book is a polemical challenge to the failure of English intellectuals properly to square up to important changes affecting Britain in the post-war world. One might have expected the man who longed for intelligent young playwrights to reinvigorate the stage to applaud the generation which stepped forward at the Royal Court, but his response to the New Wave is surprisingly diffident, largely because of their attitude to empire.

There are two main strands to Hartley's argument, but both show the same general structure. One concerns the effects of the properly established welfare state brought to maturity by the Labour Government of 1945–50. He suggests that left intellectuals were appalled to discover that the rising prosperity of the working class in the 1950s had manifested itself in consumerism rather than more 'elevated' cultural pursuits. Rightly reluctant to criticise welfare, or indeed the choices made by working people, these thinkers turned their fire on the producers of that culture. It is evident that Hartley has in mind the thinkers popularly associated with the New Left – Richard Hoggart and Raymond Williams in particular – and their contempt for the 'consumer society' and 'mass communication'. A quasi-psychoanalytic model is employed to suggest that the real source of concern is repressed, leading to the irrational parapraxis of criticising other, less relevant targets. He describes 'outbursts of futile rage over trifles' and 'aimless bursts of rage against comparatively minor irritations', offering *Declaration* as an exemplary instance.[49]

Hartley finds the same hysterical structure when the intellectuals looked outward. The diminishing of Britain's international status meant that the progressive consensus that characterised British post-war politics could not be brought to bear elsewhere in the world: 'at the very moment when a British Labour Government was bursting with good intentions, at the very period of its history when Britain appeared best suited to exercise its influence for the good, that influence was to be taken from it'.[50] No liberal-left intellectual could reasonably call a halt to decolonisation, creating a form of repression leaking out in other forms. In his claim that for some on the left the United Nations was a kind of sublimation of latent imperialism, we might look to Priestley's impeccably liberal *Home is Tomorrow*, which supports the humanitarianism of the UN in the very same tones that others used to applaud the dual mandate thesis.

But the argument has even more pertinence when we come to look at the New Wave. In 1958 Kenneth Tynan described the response of the post-war generation to international affairs: 'feelings of uselessness and impotence, which led in some to apathy, in others to a sort of derisive detachment, and in still others to downright rage. And these feelings were intensified by the knowledge that Britain no longer had a voice strong enough to forbid chaos if, by some horrific chance, it should impend.'[51]

This unusually lucid diagnosis shares with Hartley's portrait the curious mixture of symptoms and the covert longing for the military power to 'forbid' chaos. For the most part though, Hartley remarks, '*Declaration* and its contributors might themselves be the symptoms rather than the analysts of a process of which they were unconscious'.[52]

Hartley's argument helps to explain the strangely hesitant judgements we have already encountered of contemporaries responding to the New Wave. Hartley also notes the paradoxical behaviour of 'those who proclaim their desire for social and political reform' turning their thoughts so decisively to the past.[53] One defender of the Angry Young Men wrote in the *Spectator* with exasperation that they 'cannot be expected to look back to Imperial Britain'.[54] Oddly, this is precisely what many of them did.

This habit of mind is most nakedly visible in the angriest of these young men, John Osborne. *The Entertainer* (Royal Court, April 1957) centres on Archie Rice, a third-rate variety performer.[55] As many critics have argued, *The Entertainer* is one of the first 'state-of-the-nation' plays, in which 'the Music Hall is both a frame for the action and an image of Britain'.[56] The link is made by reference to the Suez crisis, which provides the backdrop to the play, and the last days of the music hall are also the last days of the benevolent trustee thesis.

One particular image aligns the music hall image with the historical context. Increasingly desperate in his quest for catchpenny ideas, Archie decides to beef up his act with a nude tableau, in the traditional posture (and some of the traditional clothes) of Britannia. She is disclosed, behind a gauze, foot up on a china bulldog, with trident and helmet, as Archie sings:

> Some people say we're finished,
> Some people say we're done.
> But if we all stand
> By this dear old land
> The battle will be won.[57]

The shabbiness of the theatrical image chimes beautifully with the shabbiness of the sentiment, creating a devastating image of Britain's humiliating exposure in the Suez débâcle.

The image is, however, ambiguous and needs to be looked at alongside other motifs in this complex play. Archie Rice's tawdry attempt to shore up his ailing music hall career with novelties has its root in his own personal malaise. The first time we see him off-stage we are told that 'whatever he says to anyone is almost always very carefully "thrown away". Apparently absent minded, it is a comedian's technique, it absolves him seeming committed to anyone or anything.'[58] This unwillingness or failure to commit signals a lack of personal feeling, which Archie famously admits in one of his few moments of self-awareness: 'You see this face, you see this face, this face can split open with warmth and humanity. It can sing, and tell the worst, unfunniest stories in the world to a great mob of dead, drab erks and it doesn't matter, it doesn't matter. It doesn't matter because – look at my eyes. I'm dead behind these eyes.'[59]

This theme – a particular obsession of the New Wave – theatrically suggests a broader vision of British culture flourishing on its surface and dead inside. The superficial flourishing is portrayed, just as Hartley suggests it would be, in terms of the shallow flashiness of consumer goods. The play also betrays the same random collection of targets for irreverent scorn, again reinforcing Hartley's claim that the real source of anger cannot quite be named. Yet piecing together the play's 'symptoms' we can lay bare the latent cause of the problem. Archie's daughter, Jean, went to the famous anti-Suez demonstration in November 1956 at the height of the crisis, but she seems more bewildered than exhilarated by the 40,000-strong crowd: 'with a lot of other people, strange as it may seem,' she says bathetically, 'I managed to get myself steamed up about the way things were going'.[60] The unenthusiastic tone of voice recalls Osborne's own in his contribution to *Declaration* where he writes, 'During the Suez Crisis I had collected signatures to a letter to *The Times!* That was the limit of my imagination then.'[61] Taken together, the image of Britain's internal collapse and a somewhat dismissive attitude to the anti-Suez campaign lines up Osborne not with the Movement for Colonial Freedom, but the thinking of Corelli Barnett, who would no doubt have shared a contempt for the liberal anger of Trafalgar Square.[62]

Hartley describes the response of left-intellectuals to Suez as one of 'hysterical rage'.[63] By this he means that what appeared to be rage at the imperialist idiocy of Eden's policy was actually motivated by a deep grief at the loss of status that the crisis revealed: 'the attack on Egypt swept aside the various veils with which he had sought to cover Britain's decline in power, and the real position was revealed in a nakedness all the more disagreeable for being exposed to a particularly frosty international climate'.[64] In the naked Britannia, then, it is not so much the patriotism that is being condemned but the emptiness of the patriotism.

A similar theme underlies *Look Back in Anger*. Osborne described himself as offering 'lessons in feeling'[65] and Jimmy Porter's scabrous attempt to provoke emotional responses from his wife and his friend, Alison and Cliff, is often seen in terms of as a desire to reanimate a complacent and emotionally moribund British public: 'Oh heavens, how I long for a little ordinary human enthusiasm. Just enthusiasm – that's all.'[66] Hartley notes that Jimmy seems extremely vague about precisely what it is he wants people to be enthusiastic *about*, and the play has provoked a small school of 'why is Jimmy angry?' criticism. This vagueness suggests again the random irascibility of these intellectuals-in-denial. While the public complacency that Osborne has in his sights is no doubt partly related to the rising affluence of the 1950s, it may also be aimed at the public's refusal to acknowledge the end of empire.

Despite the speed with which Britain dramatically yielded up its colonial territories, decolonisation played notoriously little part in any of the general elections between 1945 and 1959. Churchill, to be sure, raised the issue in a speech on atomic policy in 1950 and Mossadeq's nationalisation of the Anglo-Iranian Oil Company (a minor rehearsal of the Suez crisis) became a talking point in 1951.[67] But even in 1959, the Suez issue 'slipped with surprising rapidity into the shadows'.[68] But we should not conclude from this that British people were uninterested in empire, still less, as John Strachey optimistically claimed in *The End of Empire* (1959), that the British maturely relinquished their imperial claim in a progressive wave of maturity and altruism.[69] In part we should ascribe the lack of public debate about empire to the success of the benevolent trustee thesis, with the Commonwealth idea providing the 'indispensable painkiller' for territorial contraction.[70] The Suez crisis was a shock precisely because it disturbed this consensus, and politicians were united in their determination to forget it as soon as possible. 'I have no desire whatever to stir up unnecessary mud in this unhappy affair', declared Lord Tedder in the House of Lords. 'The sooner the subject can be neatly filed away as one for students the better.'[71] In the subsequent election the issue was already buried; the Conservatives had no desire to rake over the humiliation, and Labour kept quiet for fear of sounding 'unpatriotic'.[72]

When read in this light, several features of *Look Back in Anger* stand out. Towards the beginning of the play, Jimmy is reading the Sunday papers. He derides an article by J. B. Priestley, comparing him with Alison's father: 'He's like Daddy – still casting well-fed glances back to the Edwardian twilight from his comfortable, disenfranchised wilderness'.[73] A little later, he amplifies this image and gets pulled irresistibly into its rhetoric:

> The old Edwardian brigade do make their brief little world look pretty tempting. All homemade cakes and croquet, bright ideas, bright uniforms. Always the same picture: high summer, the long days in the sun, slim volumes of verse, crisp linen, the smell of starch ... Still, even I regret it somehow, phoney or not.

Looking back to the Raj signifies Jimmy's desire for a time where Britain had a meaning; 'if you've no world of your own', he explains, 'it's rather pleasant to regret the passing of someone else's'.[74] Alison refers to Jimmy as an 'Eminent Victorian',[75] and Alison's father, Colonel Redfern, is the only person we see Jimmy talk to without rancour and spite. Jimmy's shouts of despairing rage, his call for human enthusiasm, read more like an attempt to wake people from their quiet complacency about empire.

Hartley suggests that the leftishness which critics tended to find in Jimmy is worryingly unaligned and could in time give way to a more right-wing authoritarianism. This kind of nugatory speculation about what characters would do after a play is over would be dubious, were it not for the curiosity of *Déjàvu*, Osborne's own sequel to *Look Back in Anger*, written thirty-five years later, in which Jimmy has indeed followed his author's drift into a High Tory political stance, ranting bibulously about Europe, homosexuals and the artistic direction of the Royal Court.[76]

The simplistic division of British theatrical attitudes to empire, then, must be complicated by acknowledging two things: first, the climate of opinion in which these writers worked had changed greatly in the period under review and one cannot make easy comparisons between the work of writers before and after 1956; second, Coward, Priestley and Rattigan all made complex interventions in the debate which were not (with the exception of Coward's late *South Sea Bubble*) evidently supportive of empire. On the other side of that historical marker, we find that the exemplary Angry Young Man, John Osborne, may indeed have been animated by a certain kind of imperial nostalgia, in which the title of his most famous play expresses an anger at the present for failing to live up to the imperial standards of the past. In both plays, Osborne's desire for an authentic mode of cultural expression is aimed at a public not noticing the real decline of empire, and at the politicians who hid this decline beneath the fig leaf of benevolence. To do so, Osborne noticeably draws on moments of colonial strength to shape the attack. In his book on the Suez crisis, Hugh Thomas explicitly compares Jimmy Porter's longing for emotional bravery with Eden's adventurism in Suez.[77]

We might also think of Corelli Barnett's characterisation of British complacency in the face of imperial decline – 'sunset calm and nostalgia, in which the British nation, like an old couple in retirement enjoying the peaceful ending of the day, contemplated some sweep of English landscape and hearkened to the distant church bells'[78] – and remember that one of the most memorable images of *Look Back in Anger* has Jimmy raging violently but impotently at the church bells.

Notes

1   Noël Coward, 16 July 1946, *Diaries*, ed. Graham Payn and Sheridan Morley (London, Weidenfeld and Nicolson, 1982), p. 60.
2   W. Roger Louis, 'The Dissolution of Empire', in Judith M. Brown and W. Roger Louis (eds), *The Oxford History of the British Empire, Vol. IV: The Twentieth Century* (Oxford, Oxford University Press, 1999), p. 337.

3   Noël Coward, 6 August 1956, *Diaries*, p. 329.
4   Noël Coward, *Pacific 1860*, in *Play Parade V* (London, Heinemann, 1958), p. 3.
5   Kenneth Tynan, 'Theatre and Living', in Tom Maschler (ed.), *Declaration* (London, MacGibbon and Kee, 1957), p. 109.
6   Kenneth Tynan, *Tynan on Theatre* (Harmondsworth, Penguin, 1964), p. 60.
7   Michael Hastings, *Don't Destroy Me*, in *Three Plays* (London, W. H. Allen, 1966), p. 69.
8   John Elsom, *Cold War Theatre* (London, Routledge, 1992), p. 33.
9   Coward wrote a third Samolo play, *Volcano*, in 1955 but it was rejected by Binkie Beaumont and remained unperformed until April 2000, when it was finally premièred at the Palace Theatre, Westcliff-on-Sea, directed by Roy Marsden. The play is a return, in some senses, to the world of *Point Valaine*, set in a threatening landscape which seems abstractly to comment on the characters' actions. However, in an essay talking about the theatrical culture of the time, I have decided to exclude unperformed pieces from extended discussion.
10 T. S. Eliot, *The Cocktail Party*, ed. Nevill Coghill (London, Faber and Faber, 1974), p. 176.
11 At the Royal Court, such absurdities were eliminated. Errol John's *Moon on a Rainbow Shawl* (December 1958), Barry Reckord's *Flesh to a Tiger* (May 1958), Wole Soyinka's *The Invention* (November 1959), and *Eleven Dead at Hola Camp* (July 1959) featured partly or wholly black casts.
12 Noël Coward, *Point Valaine*, in *Collected Plays: Six* (London, Methuen, 1999), pp. 119, 172.
13 Ibid., p. 188.
14 Coward, *Pacific 1860*, p. 39.
15 Ibid., pp. 93–4.
16 Cf. J. A. Mangan, '"The Grit of Our Forefathers": Invented Traditions, Propaganda and Imperialism', in John M. Mackenzie (ed.), *Imperialism and Popular Culture* (Manchester, Manchester University Press, 1986), p. 133.
17 Radio commentator, quoted in John M. Mackenzie, '"In Touch with the Infinite": The BBC and the Empire, 1923–1953', in Mackenzie (ed.), *Imperialism and Popular Culture*, p. 176.
18 J. B. Priestley, *Home is Tomorrow*, in *Plays: Volume III* (London, Heinemann, 1950), p. 341.
19 Ibid., p. 372.
20 Terence Rattigan, *Adventure Story*, in *Collected Plays: Volume Two* (London, Hamish Hamilton, 1953), p. 107.
21 Christopher Innes, 'Terence Rattigan: The Voice of the 1950s', in Dominic Shellard (ed.), *British Theatre in the 1950s* (Sheffield, Sheffield Academic Press, 2000), p. 62.
22 Rattigan, *Adventure Story*, pp. 136–8.
23 Ibid., p. 124.
24 Ibid., p. 145.
25 Sandy Wilson's follow-up to *The Boyfriend* was *The Buccaneer* (Lyric, Hammersmith, September 1955) and used the editorial offices of a 'boy's own' paper dealing with imperial adventures as its setting. The magazine is in decline – science fiction has become the popular topic – and the musical comically attempts to stem the haemorrhage of its readers. As always, Wilson uses pastiche and quick wit to inject sharp satire into the work, and the debate about how to rescue the paper maps neatly onto generational clashes over empire.
26 Rattigan, *Adventure Story*, pp. 174–6, 190, 160.
27 Ibid., p. 177.
28 Ibid., p. 159.
29 W. K. Hancock, *Argument of Empire* (Harmondsworth, Penguin, 1943), pp. 75–6.
30 Stephen Howe, *Anticolonialism in British Politics: The Left and the End of Empire* (Oxford, Clarendon Press, 1993), pp. 108, 141, 48.
31 Eric A. Walker, *The British Empire: Its Structure and Spirit* (Oxford, Oxford University Press, 1943), p. 4.

32 Walker, *The British Empire*, 2nd edn (Cambridge, Bowes & Bowes, 1953), p. x.
33 Harold Macmillan, *Pointing the Way 1959–1961* (London, Macmillan, 1972), pp. 116–17.
34 John Darwin, 'British Colonialism since 1945: A Pattern or a Puzzle?', *Journal of Imperial and Commonwealth History*, 12:2 (1982) p. 189. See also Bernard Porter, *The Lion's Share: A Short History of British Imperialism 1850–1995*, 3rd edn (London, Longman, 1996), pp. 345–6.
35 Quoted in David Goldsworthy, *Colonial Issues in British Politics 1945–1961: From 'Colonial Development' to 'Wind of Change'* (Oxford, Clarendon Press, 1971), p. 297.
36 Corelli Barnett, *The Collapse of British Power* (London, Macmillan, 1972), p. 20.
37 Nicholas Owen, 'Critics of Empire in Britain', in Brown and Louis (eds), *The Twentieth Century*, p. 205.
38 Howe, *Anticolonialism in British Politics*, p. 301.
39 See, for example, W. Roger Louis and Ronald Robinson, 'The Imperialism of Decolonization', *Journal of Imperial and Commonwealth History*, 22:3 (1994), pp. 462–511.
40 Noël Coward, *South Sea Bubble*, in *Collected Plays: Six* (London, Methuen, 1999), p. 205.
41 Dorothy and Campbell Christie, *His Excellency*, in J. C. Trewin (ed.), *Plays of the Year 1950* (London, Paul Elek, 1951), pp. 206–7.
42 Ibid., p. 237.
43 Coward, *South Sea Bubble*, p. 228.
44 Alistair Davies and Peter Saunders, 'Literature, Politics and Society', in Alan Sinfield (ed.), *Society and Literature 1945–1970* (London, Methuen, 1983); David Cairns and Shaun Richard, 'No Good Brave Causes? The Alienated Intellectual, and the End of Empire', *Literature and History*, 14:2 (1988), pp. 194–206.
45 Tony Benn, 25 June 1958, *Years of Hope: Diaries, Papers and Letters 1940–62* (London, Hutchinson, 1994), p. 282.
46 Anthony Hartley, 'The London Stage: Drugs No Answer', in Frederick Lumley (ed.), *Theatre in Review* (London, Richard Patterson, 1956), p. 4.
47 Ibid., p. 10.
48 I must express my thanks to Stuart Ward for drawing this fascinating book to my attention.
49 Anthony Hartley, *A State of England* (London, Hutchinson, 1963), pp. 148–9, 85.
50 Ibid., p. 69.
51 Tynan, *Tynan on Theatre*, pp. 55–6.
52 Hartley, *State of England*, pp. 21–2.
53 Ibid., p. 225.
54 David H. Shipman, Letter, *Spectator*, 15 November 1957, p. 643.
55 Osborne is the key theatrical figure of the New Wave, and it is on his work that I shall focus. However, the argument can be applied more broadly. I have elsewhere suggested, for example, that Willis Hall's *The Long and the Short and the Tall* displays, Barnett-like, the dangers of moral squeamishness. See my *1956 and All That: The Making of Modern British Drama* (London, Routledge, 1999), pp. 141–2.
56 Christopher Innes, *Modern British Drama 1890–1990* (Cambridge, Cambridge University Press, 1992), p. 108.
57 John Osborne, *The Entertainer*, in *Plays: 2* (London, Faber and Faber, 1998), p. 55.
58 Ibid., p. 29.
59 Ibid., p. 66.
60 Ibid., p. 23. Later Jean and Archie both condemn this political action in contrast to 'real' feeling, pp. 64–5.
61 John Osborne, 'They Call It Cricket', in Tom Maschler (ed.), *Declaration* (London, MacGibbon & Kee, 1957), p. 67.
62 One might also note that many on the right wing of the debate were hostile to Europe, since entry into the Common Market would involve a final renunciation of the privileged tariff arrangements within the Commonwealth, and thus an irreversible surrender of empire status. Instead they looked to America, hoping that Britain might retain

a crucial world role by acting as a fulcrum between these two huge power blocs. This fairly precisely parallels Osborne's contempt for European drama and his enthusiasm for Arthur Miller and Tennessee Williams. Most New Wave plays look to America rather than Europe for their dramaturgical models. Osborne's *Personal Enemy* (1955) and Errol John's *Moon on a Rainbow Shawl* (1958) resemble Miller and Williams respectively. Cf. my *1956 and All That*, chapter 5.

63 Hartley, *State of England*, p. 69.
64 Ibid., p. 73.
65 Osborne, 'They Call It Cricket', p. 65.
66 John Osborne, *Look Back in Anger*, in *Plays: 1* (London, Faber and Faber, 1993), p. 11.
67 H. G. Nicholas and D. E. Butler, *The British General Election of 1950* (London, Macmillan, 1951), p. 304; D. E. Butler, *The British General Election of 1951* (London, Macmillan, 1952), p. 247.
68 D. E. Butler and Richard Rose, *The General Election of 1959* (London, Macmillan, 1960), p. 37.
69 John Strachey, *The End of Empire* (London: Victor Gollancz, 1959).
70 John Darwin, 'Decolonisation and the End of Empire', in Robin W. Winks (ed.), *The Oxford History of the British Empire, Vol. V: Historiography* (Oxford, Oxford University Press, 1999), p. 547.
71 Quoted in Leon D. Epstein, *British Politics in the Suez Crisis* (London, Pall Mall, 1964), p. 3.
72 Butler and Rose, *The General Election of 1959*, p. 64n.
73 Osborne, *Look Back in Anger*, p. 12.
74 Ibid., p. 13.
75 Ibid., p. 89.
76 John Osborne, *Déjàvu*, in *Plays: 1* (London: Faber and Faber, 1993).
77 Hugh Thomas, *The Suez Affair* (London, Weidenfeld and Nicolson, 1967), p. 161.
78 Barnett, *The Collapse of British Power*, p. 67.

CHAPTER FIVE

'No nation could be broker': the satire boom and the demise of Britain's world role

Stuart Ward

The quickening pace of imperial decline in the post-war era prompted a wide variety of responses in contemporary British culture. On the one hand, there are signs of anger and resentment at the apparently inexorable slide towards British impotence on the world stage, coupled with a mournful nostalgia for a more resolute and certain age. At the same time, the mounting pressure of international opinion led many to view the liquidation of empire with a sense of relief that transformed easily into self-congratulation at the successful forging of a new partnership of independent Commonwealth states. But the end of empire and the steady diminution of British power and prestige also became the source of immense laughter and ridicule. The ever-widening gap between the global reach of British national aspirations and the encroaching external realities of the post-war world provided new avenues for comic exploration of the imperial ethos and the myth of Britain's 'world role'.

This tendency became particularly marked with the emergence of the so-called British 'satire boom' in the early 1960s. From the late 1950s, changing tastes in popular British comedy had begun to generate an unprecedented appetite for mockery and ridicule of the manners, pretensions and pomposity of Britain's ruling elite – the so-called British 'establishment'. It was the 1960 Edinburgh stage revue *Beyond the Fringe* that launched the new satire craze into the public sphere, featuring an array of highly innovative sketches on contemporary issues and institutions such as capital punishment, the Cold War, the nuclear threat, the class system, the legacy of war, religion, politics and, above all, politicians. *Beyond the Fringe* expanded the boundaries of popular satire almost overnight, and spawned a string of imitators: the satirical magazine *Private Eye*, the West End night club 'The Establishment', and the highly popular BBC television programme *That Was the Week that Was*.

The satire boom has generally been interpreted as a symbol of profound changes in the dominant values of post-war British society. In particular, it has been understood in terms of the decline of tradition and deference, the rise of the 'permissive society', and the emergence of a cynical contempt towards politicians and public figures more generally. These factors, in turn, have been attributed to the steady shift from austerity to affluence in the post-war years, and the growing independence and purchasing power of the younger generation. In some respects the satire boom has been regarded as a precursor to the 'swinging sixties', arriving on the heels of the relaxation of censorship occasioned by the Lady Chatterley trial of 1960. It is these factors, combined with a prevailing sense of popular restlessness after ten years of 'smug Tory rule', that are normally said to account for the extraordinary flowering of satirical comedy in the early 1960s.[1]

While these factors should not be dismissed, they are insufficient as an explanation for the satirists' overwhelming preoccupation with Britain's dwindling role in the post-war world. What has been lacking is a sense of the broader context of British imperial decline that permeated much, if not all, of the new satirical reflection on the state of the nation. The underlying question at the heart of the satire boom, 'What's wrong with Britain?', would have been superfluous in an era of relative affluence were it not for the deep sense of loss that accompanied the transition from imperial power to island state in the post-war decades. It is argued here that much of the apparently progressive criticism of the British establishment that characterised the satire boom was in fact fundamentally rooted in a nostalgic reflection on the imperial past. Practically all of the leading comic figures of this generation – Peter Cook, Jonathan Miller, Alan Bennett, William Rushton, Christopher Booker, John Bird and David Frost – had been raised on pre-war and wartime notions of duty and service to nation and empire, only to reach maturity at a time when these ideas could no longer be sustained by the external political realities. This chapter, then, looks at the ways in which popular British comedy reflected the reorientation of an entire generation, away from the former conception of Britain's world-wide imperial destiny and towards a more modest awareness of Britain's place in the world. The end of empire provided fertile ground for new innovations in British comedy, as well-worn ideas about loyalty, service, character, authority and the civilising mission of the British race were subjected to relentless parody and ridicule. While on the face of it the satire boom had the character of a good-humoured acknowledgement of new post-imperial realities, closer examination reveals an underlying resentment towards those who had promised a more grandiose role for Britain in the post-war world.

When *Beyond the Fringe* opened in London in May 1961, its impact was immediate and wide-ranging. The theatre critic for the *Observer*, Kenneth Tynan, heralded the arrival of 'satire' on the English stage. 'Future historians may well thank me', he declared roundly, 'for providing them with a full account of the moment when English comedy took its first decisive step into the second half of the twentieth century.'[2] At the other end of the political spectrum, the conservative critic for the *Daily Express*, Bernard Levin, conveyed his profound 'gratitude that there should be four men living among us today who could come together to provide, as long as memory holds, an eighth colour to the rainbow'. As Levin saw it: 'Satirical revue in this country has been, until now, basically cowardly. First, it has picked on easy targets. Second, however hard it hit its targets ... it left its audience alone, to leave the theatre as fat and complacent as it came in.'[3] The *Evening News* described it as 'the perfect revue, for which we have all waited through so many a groaning and fatuous night'.[4] The broad impression was one of English stage revue having suddenly awoken from a long slumber – an impression that was energetically cultivated by the satirists themselves.[5] As Ronald Bergen has commented, 'Just as, a few years before ... "anger" was the word that had been buzzed round tables at dinner parties, now the word "satire" was bandied about as if it had just been coined'.[6]

Of course, satire had deep roots in British political culture, stretching back at least as far as the early eighteenth century in the writings of Alexander Pope, Jonathan Swift and Henry Fielding, and the etchings of William Hogarth. But in the context of the early 1960s, the sudden appearance of satirical revue was widely regarded as something new and invigorating. Prior to these years, the accepted standards for comic performance in the public sphere had been harnessed to a strict code of respectability. The Lord Chamberlain's Office was actively engaged in censoring stage productions whenever they overstepped the boundaries of public decency. A particularly stringent set of rules applied to public broadcasting. In 1949, for example, the BBC had compiled the so-called 'Green Book' – an official 'policy guide for writers and producers' outlining a whole range of subjects that were deemed unsuitable for broadcast comedy. Although 'satire' was not explicitly referred to, the possibilities for satirical material were severely restricted by an absolute ban on 'anything which can reasonably be construed as derogatory to political institutions', including impersonations of 'leading public and political figures'. The guidebook underlined that 'broadcasting is a part of the domestic life of the nation', and must therefore adhere strictly to the principles of good taste, decency and political impartiality. In other words, the BBC had a special responsibility to observe and uphold the prevailing ethical standards of British civic culture.[7]

These restrictions notwithstanding, some have identified the early roots of the satire boom in the immediate post-war era in the popular radio comedy programme *It's That Man Again*, which ran from 1939 to 1949. The *Guardian* described the programme as 'a laughing criticism of the mysterious "them" who rule our fortunes'. But invariably, the 'them' were depicted so mysteriously as to diffuse any genuinely political or satirical comment. As Stephen Wagg has argued, this 'meddling men from the Ministry' approach was only mildly rebellious at best, and may even have reflected a playful fondness for Britain's governing institutions.[8] A more significant influence on the satire boom was *The Goon Show*, by far the leading innovation in British broadcast comedy in the 1950s. The show was launched by BBC Radio in 1951, featuring four ex-servicemen, Peter Sellers, Harry Secombe, Michael Bentine and Spike Milligan.[9] Although *The Goon Show* did not deal explicitly in political satire, it was widely regarded at the time as subversive, both by the BBC hierarchy and the chief scriptwriter, Milligan. Among the prime objects of Goon humour were authority figures and officialdom generally, and the show specialised in sending up a whole host of hallowed British institutions. Privilege, patriotism, the parliament, the military and the Empire were all frequently lampooned. Milligan himself was in many respects a product of the Empire, having spent the first fifteen years of his life as the son of a working-class military family in the dying days of the British Raj. He has recounted how, as a child, he imbibed the ethos of imperial grandeur, delighting in the pomp and ceremony of military life on the frontier, and the deferential ministrations of native servants. But the shock of the family's return to the 'drab grey working-class misery' of Catford in the early 1930s became the source of profound disillusionment for Milligan, then in his mid-teens. It was the stark contrast between the heroic myths of empire and the sordid realities of the imperial metropolis in the inter-war years that later provided the inspiration for comic characters like Major Dennis Bloodnock, a seedy, dishonourable coward from the Rajputana Rifles, along with other characters such as Dr Osric Pureheart, the sinister Hercules Gryptype-Thynne, and the obnoxious schoolboy Bluebottle. As Milligan reflected on his childhood influences:

> If all my youth had been spent in Catford, there would have been no *Goon Show* ... But the way it happened, I had all these insights into the Imperial mish-mash of grandeur and a sort of moral decadence. I saw so much of the pretences, and the hollowness and the foolishness of people. You see, I saw it all as a child and as I grew older so much of it seemed ridiculous and hysterically funny. I found them all out there – Major Bloodnock, Osric Pureheart, all of them.[10]

The Goon Show came under the constant scrutiny of irate BBC executives. From 1952 to 1956 alone, the producer, Peter Eton, faced thirty separate attempts from within the BBC to have the show taken off the air. On one occasion, the Goons were given a stern warning after a programme in which Major Dennis Bloodnock was awarded the OBE for emptying dustbins during the heat of battle. On another occasion, the show came very close to being withdrawn for 'rank bad taste' when Peter Sellers breached the rules of the BBC Green Book by impersonating Her Majesty the Queen shooing pigeons from Trafalgar Square.[11] In 1957, Milligan locked horns again with his employers over his proposal to write 'a satirical programme' based on the recent film epic *Bridge on the River Kwai*. The Head of BBC Light Entertainment, Pay Hillyard, flatly rejected the idea, on the grounds that 'a programme of this nature could cause considerable offence, particularly to those who were closely connected with events in the far east'.[12] It was the Goons' blatant disrespect for the symbols of loyalty, patriotism, service, duty and empire which brought them into conflict with their employers, and which very nearly led to their undoing.

The implicit social critique of *The Goon Show* rarely took the form of overt satire, however. The broadcasts were more notable for their spiralling surrealist fantasy than any pointed commentary on the issues of the day. Nonetheless, Milligan did occasionally adopt the technique of basing his scripts loosely on current issues and events, but in such an oddball fashion as to evade the unwanted attention of the censor. For example, the 1953 episode 'The Ascent of Mount Everest' coincided with Hillary and Tenzing's real-life ascent that same year, gently mocking the prevailing triumphalist rhetoric of the 'second Elizabethan age'.[13] Similarly, 'The Nasty Affair at the Burami Oasis', broadcast in October 1956 only days before the Suez crisis erupted into full-scale military conflict, recounted the tale of an Arab seizure of a British oasis in the Middle East, and the efforts of the British 'Army, Navy and NAAFI' to get it back.[14] The British military hierarchy were portrayed as fumbling nincompoops, particularly in their 'devlish plan' to dispatch a gunboat to the Middle East dismantled and disguised in four-inch packets of date fertiliser. The parallel with Suez would have been unmistakable to the audience of the day, although it is difficult to assess how they might have interpreted Milligan's typically incoherent allegory. The fact that Prince Charles was the Goons' number one fan suggests that the show never quite lived up to the biting social critique that Milligan later claimed he was aiming for.[15] Nonetheless, it is interesting to note the way in which the idea of British ineffectiveness in the world was being brazenly sent up, even prior to Anthony Eden's infamous invasion of the canal zone. In that sense, the Goons were arguably the first of the post-war comedians to seize upon Britain's dwindling power and influence in the world as a source of comic invention.

Virtually all of the leading figures of the satire boom have acknowledged their enormous debt to *The Goon Show*. But while the Goons had their roots in a working-class tradition of poking fun at the pretensions of the aristocracy, the new generation of satirists were a far more genteel breed.[16]

The kind of humour exhibited in *Beyond the Fringe* emerged from the undergraduate revues of Oxford and Cambridge in the late 1950s. The Cambridge 'Footlights' club was an extremely influential testing ground for new innovations in revue comedy. In particular the 1958 Footlights revue *The Last Laugh*, directed by John Bird, abandoned the traditional staple fare of men in drag, torch songs, and whimsical gags about punts and proctors, and opted instead for a more hard-edged commentary on contemporary political themes.[17] Arguably the leading figure in the undergraduate satire craze was a child of the Colonial Office, Peter Cook. Cook's biographer, Harry Thompson, has described how 'for successive generations, the Cook family had placed service to empire above mere family considerations, representing their monarch dutifully in a variety of distant locations'.[18] Cook's grandfather had worked for the Federated Malay States Railway in Kuala Lumpur, while his father, Alec Cook, served for twenty years as a district colonial officer in the Nigerian bush. While his parents carried out their colonial duties, Cook was raised in England by nannies before being sent to Radley school. He read French and German at Cambridge, and for many years it was naturally assumed that he was destined for a promising career in the Foreign Office. His fellow *Beyond the Fringe* cast members, Jonathan Miller and Alan Bennett, were equally intent on pursuing respectable careers in medicine and medieval history respectively. The list of Oxbridge comedians who made a name for themselves during the satire boom of the early 1960s is remarkable: David Frost, John Bird, Eleanor Bron, John Fortune, John Wells, Christopher Booker, Richard Ingrams and Timothy Birdsdall (in addition to the *Beyond the Fringe* cast). In that sense, the new wave of satirists were exemplars of the same privileged elites they parodied.

Beyond the Fringe was not itself an undergraduate revue, but rather an attempt to bring together the best of the Oxbridge revues of that era, with Cook and Miller bringing their experience (and material) from the Cambridge Footlights revues, and Alan Bennett and Dudley Moore providing an Oxford flavour. It was conceived as the main event at the 1960 Edinburgh Festival, primarily as a means of outshining the competition of the increasingly popular Edinburgh 'fringe' (hence the title). By the time it reached London the following spring it was widely regarded as a major breakthrough in British satire, partly because of the minimalist staging (having departed from the brightly lit sets, elaborate makeup, and general air of frivolity of traditional stage revue) but mainly because of the overtly political nature of the material. It was primarily Bennett and Miller who pushed the show in a self-consciously satirical direction, while Cook and Moore were more sensitive to the problems inherent in staging undergraduate humour for a wider public – problems that seemed even more acute when the four performed to outraged audiences in Brighton in the lead-up to the London opening.[19] Not all of the material was self-consciously satirical, but the overwhelming impression conveyed was that of a major assault on the values, social mores and pretensions of the day.

In particular, *Beyond the Fringe* caricatured a wide array of stereotypical authority figures. The hermetically sealed world of the Oxbridge don was deftly sent up in a philosophical dialogue of escalating absurdity ('Are you using "yes" in the affirmative sense here?'). In 'Take a Pew', an Anglican priest delivered a typically patronising sermon consisting of pompous platitudes and earnest reflections on the obscure biblical text: 'My brother Esau is an hairy man, but I am a smooth man'. More controversial was the 'Aftermyth of War' sketch, where a Royal Air Force commander called on one of his loyal airmen to lay down his life: 'We need a futile gesture at this stage. It will raise the whole tone of the war.' And in a sketch developed during the Broadway run of *Beyond the Fringe*, the First Deputy Head of New Scotland Yard, Sir Arthur Gappy, imperiously expounded his theory that the Great Train Robbery of 1963 was in fact the work of thieves: 'The whole pattern is extremely reminiscent of past robberies where we have found thieves to be involved'.[20]

It was the idea of character and breeding as the key to political legitimacy that was most brazenly sent up in *Beyond the Fringe*. This was a particularly pertinent theme to the kind of educated middle-class and upper-middle-class sensitivities of the *Beyond the Fringe* cast, all of whom had been raised on the ideals of good manners and gentlemanly conduct. Generations of British public schoolboys had been imbued with the myth that it was the force of character that enabled small clusters of British patriots to rule large swathes of territory and command the respect and obedience of inferior races. Self-restraint, loyalty, stoicism, sacrifice, a devotion to nation and empire, a capacity to command, and a sense of duty and service were the mainstays of the British imperial ideal. Yet it was these very qualities that the new generation of satirists held up to contempt and ridicule. The ideal of restraint, self-control and subordination of the self, far from representing the pillar on which Britain's greatness was founded, were shown to result in the kind of repressed, inept and degenerate characters so skilfully rendered by the *Beyond the Fringe* cast.

The comic creations of *Beyond the Fringe* were so effective as satire because they conveyed the sense of a ruling elite completely out of touch with their own (and the nation's) shortcomings. This was perhaps most succinctly conveyed in the 'Civil War' sketch, where a panel of dithering Whitehall mandarins addressed a public meeting, carefully outlining the preparations they had made in the event of a nuclear holocaust:

> What can we do from a practical point of view in the event of a nuclear attack? Well, the first golden rule to remember about hydrogen warfare is to

be *out* of the area where the attack is about to occur – get *right out* of the area because that's the danger area, where the bombs are dropping. Get right out of it – get right out of it – if you're out of it you're well out of it, if you're in it, you're really in it.

Earlier in the sketch, the public were reassured about their chances of escaping injury:

Now, we shall receive four minutes warning of any impending nuclear attack. Some people have said, 'Oh my goodness me – four minutes? that is not a very long time!' Well, I would remind those doubters that some people in this great country of ours can run a mile in four minutes.

The reference to Roger Bannister's record-breaking four-minute mile served to highlight the way in which any British triumph, however trivial, might be used to screen out the harsh realities of Britain's relative helplessness in the changing political configuration of the post-war world. As Cook's contemporary John Bird reflected years later, the Bannister joke 'brilliantly clamped its teeth on that era's self-delusion and hopeless nostalgia for power and glory'.[21]

It is precisely this context that is vital for understanding the emergence of the satire craze in the early 1960s. *Beyond the Fringe* came on the scene at a time of widespread public discussion and debate about the 'state of the nation'. A succession of learned publications, from Hugh Thomas's 1959 collection *The Establishment: A Symposium*, to Anthony Hartley's *A State of England* in 1963, all posed the fundamental question: 'What's wrong with Britain?' Other titles of that era such as *The Stagnant Society* (1961), *Suicide of a Nation?* (1963) and *Great Britain or Little England?* (1963) revealed a growing dissatisfaction with the way the nation was governed.[22] It was these ideological currents that directly informed the kind of 'anti-establishment' satire that was the hallmark of *Beyond the Fringe*. Christopher Booker has recognised that the underlying message of the satirists 'was simply that of the "What's Wrong With Britain" journalists – only carried to a newly irresponsible, unreal and more destructive level'.[23] No less than the Prime Minister of the day, Harold Macmillan, was held up to unprecedented mockery and ridicule. Macmillan had taken over the prime ministership from Anthony Eden in 1957 in the immediate aftermath of the Suez fiasco. Much of his tenure in office had been devoted to restoring Britain's damaged international prestige and reversing the downward trend in British power and influence in the world. His task in this regard was made all the more complicated by the transformation of the Empire into a new multi-racial Commonwealth, which proceeded apace in the late 1950s and early 1960s. In this climate, Macmillan's attempts to play the role of world statesman were seen by many as ineffective and inappropriate – particularly in so far as he imagined himself in the role of 'honest broker' between the superpowers. Although the early years of his premiership were highly successful in electoral terms, by the early 1960s Macmillan had come to personify the growing sense of national malaise. Thus, a receptive climate awaited Peter Cook's lampoon of the Prime Minister in *Beyond the Fringe* in a sketch entitled 'TV PM':

> Good evening. I have recently been travelling round the world, on your behalf, and at your expense, visiting some of the chaps with whom I hope to be shaping your future. I went first to Germany, and there I spoke with the German Foreign Minister, Herr ... Herr and there, and we exchanged many frank words in our respective languages; so precious little came of that in the way of understanding ...
>
> I then went on to America, and there I had talks with the young, vigorous President of that great country, and danced with his lovely lady wife. We talked of many things, including Great Britain's position in the world as some kind of honest broker. I agreed with him, when he said that no nation could be more honest; and he agreed with me, when I chaffed him, and said that no nation could be broker.

At a time when public impersonations of leading political figures were not regarded as an acceptable part of a comedian's repertoire, this particular sketch represented a radical new departure. As Michael Palin has reflected: 'It is not easy nowadays to convey the sensational audacity, the explosively liberating effect of hearing the Prime Minister of the day impersonated'.[24] The distinctive feature about Cook's routine was its overwhelming preoccupation with Macmillan's performance on the world stage. Throughout the performance, he would stand next to a globe which he used from time to time to point out – hopelessly incorrectly – the various destinations he had visited. This served as a none too subtle metaphor for the decline of British global mastery, and more importantly, the folly of those who, like Macmillan, remained unreconciled to a more modest British role in world affairs. The entire routine relied implicitly on the audience's familiarity with long-established myths about Britain's preordained role as a leading world power. It was against the grandiose vision of 'Rule Britannia' that Macmillan seemed such an inept and inadequate world statesman – a symbol of the unrealised expectations of an entire generation. In that sense, the leading figures of the satire boom were by no means social revolutionaries as is often suggested. On the contrary, the cast of *Beyond the Fringe* have all disclaimed any radical social intent, particularly Jonathan Miller, who complains that he has been 'lumbered with the satire tag' ever since. In a similar vein, Peter Cook has claimed that his Macmillan routine was extremely affectionate, and confessed that he was 'a great Macmillan fan'.[25] This merely underlines the conservative ideological basis of much of the satirical material of this era. The likes of Cook and Miller were not out to change the social or political order radically, but to mock the shortcomings of those who had allowed so much change to rock the material and political bases of British power and prestige.

The success of *Beyond the Fringe* prompted a spate of spin-off ventures, largely at the instigation of Cook. Within five months of the London opening of *Beyond the Fringe*, Cook opened a satirical nightclub in the West End which he ironically christened 'The Establishment'. The club format enabled him to evade the censorious gaze of the Lord Chamberlain's office, thus providing a venue 'where we could be more outrageous than we could be on stage'.[26] The nightly satirical show featured some of the leading names of the 'satire boom' – John Bird, John Wells, John Fortune, Eleanor Bron, as well as occasional late night appearances by Cook himself. Around the same time, the satirical magazine *Private Eye* was launched by an old Cambridge associate of Cook, Christopher Booker, together with part-time Establishment club performer William Rushton. A series of political scandals in 1963 provided *Private Eye* with a wealth of raw material for casting derision on the moral bankruptcy of the Macmillan Government. The Vassal affair, involving homosexuality, blackmail and security risks in the civil service, was soon followed by the infamous Profumo scandal in which the Minister for War, John Profumo, was forced to resign over his affair with Christine Keeler (who was also involved at the time with a Russian diplomat). Within a week of Profumo's denunciation in the House of Commons in March 1963, *Private Eye* published a double-spread cartoon by Timothy Birdsdall (yet another of the Cambridge Footlights generation) depicting Macmillan as a debauched Roman emperor reclining among naked women and mincing homosexuals clad in togas and bowler hats, while the Empire crumbled around him. The accompanying text by Christopher Booker was a clever pastiche of Edward Gibbon's *Decline and Fall of the Roman Empire*:

> By the early days of the year 1963, the twilight of the British Empire provided a sorry spectacle of collapse and decay on every hand. It is evident from history that there is no nation which, having extended its sinews and vigour in the conquest and administration of empire, maintains its previous standards of morality and efficiency in the prosecution of its remaining activities.

The text referred to the Profumo affair only in a passing allusion to 'the Chief of the Praetorian Guard, Sextus Profano' and his acquaintance with Christina – 'a beautiful girl known well to many of the great figures of society despite her lowly origins'.[27] But the broader point was a perceived link between the moral decrepitude of an aloof and elitist government at home, and the dwindling power and prestige of the British Empire abroad.

By far the most significant development in the booming satire craze was the BBC's decision in 1962 to launch a late night satirical programme, structured around a 'news of the week' format. The appointment of Hugh

Carleton-Greene as Director General of the BBC in 1960 is widely thought to have coincided with a relaxation of the strict code of good taste that had predominated in BBC broadcasting policy since the 1920s. The idea for television satire was obviously inspired by the success of *Beyond the Fringe*, although Carleton-Greene himself merely explains that he had 'a vague idea ... that in the atmosphere of the early '60s, it would be very good to have a programme which did something to prick pomposity, and show politicians and others in their true character'.[28] The BBC chose the late Saturday time slot because this seemed to be a time when people were 'more aware of being persons and less of being citizens, than at any other time of the week. It is therefore the best time ... to relieve the pressure of earnest concern and goodwill which presses down on us for the rest of the week.'[29] The show was given the title *That Was the Week that Was* (normally abbreviated to *TW3*), and was broadcast live in front of an enthusiastic studio audience. It was hosted by yet another of Cook's followers from his Cambridge days, David Frost, backed up by a team of young writers and performers including Roy Kinnear, Lance Percival, Kenneth Cope, William Rushton and Millicent Martin. The programme consisted of mock news reports, songs, sketches and monologues, targeting the by now familiar objects of ridicule – parliament, politicians, the aristocracy and the British 'establishment' in general. While it instantly attracted a hoard of devoted viewers, it also became the subject of unprecedented public complaint and internal discord in the BBC.

Again, Britain's fall from world power status provided a rich vein of comic invention, which was taken up in one form or another in almost every week the show went to air. In one programme, for example, Frost ironically read out a list of 'the colonies we've still got – Fiji, Mauritius, Swaziland, the New Hebrides Condominium ...'.[30] This theme came strongly to the fore in December 1962 when former US Secretary of State Dean Acheson bluntly stated in a major public speech that Great Britain had 'lost an Empire, but had not yet found a role'. In many respects, Acheson had neatly captured the mood of post-imperial crisis within the British establishment, but his comments were deeply resented by the older generation in Britain, and a minor furore broke out in the British press. The response of *TW3*, however, revealed a more resigned attitude among the new breed of satirists:

Frost:	This has also been the week of Dean Acheson's sensational outburst, when he said:
Percival:	(as Acheson) Having lost her Empire, Britain is not quite as important in the world as she used to be. She cannot remain totally independent.
Frost:	Acheson's wild words caused an international furore:
Rushton:	(As Macmillan, on the phone) Ah, about this Acheson thing Jack,

er its Harold here ... Harold Macmillan ... M.A.C. ah! I'm call-
ing from London. Now lookie here, this thing doesn't represent
the views of your government, does it? ... Oh ... well goodbye
then.

Frost: The British people are angered and hurt by this vicious personal
            affront.

Cope: Disgraceful, disgusting ... what did he say? ...

Kinnear: Let Mr. Acheson answer this question: How many gold medals
            did the United States get in the Empire Games?

Rushton: Nonsense! Many of the greatest miracles of modern science stem
            from Britain. Radar, penicillin, the hovercraft ... radar, the steam
            engine, penicillin, the spinning jenny ... radar. And didn't Brit-
            ain produce the great transistor valve?

Frost: No. But whichever way you look at it, understand this Mr.
            Acheson: British leadership follows the world![31]

Far from resenting Acheson's statement, *TW3* found far greater amusement in mocking the pomposity and self-delusion of those in Britain who
continued to think of Britain in terms of imperial grandeur. Macmillan
was again portrayed as insignificant and ineffective in the eyes of the
world, this time by William Rushton. The mock retort to Acheson: 'How
many gold medals did the United States win in the Empire Games?' clev-
erly conveyed the idea that the Empire itself – once the most important
pillar in Britain's claim to world greatness – had become a small and rather
insignificant club in the broader, global scheme of things. It also implied
that the public school games ethic that had for so long fostered the ideals
of imperial service and leadership was all that remained of the imperial
ideal. The entire sketch pointed to the unavoidable fact that the old myths
about Britain and the world were simply no longer tenable. But implicit in
this technique was a trenchant criticism of those who had brought Britain
to such a sorry state, in their failure to address the steady slide in Britain's
political, economic and technological primacy in the post-war world. In
this sense, the sketch represented an attack on the stubborn complacency
of a ruling elite that continued to revel in the glories of the past, thus
blinding the nation to the urgent challenges of the present. This would
suggest that the new generation of satirists were by no means so entirely
reconciled to the new global realities as their good-humoured tone might
otherwise indicate.

This attitude to the end of empire took other forms that raise even
further questions about the extent to which the satire movement had truly
distanced itself from the allure of the imperial imagination. For example,
the first edition of *TW3* in November 1962 included a segment entitled
'Party Political Broadcast' which featured private soldiers standing as independent parliamentary candidates. Roy Kinnear, in the role of 'Lieutenant

Corporal Wallace A., Royal Signals', presented the new Party's political platform in the clipped cockney tones of the lower military ranks:

> Our shadow Secretary for Commonwealth Affairs is Provost-Sergeant Macmichael J., who has done extensive tours of the Commonwealth under discussion and is in fact married to a wog bint. So what Jock doesn't know about these hot countries is not worth knowing ... Our Shadow Colonial Secretary, Signalman Cooney, who is himself an Anglo-Banglo, proposes to go on a goodwill mission to all these nig nog countries and chat up the blackies as if they was man to man. As Signalman Cooney so shrewdly puts it, you've got to live with the darkies, therefore, you might as well look as if you was good mates – and I endorse this policy.[32]

This example illustrates the notoriously unstable nature of comedy as a historical source. There are a range of positions from which audiences might have derived amusement from Kinnear's performance. On the one hand it could easily have been interpreted as an attack on the knee-jerk racist attitudes of a stereotypical working-class servant of the Empire. 'Racism' in a general sense was the frequent target of *TW3* sketches, although these tended to be aimed more at racial problems in South Africa and the United States than in Britain. It was often these sketches that blurred the distinction between satire and sermonising, bludgeoning the message home in a fashion that often allowed little room for humour or wit. The 'Party Political Broadcast', by contrast, was more subtle in the sense that it drew on a certain manner of speech, behaviour and attitude that might conceivably have conjured up an ambivalent fondness for the character depicted by Kinnear. Similarly, Kinnear's dialogue was illustrated by a snapshot depicting a lanky sergeant in tropical kit that was hand-signed 'Roll on Blighty'. So while the basic views espoused by Kinnear's corporal may have been repugnant to typical *TW3* viewers, the language and imagery in which they were conveyed might conceivably have tickled a nostalgic nerve in that same audience, in much the same way as the bumbling military figures of the 1968 film *Carry on Up the Khyber*, or television series such as *Dad's Army* and *It Ain't Half Hot Mum* in the 1970s.

This underlying ambivalence was most clearly in evidence whenever the satire boom turned its attention to specific colonial issues. Peter Cook wrote two pieces for *Beyond the Fringe* which had their origins in the lively discussions in the Cook family about decolonisation in Africa.[33] The first, entitled 'Black Equals White', featured an interview by Cook with the leader of the 'Pan-African Federal Party', Mr Akiboto Nobitsu (played by Jonathan Miller). This theme provided further ammunition for ridiculing the complacent self-satisfaction of British imperial elites, as in the following exchange:

Miller: There can be no progress, Mr Edwards, until you Englishmen stop looking down your noses at us Africans.

Cook: (looking down his nose) Yes, I *think* I see what you mean ...

But this in no way implied any special sympathy for the cause of colonial nationalism, which Cook regarded as equally worthy of scorn:

Cook: Mr Nobitsu, how do you view the imprisonment of your colleague, Mr Bandabaku?

Miller: The imprisonment of Mr Bandabaku is a most immoral, disgusting and illegal act and definitely not cricket. It is an outrageous and despicable act, and I am in favour of it as it lets me get on with a little bit of agitating on my own.

Cook: Mr Nobitsu, do you in any way condone the violent methods used by your party to further their ends?

Miller: By 'violent methods', Mr Edwards, I presume you are referring to the isolated and sporadic outbreaks of entire communities being wiped out?

Cook: Yes, I did have that in mind.

Cook's contempt for colonial nationalism was most clearly conveyed in Mr Nobitsu's solemn declaration: 'One man, one vote, that is essential – especially for the nine million black idiots who vote for me'. This sketch was in many ways typical of contemporary attitudes, and represented the other side of the coin of the prevailing rhetoric about the benefits of a new, multi-racial Commonwealth – namely, a deep cynicism towards the self-interested motives of supposedly 'nationalist' leaders, and a profound scepticism about the possibilities of genuine democracy in Africa. As Jonathan Miller conceded years later: 'The sketch reflected a right wing attitude on [Cook's] part, in a way which is of course quite unperformable now. It reflected his own experience as a child of someone who had served in black Africa, a contempt for the hypocritical self-serving of black leaders.'[34]

Indeed the sketch was already regarded as 'unperformable' by the time the show reached Broadway in 1963, where it was quietly removed from the programme. In all likelihood, this had as much to do with the change in venue from an upper-middle-class British public to a New York audience more attuned to racial sensitivities in the early civil rights era. The sketch was later substituted by Cook's second foray into colonial politics in the autumn of 1963, around the time of Kenyan independence. The new sketch again took the form of an interview, this time with the Duke of Edinburgh (also played by Jonathan Miller):

Cook: Prince Philip has recently returned from Africa where he has been celebrating the independence of Kenya.

Miller: Well, not exactly – *they* were.

Cook: They were what?
Miller: They were doing the celebrating, not me.
Cook: I see.
Miller: I was there in a symbolic capacity.
Cook: What were you symbolising?
Miller: Capitulation. Mind you, of course, I was very well received. Mr Kenyatta himself came to the airport to greet me and shook me very warmly by the throat as I got off the plane.
Cook: Of course, Mr Kenyatta was at one time imprisoned by the British, wasn't he?
Miller: Yes, well, that was when we thought he was a Mau Mau terrorist. Now of course we realise that he was a freedom fighter.
Cook: What precisely is the difference?
Miller: Very hard to tell as a matter of fact, especially when you're being disembowelled by one. That, I gather, was how the confusion first arose.
Cook: Yes, I imagine there must have been some confusion in the minds of the disembowel-ees at the time. Do you feel that Kenya is ready for independence?
Miller: Oh yes, I think so. But there'll still be many links with Great Britain. For instance, Mr Kenyatta assured me that he still intends to keep my wife on the stamps.
Cook: That is an encouraging sign of continuity.

Once again this sketch adopted the technique of ridiculing the rhetorical cant about the fundamental 'continuity' in the transition from empire to Commonwealth, while at the same time retaining an undisguised disdain for the idea of African independence. The joke about British 'capitulation' was particularly pertinent at a time when the Government was seeking to present decolonisation in Africa as the culmination of the imperial mission – the deliberate conferral of independence on peoples who had imbibed the benefits of British civilisation and proven themselves ready for self-government. Likewise, Kenyatta's assurance that he would keep the Duke's 'wife on the stamps' suggested that the promise of continuity – of Britain's ongoing influence in the affairs of the new Commonwealth countries – already had a vague sense of anachronism about it. None of this, however, implied anything resembling anti-colonial politics. On the contrary, the cynical blurring of the distinction between the terrorist and freedom fighter reflected a deep scepticism about the legitimacy of colonial nationalist leaders more generally. The clear implication of the sketch was that the British Government had capitulated to brute force in Kenya, and sought to reconcile Britain's abject humiliation by recasting their adversary in the guise of a respectable world leader – a view that was prevalent in Britain at the time among conservative voters in particular. Only months before Kenyatta was set free from prison in July 1961, the

Foreign Secretary, Lord Home, had warned Macmillan that to release Kenyatta would spark 'a revolt in the Conservative Party' and that it would in any case be 'utterly repugnant to decent minded people'. [35] Peter Cook's sketch indicates that the sense of repugnance at Kenyatta's unseemly metamorphosis continued to rankle some two years after the event.

In fact, Kenyatta became a favourite object of ridicule among satirical performers during these years. At Peter Cook's 'Establishment' club, John Bird regularly assumed the persona of the Kenyan leader, outlining his elaborate plans to invade the British Isles while ostentatiously waving a flywhisk in mock Kenyatta fashion. He performed a version of this routine on BBC television in November 1964 on a programme designed to take up the mantle of *TW3* that was curiously entitled *Not So Much a Programme, More a Way of Life*:

> So then, let us be surgin' forward under de leadership of de party ... Tomorrow mornin', while all England is snorin' and slumberin', thousands of highly trained soldiers of the Kenya Army will be landin' on de beaches. Crack units of de Fourth Battalion de Nairobi Poison Spears will be creepin' about and seizin' key government buildin's, with the aid of their fatal plungin' movements of their machete knives, arrestin' de chief officers of state – the Queen, the Prime Minister, the Archbishop of Canterbury, and de most powerful of dem all, the greasy eminence behind de Throne – the notorious Warden of All Souls. Britain will be ours. No doubt there will be the occasional bloodbath. But, I always say, you can't make an omelette without layin' eggs. I myself will temporarily assume the office of Queen until a reliable native replacement can be found. [36]

As Bird's Kenyatta explained, Africans must not condemn the British way of life, 'just because it is not like ours'. But nevertheless, Africa had a duty to raise the living standards of underdeveloped nations like Britain, and this, he claimed, could only be carried out through a full-scale invasion. Again, a fundamental ambiguity about colonial politics was clearly in evidence. On the one hand, Bird was undoubtedly trying to comment on the paternalism of colonial discourse – showing up the full absurdity of the 'white man's burden' by inverting its context. But at the same time, he seems to have fully shared Peter Cook's scepticism about the readiness of Africa for self-government, and in particular the appropriateness of someone like Kenyatta for the role of colonial liberator. And it was arguably this latter aspect of his routine that was most immediately apparent to the viewer, given the colourful props and elaborate mockery of African English. It was certainly the aspect of his routine that was most apparent to the Kenyan High Commissioner, who complained bitterly to the BBC for broadcasting such a blatant insult to the Kenyan President. In Bird's defence, Roger Wilmut has argued that the Kenyans misunderstood the fundamentally anti-colonial tone of the sketch. [37] But in reality, Bird's sketch was neither exclusively anti-colonial nor solely a parody of colonial liberation – it was both.

Here lies the core ambivalence in the British response to imperial decline. The satirists were a product of their times, and their instinctive aversion to the new assertiveness of colonial nationalist leaders went hand in hand with their disdain for the pretensions and failings of Britain's governing elites. Indeed, it was in the abject failure of Britain's post-war aspirations to great power status that the 'pretensions' of the establishment were most painfully exposed. As Peregrine Worsthorne observed in 1959, a social system that seemed appropriate at a time when Britain reigned over a vast empire would look very different when the material and political foundations of British power collapsed. 'Everything about the British class system', he concluded, 'begins to look foolish and tacky when related to a second class power on the decline.'[38] It is no coincidence, therefore, that the pomposity and inadequacy of Britain's ruling classes became subject to widespread public amusement at a time when the demise of Britain's imperial mission seemed most glaringly apparent. As Jonathan Miller commented in the *Observer* in October 1961:

> Good manners have suffocated English satire more effectively than any secret police. The smug courtesy of the public school sixth former, neatly adjusted to the demands of loyal service in a growing Empire, takes all the life-blood out of satire. John Osborne, Nigel Dennis, Pinter and Simpson have gone a long way towards blowing the top off this fifth form at St. Dominics. The sturdy, sterling figure of the school prefect is at last becoming an object of ridicule.[39]

What Miller didn't recognise was that it was precisely the collapse of the imperial superstructure that rendered these values open to the kind of public ridicule he so passionately advocated. It is again no coincidence that the strongest criticism of the imperially minded 'school prefect' came from the very quarters where the imperial ethos had been so firmly embedded – the public schools, Oxbridge, and the BBC. The events of the post-war era had shattered the myth of Britain's imperial destiny in a way that was particularly traumatic for the younger generation of would-be colonial administrators. It is no surprise that the social trappings of imperial rule began to seem particularly absurd to those who felt most betrayed by the 'illusion of permanence'. The young satirists of the early 1960s, far from advocating a more modest British role in the world, were railing against a British ruling elite that had failed to secure the promise of the imperial inheritance.

By the end of 1963, the satire boom had burst. *TW3* had been prematurely cancelled so as to avoid charges of BBC bias in the 1964 election. The 'Establishment' nightclub had fallen under new management, and no

longer attracted the fashionable crowds of 1961–62. *Private Eye* had suffered a massive drop in circulation from a peak of 80,000 in mid-1963 to a
mere 20,000 the following year.[40] When Peter Cook and Dudley Moore
returned from the New York run of *Beyond the Fringe* to launch a new
television series, they went out of their way to stress that the show would
in no way deal with contemporary political issues.[41] Satire had become a
tired cliché, and when the BBC sought to revive the craze in late 1964 with
Not so Much a Programme, More a Way of Life (also anchored by David
Frost) the result was disastrous and short-lived.

Nonetheless, within the space of only three years the satire boom had
radically redefined the parameters of appropriate material for broadcast
comedy, and perhaps even redrawn the boundaries of what might be
regarded as funny. Many of the innovations of the satire boom became
comic conventions that have since reappeared many times over in popular
films and television series such as *Monty Python's Flying Circus*, *The
Goodies*, *Ripping Yarns* and the *Blackadder* series. But even more significantly, the satire boom played an important role in shaping popular attitudes towards an imperial nation in decline. The idea that the British race
was ordained to spread British culture and civilisation around the globe
had been one of the core ideological precepts of British national identity
for more than a century. Reconciling this grand national vision with the
encroaching realities of the post-war world involved a traumatic adjustment of national aspirations, and a major realignment of national assumptions. The comic relief provided by the satirists' relentless parodying
of Britain's flagging fortunes in the post-war world provided a welcome
pressure valve whereby these dramatic changes in the national self-image
could be rendered less threatening. Moreover, in subjecting leading political figures and civic institutions to public ridicule, the satire boom undermined the automatic deference and respect that had traditionally occupied
the core of British civic culture.

But in laughing at the changes that had been forced on Britain in the
post-war years, the satirists were by no means articulating a sense of popular indifference towards the end of empire. Just as the 'Angry Young Men'
of the 1950s directed their 'anger at the present for failing to live up to the
imperial standards of the past',[42] so too the satirists of the 1960s poured
scorn on those who had promised a more grandiose role for Britain in the
post-war world. Or as David Frost commented years later: 'We were the
Exasperated Young Men – exasperated by Britain's recurring failures, by
hypocrisy and the shabbiness of its politics'.[43] While the satire boom
heaped endless ridicule on the outdated habits, outlook and pretensions of
imperial Britain, this amounted to little more than a lament for the material and political substance that had once underpinned a more exalted
image of the 'British world'. Kenneth Tynan noted at the time that the new

breed of satirists were 'anti-reactionary without being progressive' – scathing in their criticism of the pomposity and cant of the British establishment, but offering nothing by way of an alternative. This political no-man's-land derived on the one hand from a deep sense of disillusionment with the downward trend in Britain's global fortunes, coupled with a keen awareness that a return to the glory days of empire was neither a credible alternative nor a particularly desirable one. In that sense, the satire boom was a striking manifestation of the deep sense of ambivalence that permeated British culture in the age of imperial decline – evincing at one and the same time an overweening pride, self-deprecatory shame, and a feeling of powerlessness to embrace a post-imperial future.

Notes

My thanks go to Ewan Morris and Hsu-Ming Teo for their detailed comments on an earlier draft of this chapter.

1   Ronald Bergen, *Beyond the Fringe … and Beyond* (London, Virgin, 1989) p. 25. Other studies that have interpreted the satire boom exclusively in terms of domestic politics and social currents include Humphrey Carpenter's *That Was Satire That Was: The Satire Boom of the 1960s* (London, Victor Gollancz, 2000); Stephen Wagg, 'You've Never Had it So Silly: The Politics of British Satirical Comedy from *Beyond the Fringe* to *Spitting Image*', in Dominic Strinati and Stephen Wagg (eds), *Come on Down?: Popular Media Culture in Post-War Britain* (London, Routledge, 1992), pp. 254–84; Roger Wilmut, *From Fringe to Flying Circus* (London, Methuen, 1980); Kenneth O. Morgan, *The People's Peace* (Oxford, Oxford University Press, 1992), pp. 208–9; Robert Hewison, *Culture and Consensus: England, Art and Politics Since 1940* (London, Methuen, 1995), p. 128.

2   Kenneth Tynan, 'English Satire Advances into the Sixties', *Observer*, 14 May 1961.

3   *Daily Express*, 11 May 1961.

4   Quoted in Harry Thompson, *Peter Cook: A Biography* (London, Hodder & Stoughton, 1997), p. 109.

5   See for example the article by *Beyond the Fringe* cast member Jonathan Miller, 'Can English Satire Draw Blood?', *Observer*, 1 October 1961.

6   Bergen, *Beyond the Fringe*, p. 22.

7   The 'Green Book' is reprinted in full in Barry Took, *Laughter in the Air: An Informal History of British Radio Comedy* (London, Robson, 1981), pp. 86–91.

8   Wagg, 'You've Never Had It So Silly', p. 256.

9   Bentine left the show in 1953, and the remaining three continued until 1960.

10   Pauline Scudamore, *Spike Milligan: A Biography* (London, Granada, 1985), p. 270.

11   Peter Eton, Introduction to Spike Milligan, *The Book of the Goons* (London, Robson, 1974), p. 10.

12   BBC Written Archives Centre (hereafter WAC), R19/1672/1, Pat Hillyard to Pat Dixon, 13 November 1957; Hillyard to Milligan, 19 November 1957. Milligan eventually produced his River Kwai script as a private recording venture in 1962 entitled *Bridge Over the River Wye*, with the help of *Beyond the Fringe* cast members Jonathan Miller and Peter Cook.

13   See the chapter by Peter H. Hansen in this volume.

14   The term NAAFI referred to the 'Navy, Army and Air Force Institutes', which ran the servicemen's canteens.

15   Scudamore, *Spike Milligan*, p. 158.

16 As Milligan put it, 'The Goons gave me a chance to knock people who my father and I as a boy had to call "sir". Colonels, chaps like Gryptype-Thynne with educated voices who were really bloody scoundrels.' Quoted in Bergen, *Beyond the Fringe*, p. 38.

17 On the traditional fare of the Footlights Revue, see Robert Hewison, *Footlights! A Hundred Years of Cambridge Comedy* (London, Methuen, 1983).

18 Thompson, *Peter Cook*, p. 1.

19 Ibid., pp. 93–4. On the hostile reception in Brighton see Bergen, *Beyond the Fringe*, pp. 17–19.

20 Quotations from *Beyond the Fringe* are taken from Roger Wilmut (ed.), *The Complete Beyond the Fringe* (London, Methuen, 1987).

21 Quoted in Thompson, *Peter Cook*, p. 93.

22 See the discussion of these texts in the Introduction to this volume, pp. 9–11.

23 Christopher Booker, *The Neophiliacs* (London, Collins, 1969), p. 166.

24 Quoted in Thompson, *Peter Cook*, p. 109.

25 Quoted in ibid., p. 111.

26 Peter Cook, quoted in ibid., p. 120.

27 This item was reprinted in Richard Ingrams (ed.), *The Life and Times of Private Eye* (Harmondsworth, Penguin, 1971), pp. 76–7.

28 Quoted in Michael Tracey, *The Production of Political Television* (London, Routledge & Kegan Paul, 1977), p. 75.

29 WAC, T16/589, Donald Baverstock to Stuart Hood, 15 November 1962.

30 Quoted in Carpenter, *That Was Satire*, p. 239.

31 British Film Institute, London, 8.038.233AA, *TW3*, 8 December 1962.

32 WAC, T32/1649/1, *TW3*, Gen 1962.

33 Thompson, *Peter Cook*, p. 106.

34 Quoted in ibid.

35 Quoted in Richard Lamb, *The Macmillan Years* (London, John Murray, 1995), p. 227.

36 Quoted in Wilmut, *Fringe to Flying Circus*, pp. 77–8.

37 Ibid., p. 77.

38 Quoted in David Cannadine, *Class in Britain* (London, Penguin, 2000), p. 159.

39 Miller, 'Can English Satire Draw Blood?'.

40 Ingrams, *Private Eye*, p. 17.

41 Thompson, *Peter Cook*, p. 179.

42 See the chapter by Dan Rebellato in this volume, p. 87.

43 Quoted in Carpenter, *That Was Satire*, pp. 214–15.

CHAPTER SIX

The imperial game in crisis:
English cricket and decolonisation
Mike Cronin and Richard Holt

In 1993, the then British Prime Minister, John Major, made a speech encapsulating his policies concerning further European integration. This quickly came to be seen as a regressive representation of how an out-of-touch Conservative Party understood England. Major was concerned to define abiding English values, stating that 'fifty years from now, Britain will still be the country of long shadows on county grounds, warm beer, invincible green suburbs, dog lovers and pools fillers'.[1] To many it seemed incredible that a prime minister, entering negotiations that would shape Britain's future relationships with Europe, was sketching an image of Britain that was centred around the county grounds of English cricket. For the late twentieth century, the image was anachronistic and, for much of the population, completely irrelevant. Major's belief that his image of Britain would be alive and well into the middle of the twenty-first century appears difficult to sustain. In the same way that the brewers of warm beer are under threat from the purveyors of cold bottled lager, so cricket, especially at the county level, is lurching from crisis to crisis, with its long-term future far from assured.

The importance of Major's speech was not its forecast for the future but its vision of the past. Its resonance came from its use of cricket, among other things, to create an image of England (and not Britain). This image, although lost or forgotten to most English men and women, was alive and well in the hearts and minds of an ageing middle and upper class, predominantly drawn from the Home Counties, who were still nostalgically attached to the imperial vision.[2] Major was attempting to roll back the years. In approaching his negotiations on European integration, he was arming himself, and bolstering his supporters, with an England that was not only opposed to a European superstate but indulged in a collective amnesia, especially when it came to the unifying role of cricket within the imperial family of nations. England was painted and imagined in Major's speech as a great and important nation, and it was cricket that was chosen as the shorthand metaphor to represent such a belief. If the speech had been made in the 1950s, a time 'when the authority of England and its empire was almost at one with Nineveh and Tyre [and] English sport and its vocabulary were helping shape the modern world',[3] no one would have criticised Major's dreamings. In the passage of four decades, however, Britain has lost its Empire and its place in the world. Cricket has ceased to be a signifier of imperial cohesion, and the game has slipped in the nation's affections.

Throughout the twentieth century cricket has been viewed as a sport that represents the centrality of England and English values at the heart of a family of colonial nations. In 1973, a book celebrating what was best about Britain was able to offer the opinion that 'cricket is the most peculiarly English of the major sports … [it has] a whole history, a whole philosophy … cricket is one of the intangibles which hold the countries formerly constituting the British Empire together'. If such a legacy wasn't enough for the game, the authors also expressed the opinion that 'the capacity to lose gracefully has been transmitted from the British Isles to other parts of the world and is one of the major contributions England has made to global goodwill [and has] cemented relations between countries with little else in common'.[4] To go back much earlier in the century to 1926, a sporting editorial declared in a similar vein: 'Profound is the chain of Empire through the agency of sport. The playing fields have done more to cement the bonds of Imperialism than many a diplomatic conference.'[5] The world of cricket was often presented as a microcosm of England itself – and more widely of the British Empire – where social order and prosperity were guaranteed by enlightened patrician government. Cricket was widely held to embody the authority of the English gentleman, whose paternalism would guarantee both domestic and imperial harmony. This vision of a benign hierarchy rooted in English rural tradition and extending around the imperial world gave cricket a unique prestige and authority among English sports in the first half of the twentieth century.

All this changed abruptly in the 1960s and 1970s. The general recognition of cricket's symbolic role in sustaining English and imperial tradition almost disappeared. This left an ageing social elite to mourn the passing of the amateur era and created a lively market for cricket memorabilia and nostalgic literature. The gentlemen who still ran the game were increasingly portrayed as relics of a bygone age. They were out of touch with the public mood and best confined to the pages of the *Daily Telegraph*, whose veteran cricket correspondent, E. W. Swanton, was a bulwark of the old order just as the BBC's Brian Johnson was its licensed jester. Cricket was no longer taken seriously as a force for social or imperial solidarity. Its code of sportsmanship and morality was increasingly ignored or derided. The England–Australia test matches were no longer the pre-eminent sporting event in England. Cricket had lost its special place in English sport and in English life.

Why was this? The complex factors which influenced the actual playing of the game cannot be examined in detail here. It is not so much the state of the game itself as the *perception* of cricket as an embodiment of England and empire which is significant for understanding the impact of imperial decline. Cricket was so deeply implicated in the imperial project that the collapse of empire inevitably influenced public attitudes to the game. But how did this happen? There is no simple correlation between the declining importance of the game and the pace of decolonisation. Understanding how the game appeared to lose its authority and become part of John Major's 'heritage' England requires two approaches. The first looks at the ideological baggage cricket brought with it and how the 'village cricket' vision of England was received in an era of affluence, greater equality and a less deferential social structure. The second examines the difficulty of seeing cricket as a source of imperial consensus during the process of decolonisation and conflict within the Commonwealth.

Cricket and the myth of England

Cricket began as a southern rural sport. Its symbolic home was Hambledon, a Hampshire village where the nobility mixed with local farmers on the cricket field in the later eighteenth century. Dominance of the game moved from Hampshire to London and the Marylebone Cricket Club (MCC), which gradually increased its power over touring teams of professional cricketers and the emerging English county sides during the nineteenth century. It was not until the 1880s and 1890s, however, that the modern structure of the game finally took shape organised around a county championship and regular international games or 'test matches' against Australia and South Africa. By this time cricket was the most widespread sport in England. Unlike football or rugby it was played in all regions of the country from the industrial urban landscapes of Lancashire and Yorkshire to the wisteria-clad clubhouse at Taunton. No accurate estimate of the number of clubs is available. Like golf and horse racing, cricket was regulated by a gentlemen's club which established rules but did not set up a national administrative structure to govern clubs and count them. However, it is clear that cricket clubs were exceptionally common and widespread on the eve of the Second World War. Research by Jack Williams on press coverage of inter-war cricket found 430 clubs in Middlesex in 1939 and 334 in Surrey. The number of clubs in Bolton and its surroundings varied from 140 to 180 in the 1930s and Birmingham had over 300.[6] Yet the urban success of cricket did not eclipse its rural roots. Even thinly populated Herefordshire had 60 teams and the sport was widely played in remoter counties like Cornwall and Northumberland.

The 1960s saw a profound change in patterns of playing and spectating. Affluence brought choice into leisure and choice brought diversity. The sporting public was no longer restricted to watching football and cricket on winter and summer weekends as they had been between the wars. Some 3,472 cricket matches were played in the parks of Birmingham in 1955 but only 2,268 in 1965.[7] Cricket suffered from the success of golf as a summer sport, which grew from half a million to over a million players from the mid-1950s to the mid-1960s, drawing away potential middle-class spectators and players. There was a decline in the number of youth teams playing cricket on public parks, which was a bad sign for the sport. One estimate suggested there were between 10,000 and 12,000 cricket clubs in England and Wales in 1965 but in the 1980s the National Cricket Association claimed no more than between 4,000 and 6,500 (against around 40,000 football clubs). On the spectator side, crowds fell sharply in county cricket from the highpoint of the late 1940s as television, the car and rising incomes provided new leisure and sporting opportunities. Around two million tickets were sold for county cricket matches in 1950. This fell to a million in 1960 and a mere 659,000 in 1965.[8]

Clearly the circumstances of daily life were changing and cricket no longer enjoyed a captive audience. But this alone cannot explain its declining influence. Football spectator numbers also declined sharply but the national importance attached to football did not. On the contrary, success in international football took on the importance that had formerly been attached to cricket, especially after England won the World Cup in 1966. When Len Hutton led the England team that re-captured the Ashes in 1953 there had been a huge public response. Hutton's victory and Compton's winning runs were seen as a patriotic triumph in the coronation year to rank almost alongside the conquest of Everest. Yet when Ray Illingworth went to Australia in 1970–71 and returned with the trophy, there was little public rejoicing. Winning back the Ashes no longer seemed so important. Although there were some exciting cricketers playing for England in the 1970s, like Tony Greig and Ian Botham, the image of the game continued to decline. It had lost much of its popular appeal to the young, and attempts to revive its fortunes via one-day matches and sponsorship risked losing some of the old guard.

It was not simply changes in the habits of playing and watching or a lack of talent or success which had stripped English cricket of its central place in English culture. From the 1950s, BBC television gave ball by ball coverage of most domestic test cricket, which arguably could now reach a far wider public than ever before. Disillusionment with English cricket went deeper. The sport was a victim of profound changes in popular values and attitudes, which swept aside so much of the conventional Victorian culture of respectability.

The game of cricket had long been part of this wider social vision of England, which was not only dear to the public school elite but adopted by the lower middle classes and many of the respectable working class.[9] Cricket was not only England's 'best loved game', it was also 'more than a game'. It was held to embody a style of behaviour and system of values that were distinctively English. The Welsh and Scots also played cricket but not with the same seriousness and did not incorporate the game as part of their national identity. Great importance was attached to a code of honour and good manners. The term 'not cricket' was widely used to mean anything underhand or unfair. Cricket involved self-control, instant acceptance of the umpire's decision, obedience to the captain and respect for the other team.

Cricket's upper-class ethic was underpinned by a system of social hierarchy within the game. Social relations in cricket were explicitly hegemonic. Unlike rugby, which segregated the classes, cricket brought them together in a manner which was both striking and distinctive. The sport was run by an amateur group, largely composed of ex-public schoolboys, known as 'the gentlemen'. The gentlemen governed professional cricketers, who were called 'the players'. Professionals, who were largely working-class, were permitted to play with their social superiors on the condition that an elaborate code of conduct was maintained to establish their relative status. They normally travelled, lodged and changed separately. They sometimes entered the ground by different gates and if the same gate was used professionals were expected to allow the amateurs to enter the field first. Professionals were expected to call amateurs 'Sir' or 'Mr' and were identified on the scorecard by having their initials placed after their name. Professionals were not allowed positions of authority within the team as captain or within the county or the MCC. The principle was that only an amateur could be in command. Professionals were expected to acquiesce in these arrangements on the basis of the amateur's superior education, manners and leadership qualities.[10]

Both the First and the Second World Wars weakened the economic and cultural power of the English gentleman. In the Edwardian years around 40 per cent of county players were amateur, but this figure fell to around 20 per cent by 1939 and 15 per cent in the 1950s. However, the decline of the English gentleman was only one element in the story of cricket's changing significance. Perhaps more important was the decline of deference. Working-class politics in the 1930s had been more concerned with employment than attacking Baldwin's cosy vision of an Anglican cricket-playing England. But by the 1950s, attitudes had changed as full employment together with the achievement of the welfare state and wider educational opportunities produced a youth culture that was anathema to the values of hierarchy and imperial ideology promoted by a game like cricket. In a Britain which had relinquished that symbol of national and imperial service – an enforced period spent in the armed forces – many of the traditional values, which had controlled and tempered youthful freedom, were decreasing in their importance. Compare the 'Boys' Own' heroes of the 1950s like Len Hutton, the Yorkshire professional who was knighted and settled down in Surrey, or Peter May, of Charterhouse and Cambridge, who was 'something in the City', with sporting idols of the 1960s such as George Best. Cricket, a game that had been so closely attached to the ideals of empire, fair play and gentlemanly behaviour, became deeply unfashionable.

This shift in public sentiment, which was most apparent in the young, made the long-standing privileges and 'perks' of the amateur elite untenable. The rigid distinction between amateurs and professionals was finally becoming an embarrassment. It is striking that the socially divisive structure of the sport had gone almost unnoticed between the wars. Despite the landslide victory of a Labour Government and the introduction of the principle of equality into health and pensions, there was no social reform at Lord's. Clement Attlee was, after all, very much a gentleman and a cricket lover. The social distinction between gentlemen and players was maintained as part of the natural order of things. Although Hutton was appointed to the England captaincy in 1952, the counties continued to insist on appointing amateur captains, some of whom could not hold their place in the side on merit. 'Down the century the Yorkshire committee had offered many examples of comic ineptitude and bigotry', as Benny Green remarked. But nothing could 'approach its refusal to appoint the England captain as its own captain'.[11] When Yorkshire appointed its second team captain, Ronnie Burnett, to captain the first team in 1958, one of the senior professionals went to the *Daily Mail* with an article headlined 'We're Carrying the Captain'.

Snobbery masquerading as tradition and wisdom was increasingly criticised both in the press and by leading amateurs like the Rev. David Sheppard, the future Bishop of Liverpool, and Peter May, Hutton's successor as England captain. The MCC put up stiff resistance to abolishing social distinctions and damaged the sport's reputation in the process. Press criticism and public ridicule of the MCC mounted. The MCC's increasingly 'fuddy duddy' image came across in the BBC's new satirical look at Britain, *That Was The Week That Was*, with William Rushton dressed in the robes of nobility singing: 'All you have to do is be a Duke like me, and you can be the President of the MCC'. The Duke of Edinburgh, in fact, had been MCC President in 1949 (and again in 1974), and the post was held by the Duke of Beaufort in 1952. When the Duke of Norfolk got the job in 1957, he chaired a committee which permitted the payment of amateurs for loss of earnings whilst on tour. The aim was to re-invigorate and legitimise the role of the imperial amateur rather than to do away with it. But it was no use. The economic pressures on amateurs – taxation, new business practices and career structures – proved too great. This, along with public criticism of class distinction, finally swung the debate within the MCC. The key figure here was the distinguished cricket historian and public schoolmaster Harry Altham, the MCC Treasurer from 1950 to 1963 and President in 1959, who feared that the public school amateur would soon disappear if payment continued to incur a loss of social status. Hence when the final decision to abolish the social distinction between gentlemen and players was taken on 26 November 1962, it was as much a matter of offering the gentleman a future in the game as recognising a wider shift in class relationships.

Hypocrisy had long been the charge made by the new generation of post-war players against some of the 'old school' of amateurs. 'Shamateurism' was well established in cricket and perfected by W. G. Grace. Amateurs could retain their status whilst being paid as club secretaries or drawing generous expenses. This had always been a grievance among professionals, who knew that some amateurs made more money out of the sport than they did whilst continuing to enjoy the status accorded to a gentleman. The whole structure was eaten through with hypocrisy. There had been occasional public criticism of this practice in the press or by the few professionals who dared risk their careers and their benefit matches by speaking out. It was not until the 1950s that the press began to take up the issue seriously. Trevor Bailey, the Cambridge, Essex and England amateur, admitted that he could not afford to be a professional, whilst Jim Laker, the star of English spin bowling, considered the possibility of becoming an amateur in order to increase his income.[12] Amateurs increasingly were unable to live up to their self-professed ideals and the press and public were becoming more aware of the fact. Television was a factor here. Though the BBC was very much complicit in the amateur project and generally kept controversy out of cricket broadcasting, inevitably the amateur issue arose from time to time. Influential figures favoured the abolition of the distinction and leading amateurs became increasingly reluctant to defend the status quo, especially on television. However, by the time the abuses had been removed, it was too late to reinvent the sport as modern or meritocratic.

This critique of cricket fitted into a much wider attack on what came to be called 'the establishment' in the late 1950s and early 1960s. The younger, well-educated middle classes, including many from public schools and Oxbridge, were increasingly critical of the innate conservatism of English society. Inefficiency and snobbery were two of the main targets, but the wider agenda was to open up the key national institutions to merit in all its forms. The social consensus upon which cricket was built seemed suddenly absurd and old-fashioned, rather like the last Tory Prime Minister of the period, Lord Home, who was a great follower of the game. England had to change and cricket was too implicated in the old order of things to survive the shift to a more open, competitive, permissive and post-imperial democracy.

Cricket and the myth of empire

Just as amateurs believed in England as a benign hierarchy based on a paternalism relatively undisturbed by the forces of democracy, so too they espoused the civilising mission of the Empire. English sportsmen with a sense of 'fair play' and a flair for leadership would look after the natives for their own good. At first this did not involve direct sporting contacts with subject peoples. Cricket was at first a game for the white Empire (and was also quite widely played among the social elite in the United States). From the 1880s test matches were arranged against Australia for the Ashes and this competition was the most important sporting event in England by 1900. The game was taken up by the anglophone whites in South Africa who made up the third force in cricket. In 1909 the Imperial Cricket Conference was formed. It was made up of the MCC, the Australian Board of Control and the South African Cricket Association and drew up the rules for international test cricket. In 1926, New Zealand, the West Indies and India joined this 'family of cricket nations'.[13] West Indies cricket at that time was still white-dominated and Indian cricket was run by the princes, who were incorporated into the Raj and given a kind of honorary English identity through their love of the game.

The role of the MCC cannot be underestimated when considering the growth and development of imperial cricket. The MCC was the embodiment of the game and its values, and as such became the arbiter and protector of cricket. The MCC deliberately controlled the spread of the game, and projected its own imperial vision for cricket through that process. The MCC tours of the West Indies in 1925–26 and 1929–30, which took place either side of the West Indian entry into the Imperial Cricket Conference, underpinned the formal acceptance of a new Cricket Board into the empire club. Equally, the 1926–27 tour of Ceylon signalled that while that nation was not yet ready to join the elite group, it was considered a part of the wider imperial mission. The intense cricket rivalry between England and Australia led to a confrontation in 1932 over the English captain's decision to bowl at the body of the Australian batsmen. Once the dust had settled, great efforts were made on both sides to repair the damage. Cricket was too important to be left to the tactical whims of gentleman cricketers, however distinguished.[14] In the decades leading to the outbreak of the Second World War, cricket became entrenched as one of the cornerstones of Englishness and the accompanying centrality of the Empire within such a vision. Cricket, the test matches that were played between England and her colonial nations, and the values of fair play that were enshrined in the game, all combined to make the sport a powerful symbol of empire.

In the wake of all the upheavals of the Second World War, cricket seemingly emerged as strong as ever. The 1950s are seen as a golden age of domestic cricket, and the test matches against the various touring nations demonstrated how strong the imperial bond was. The world, however, was changing rapidly. India gained independence in 1947, and the late 1950s saw the beginnings of a new wave of decolonisation in Africa. World politics were dominated by US–Soviet rivalries and the Cold War. Imperial politics were sidelined with startling rapidity, a shift that was re-emphasised during the Suez crisis. Britain began to make tentative overtures to the newly formed European Economic Community in the late 1950s.

Britain's changing place in the world and the shift in imperial relations were visibly manifested on the cricket pitch during the post-war era. Whereas the England victory in the 1966 football World Cup final was seen as a vindication for the continued vitality of the nation on the world stage, cricket seemed to offer a steady stream of evidence to the contrary. In 1950 England lost its first test match series against the West Indies on home soil. *Wisden*, however, did not take this as an omen of imperial decline. Even Learie Constantine, the great inter-war West Indian batsman and future knight and peer, put England's defeat down to the long-term disruption of war rather than the creeping disintegration of empire. On the contrary, English cricket was buoyant. Hutton's successful Ashes side of 1953 was followed by victories against Australia in 1955 and 1956. A powerful performance against the West Indies side in 1957, with the amateurs May and Cowdrey breaking the record for an England partnership in the first test, seemed to show that the gentleman could still compete at the highest level.

However, after this indian summer of the amateur, the prestige and popularity of the England test team went into sharp decline. Australia routed England in 1959 and again in 1961. In the same year an England touring team was defeated by India. In 1963 the West Indies won a decisive victory in England and confirmed their status as a world-class team led by Gary Sobers. A dismal series of draws against the Australians the following year seemed to underline the fact that the England team was no longer successful or entertaining. Despite some flourishes from 'Lord' Ted Dexter, the post-war glory days of Compton had gone. Test cricket was becoming dull with a large number of drawn games and a relative lack of quality players. England no longer expected to win against the West Indies, even at home, and by 1971 England lost at home to India. Where previously the English team had always been regarded alongside Australia as the dominant world side, it was now no longer supreme and looked distinctly vulnerable. Confidence in English cricket seeped away just as imperial confidence was on the wane. When Major Rowland Bowen published *Cricket: A History of its Growth and Development Throughout the World* in 1970, he was under no doubt that the decay of English cricket was as inevitable as the decline of the British Empire. The key cricketing events of 'the season' such as the Eton and Harrow game or the University match were no longer endowed with such significance. The MCC was not amused at this heresy, though privately it could hardly deny there was a certain truth in Bowen's polemic.

English football, by contrast, with the possible exception of the famous Hungarian victory at Wembley in November 1953, was immune until well into the mid-1970s from value-laden judgements about the state of the nation.[15] One wonders how far this was due to the kinds of teams England faced on the football field. The majority of football nations were outsiders, that is, non-Commonwealth nations. English cricket was perhaps used far more readily as a yard-stick of the nation's place in the world because the opponents within the game were from the inner circle of empire. Imperial nations were supposed, according to long-held prejudices, to play the English way. And this paternal structure implied an expectation of a high English success rate on the field. Imperial cricket in the decades after the war failed to deliver such results, as all of the major colonial cricket-playing nations defeated England both at home and on English soil. As colonial nations emerged as independent sovereign states, their rationale for playing cricket changed in subtle ways. Prior to the Second World War, all imperial nations had shared a belief in cricket's role as a transmitter of the virtue and fellowship of empire. With the advent of the post-colonial world, there was a collapse of imperial consensus. While other nations found a new message in cricket – the promotion of nationalism – English cricket could not reinvent itself in the same way.

A sense of this declining position was reflected in the changing pattern of international cricket encounters. In the period between the two wars, England played a combined total of 100 test matches against New Zealand, South Africa, the West Indies and India. By contrast, Australia played only 29 tests against the same opposition in the corresponding period. In the 1946–71 period, England played 154 tests against these four countries plus Pakistan, compared to Australia's 88. Thus, although England was still an important centre for world cricket, the balance had clearly shifted away from an entrenched anglocentric focused sport and a bilateral form of competition (England versus the Empire), to a multilateral contest involving all nations on an equal footing.[16]

The retreat from imperial certainty was felt across a wide range of British institutions. It is clear that the City of London, for example, was in a state of crisis following the end of the war, and that adjusting to the new world where its position of unquestionable dominance was at an end would be hugely problematic. As David Kynaston concluded of the period, 'the square mile found itself at its lowest peacetime ebb in living memory'.[17] The City of London, indeed the whole financial services sector, succeeded in renegotiating its position in the world in the post-war years. This process has been thoroughly explored by Cain and Hopkins, who argued that while 'the end of the British Empire removed one of the props of the gentlemanly order … it did not bring about the fall of the City, which may help to explain why the trauma of decolonisation was psychological rather than economic'.[18] The City of London, it is clear, was able to transform itself from a structure that relied on the certainties of gentlemanly capitalism. The links between the City and the MCC were close. Many leading merchants and brokers were members of the MCC, but unlike the City of London, the gentlemanly administrators of the MCC found it harder to dominate the post-colonial structure of the sport. The Imperial Cricket Conference changed its name to become the International Cricket Conference, although the MCC continued to provide the chairman and the secretary. The running of test and professional cricket was removed from the MCC in 1968 with the formation of the Test and County Cricket Board, and the National Cricket Association was formed in 1965 to run the amateur game. The MCC remained responsible only for framing the laws of the game itself.

The problem for English cricket in the post-war and post-colonial era was how to modernise and adapt. Cricket's very strength, and hence its mobilisation by John Major as a political tool, was, and remains, its traditions. The game has always looked to the past and its bedrock certainties, rather than to the future and to new modes of operation and activity. As Brian Stoddart has argued: 'Cricket devotees need to be convinced that new forms fit their social world. Attempts to attract new crowds frequently founder upon this point. Cricket survives and flourishes because those who follow it find meaning within its playing and representational text.'[19]

The custodians and supporters of the game believed in the social importance and conventions of cricket. Every time any of the certainties upon which cricket was based collapsed in the second half of the twentieth century, the further those charged with steering the game put their heads in the sand and became yet further entrenched. The followers of English cricket wanted it to be forever the summer of 1947. The more that the world around them changed, and old certainties disappeared, the more they clung to the faded sepia images of former greatness. Unlike the City, and other central institutions in English life, cricket failed to look ahead and adapt fully. Right until the end of the century, for example, a structure survived which had no system of promotion or relegation and privileged the ancient universities far beyond their playing strength. Cricket came to be seen as an English anachronism, a place of refuge for those who still longed for a place called England.

The reasons for the failure of cricket to adapt to its new surroundings, and hence the steady decline of the game and its importance, can be found within wider changes in post-war British society. David Cannadine has argued that changes in the nature of the British social order in the post-war era were a product of imperial decline. 'The British did not see themselves – indeed could not see themselves – in the same way without an empire as they had done when they possessed one … the British Empire had not just reinforced ideas and perceptions of hierarchy by exporting it overseas: it had also reinforced these ideas and perceptions at home.'[20] The development of cricket had mirrored the growth of empire. As the game took off in far-flung corners of the globe, it reinforced the value of the game and the sense of importance that the English attached to it. With the retreat from empire, and the growth of colonial nationalism, the bonds with home were broken.

There was no simple pattern to the collapse of imperial consensus. During the era of Macmillan and Menzies, the spirit of colonial cricket was alive and well. On one occasion at an Australia Club dinner in 1959 the two prime ministers made no less than fourteen references to test cricket during their after-dinner speeches. Robert Menzies believed that cricket underpinned the positive values of British cultural life. In 1963 he remarked that cricket was 'part of Australia's rich British inheritance' in which the two countries are part of the 'same blood and allegiance and history and instinctive mental process'.[21] The Menzies vision stretched beyond Anglo-Australian sporting links as he was a believer in the Commonwealth mission. He saw cricket as a way of advancing 'his status within the Commonwealth'.[22] Such an idea was borne out in 1954 when the Australians toured the West Indies. In the wake of England's disastrous tour of 1953 which had been 'a social disaster at a delicate stage in the Caribbean's late-colonial political development',[23] Menzies argued that a tour of the West Indies would be of 'great diplomatic value'.[24] Menzies' belief in cricket, its values and its role in colonial relations, however, was increasingly at odds with the changing pattern of Australian life and the emergence of a more strident domestic nationalism associated in particular with the Labor Party and the personality of Gough Whitlam. In cricket terms this was expressed in the decline of the more polite anglophilic style of Bradman and the rise of a more combative, 'anti-pom' attitude associated with the Chappell brothers in the 1970s and the ferociously aggressive bowling of Lillee and Thompson. It was one thing for Don Bradman, the grandson of a Suffolk artisan, to destroy the England team whilst praising England and all her works. It was another to be battered by a verbal and physical assault from a ruthless competitor like Ian Chappell who seemed to have very little affection for the 'old country'. The new tone was most memorably conveyed by the ageing Robert Menzies, who complained in 1976 that his 'beloved cricket is being marred by "streakers" and boisterous rowdiness … more in keeping with a football crowd than a cricket match'.[25]

Similarly, in the West Indies nationalism and colonial liberation found popular expression in the playing and watching of cricket.[26] Cricket was used successfully to challenge the ethos of empire, and to reinvent the game as something that was nation-specific rather than generically imperial. The classic formulation of the complex relationship between cricket and colonial independence is to be found in *Beyond a Boundary*, published in 1963 by the radical black historian, social critic and cricket-lover C. L. R. James.[27] Part autobiography, part ethnic and political analysis, James stresses how deeply cricket permeated anglophone West Indian culture and how the ideology of 'fair play' was appropriated by the emergent independence movement. The insistence on having a white captain in an otherwise non-white team symbolised the power of coloniser and colonised into the late 1950s, just as the restriction of the captaincy to amateurs had demonstrated the residual strength of post-war paternalism in England itself. Frank Worrell, one of a number of outstanding and long-established black West Indian players, was finally given the captaincy after a prolonged struggle and led the West Indies in a marvellous tour of Australia in 1961. He then came in triumph to England in 1963, leading his team to a famous victory in the series. Worrell was a dignified, stylish and sportsmanlike figure in the cultural mould of the English gentleman, who had a degree in economics from Manchester University (gained whilst playing for Radcliffe in the Lancashire league). Worrell was knighted in 1964 in a striking acknowledgement of the political importance of the game and a memorial service in Westminster Abbey was held after his tragic death in 1966 from leukaemia. The British establishment had switched from a strategy of ingrained opposition to black emancipation to one of acceptance and incorporation with remarkable speed.

If the rise of post-colonial nationalism in cricket demonstrates how a sport became a vehicle for breaking the imperial consensus, the issue of South Africa destroyed any lingering sense that cricket could act as an expression of imperial influence or control. The South Africans' tour of 1960 had met with protests around the games while David Sheppard refused to play and John Arlott refused to commentate.[28] The MCC believed that 'normal' cricketing relations with South Africa should continue, irrespective of any political considerations. Such a stance caused divisions within the imperial cricketing family, as most nations had chosen to reject official sporting links with South Africa. In 1968, the MCC refused to select Basil D'Oliveira, the Cape coloured player based in England, to play against South Africa, although D'Oliveira had just made 158 for England against Australia. David Sheppard and the future England captain Mike Brearley called an extraordinary general meeting to censure the selection committee. The South African Government would not allow a mixed-race team into the country, and it was duly banned and the tour cancelled. In 1970, the MCC, continuing its policy of sporting normalcy, extended an invitation to the South Africans to tour England. In the face of mass protests, a damaging boycott of the 1970 Commonwealth Games in Edinburgh and intense political pressure, the tour was cancelled.

The attempts of the MCC to engage South Africa in test matches when the rest of the world was turning its back on the apartheid nation was the last stand for a belief in cricket's role as the cement of the imperial consensus. The MCC took the line that it would be damaging to world cricket if the South Africans were excluded, and that politics were being unduly allowed to interfere with the game. South Africa had been, so argued the MCC, a loyal member of the Empire and of the cricketing family, and that local difficulties in the form of race relations should not be allowed to interfere with the wider goal of imperial cohesion.[29] The D'Oliveira issue, and the arguments that surrounded the proposed 1970 tour, demonstrated how far the MCC was out of step, and the extent to which the imperial consensus in the values and traditions of cricket as a tool of empire had been eroded. The lack of power of the MCC after the reforms of the late 1960s and the strength of the non-white cricketing nations revealed the extent to which the game had become thoroughly post-colonial.

In 1964 the Australians toured England and won the Ashes. By the early 1960s, the sense of resigned post-mortem that so regularly surrounds English test defeats today, was already in evidence. In his record of the series, Denzil Batchelor attempted to understand why England had lost on home ground, and what, if anything, could be done to stop the rot. He began by examining the loss of competitive spirit within the England team. 'Why can't we find the great players today? Why do we lack cricketers, and above all batsmen, fit for the big occasions? It isn't the technique that is lacking. It is, plainly and briefly, guts. Has the Welfare State sapped our initiative and self-reliance?'[30] Batchelor argued that the loss of a competitive edge was not confined to cricket, but could be found across British society and throughout its international sport. To remedy the situation, the cricketing authorities had to reform the game, introduce more knock-out competitions, grasp the opportunities afforded by professionalism and play the game in a spirit of inflexible antagonism in the manner of a boxer.

Batchelor, it seems, had perhaps already reconciled himself to the end of empire, the value-free use of cricket within colonial relationships and the demise of English supremacy. He warned that if cricket was not prepared to modernise and become competitive, the future of the game would be that which his great-grandfather had enjoyed: 'On velvety lawns shadowed by immemorial elms, beneath a ladder of lark song whose top rung must surely be heaven; village against village, tea and plum cake prepared by the ladies, and beer at *The Green Dragon* when stumps are drawn and before choir practice'.[31]

Batchelor was using the same rural imagery of an imagined England to forecast the demise of cricket during the era of decolonisation which John Major would use for different reasons thirty years later. Rather than understanding Batchelor as an advocate of a brighter cricketing future, however, one wonders whether we should interpret his arguments in a similar context to that of Major. Men like Batchelor, like so many of the cricketing hierarchy in the late 1950s and early 1960s, had no desire to embrace a post-imperial world. Rather, by clinging onto and supporting the values of their game, the English game, they cast derision on their political and cultural opponents who had let England's place in the world slip. For Batchelor, as perhaps for Major, the rural idyll of cricket represented a place from which England should still lead the world. The themes that were played out in Britain, and in its relationship with the Empire and Commonwealth in the years following the Second World War, were mirrored in cricket. A game that had come to symbolise the championing of British values across the Empire in the late nineteenth and early twentieth centuries, became instead the signifier, for many, of all that was wrong with an England struggling with the demands of a post-imperial world, and unsure of its identity or its role. Cricket, from the 1950s, was the carrier of imperial values and traditions in an England that had ceased to dominate. There was no longer one cricketing message, but instead a series of competing values and symbols, the majority of which challenged imperial consensus.

Notes

The authors wish to acknowledge the valuable and generous support of the editor, Stuart Ward, in discussing and developing this article. His assistance has far exceeded the usual critical help offered by an editor to contributors, and we are much in his debt.

1   Quoted in Jeremy Paxman, *The English: A Portrait of a People* (London, Penguin, 1999), p. 142.
2   For a discussion of the class debate and modern cricket and other sports see Andrew Adonis and Stephen Pollard, *A Class Act: The Myth of Britain's Classless Society* (London, Penguin, 1998), pp. 229–39.

3   Ross McKibbin, *Classes and Cultures: England 1918–1951* (Oxford, Oxford University Press, 1998), p. 385.
4   Peter Grosvenor and James McMillan, *The British Genius* (London, Coronet, 1973), pp. 514–16.
5   *Athletic News*, 6 September 1926, quoted in Jack Williams, *Cricket and England: A Cultural and Social History of the Inter-War Years* (London, Frank Cass, 1999), p. 13.
6   Jeffrey Hill and Jack Williams, *Sport and Identity in the North* (Keele, Keele University Press, 1996), p. 115.
7   Walter Winterbottom, 'The Pattern of Sport in the United Kingdom', 9 July 1966, Appendix 1, Copy kept in Sport England Information Centre.
8   Ibid., p. 22.
9   On the mythology of English cricket see especially Derek Birley, *The Willow Wand: Some Cricket Myths Explored* (London, Simon and Schuster, 1989) and Mike Marquese, *Anyone But England: Cricket, Race and Class* (London, Two Heads Publishing, 1998).
10 Malcolm Marshall, *Gentlemen and Players: Conversations with Cricketers* (London, Grafton, 1987).
11 Benny Green, *A History of Cricket* (London, Barrie and Jenkins, 1988), p. 254.
12 D. Mosey, *Laker: Portrait of a Legend* (London, Macdonald/Queen Anne, 1989), p. 65.
13 Roland Bowen, *Cricket: Its History and Development Throughout the World* (London, Eyre and Spottiswoode, 1970), pp. 320–33.
14 See Ric Sissons and Brian Stoddart, *Cricket and Empire: The 1932–33 Bodyline Tour of Australia* (Sydney, Allen & Unwin, 1984).
15 On the Hungarian victory see Brian Glanville, *Soccer Nemesis* (London, Secker & Warburg, 1955).
16 R. S. Whittington, *An Illustrated History of Australian Cricket* (Melbourne, Lansdowne Press, 1972).
17 David Kynaston, *The City of London, Vol. III: Illusions of Gold, 1914–1945* (London, Chatto and Windus, 1999), p. 510.
18 P. J. Cain and A. G. Hopkins, *British Imperialism: Crisis and Deconstruction, 1914–1990* (Harlow, Longman, 1993), pp. 313–14, and for a recent assessment of the idea of gentlemanly capitalism, see Raymond E. Dumett (ed.), *Gentlemanly Capitalism and British Imperialism: The New Debate on Empire* (Harlow, Longman, 1999).
19 Brian Stoddart, 'At the End of the Day's Play: Reflections on Cricket, Culture and Meaning', in Brian Stoddart and Keith A. P. Sandiford (eds), *The Imperial Game: Cricket, Culture and Society* (Manchester, Manchester University Press, 1998), p. 156.
20 David Cannadine, *Class in Britain* (New Haven, Yale University Press, 1998), p. 159.
21 Quoted in Douglas Booth and Colin Tatz, *One-Eyed: A View of Australian Sport* (Sydney, Allen and Unwin, 2000), p. 156.
22 Quoted in Richard Cashman, *Paradise of Sport: The Rise of Organised Sport in Australia* (Melbourne, Oxford University Press, 1995), p. 121.
23 Brian Stoddart, *Saturday Afternoon Fever: Sport in Australian Culture* (Sydney, Angus and Robertson, 1986), p. 66.
24 Quoted in Booth and Tatz, *One-Eyed*, p. 159.
25 A. W. Martin, *Robert Menzies: A Life, Vol. 2, 1944–78* (Melbourne, Melbourne University Press, 1999), p. 562.
26 Hilary McD. Beckles, *The Development of West Indies Cricket, Vol. 1: The Age of Nationalism* (London, Pluto Press, 1998), p. xviii. See also Hilary McD. Beckles and Brian Stoddart (eds), *Liberation Cricket: West Indies Cricket Culture* (Manchester, Manchester University Press, 1995).
27 C. L. R. James, *Beyond a Boundary* (London, Hutchinson, 1963).
28 See Martin Polley, *Moving the Goalposts: A History of Sport and Society Since 1945* (London, Routledge, 1998), p. 30.
29 For coverage of the MCC and South African stance on the 1968 and 1970 tours, see Christopher Merrett and John Nauright, 'South Africa', in Stoddart and Sandiford (eds), *Imperial Game*, pp. 70–3.

30 Denzil Batchelor, *The Test Matches of 1964: England v Australia* (London, Epworth Press, 1964), p. 156.
31 Ibid.

CHAPTER SEVEN

Imperial heroes for a post-imperial age: films and the end of empire

Jeffrey Richards

The Diamond Jubilee of Queen Victoria in 1897 has been seen in retrospect as the apogee of the British Empire. It is a remarkable fact that an empire that encompassed a quarter of the globe, and one that was ubiquitous in culture high and low, official and unofficial, has within a century largely vanished from the popular historical consciousness. This was graphically confirmed in 1997 when, to mark the centenary of the Diamond Jubilee, the *Daily Telegraph* commissioned a Gallup Poll to discover the current extent of popular knowledge of Britain's imperial history.[1] The results were revealing. Asked in which country General Wolfe and General Gordon died, 81 per cent and 80 per cent respectively either did not know or got it wrong. Asked what countries Robert Clive and Cecil Rhodes were associated with, 65 per cent and 77 per cent respectively either did not know or got it wrong. Asked who wrote the poem *Gunga Din*, 79 per cent did not know or got it wrong, and the answers included Richard Attenborough, Roald Dahl and Mahatma Gandhi. More than half of the respondents were unaware that the USA had once been part of the British Empire and 47 per cent thought Australia was still a British colony. When the answers were broken down by age group, it was discovered that amongst the minority getting the answers right, the highest proportion were in the age group over 50. For the young the British Empire is now quite as remote as the Roman Empire. Perhaps even more so, as Roman Britain is regularly taught in schools, the British Empire rarely.

Anecdotal evidence supports this survey. I recently asked a succession of third-year tutorial groups of university students if they could name a nineteenth-century imperial hero. None of them could and when I suggested the names of Gordon and Livingstone, they had quite simply never heard of them. This state of affairs has developed only since the 1950s. When I was growing up and going to school in that decade, these imperial figures were all familiar to us not just from school textbooks but also from films, television and comic books. In the early 1950s, although India had been given its independence, the African Empire remained and memories of the Second World War in which the British Empire as a whole had participated in the struggle against fascism were still fresh. Britain had witnessed an imperial coronation in 1953, the Empire Games were still staged every four years and imperial honours were awarded twice a year.

The history and meaning of the Empire has long been conveyed by the cinema. The 1930s had seen a flourishing genre of imperial films produced both in Britain and in Hollywood. There were romanticised biopics of imperial heroes: *Clive of India* (1935), *Rhodes of Africa* (1936), *Stanley and Livingstone* (1939). There were the classic celebrations of the African district officer such as *Sanders of the River* (1935) and above all there were the scarlet and gold heroics of the North-West Frontier of India, in which the British army maintained peace, order and good government and the dashing heroes accomplished rousing deeds of derring-do: *The Lives of a Bengal Lancer* (1935), *Charge of the Light Brigade* (1936), *Wee Willie Winkie* (1937), *The Drum* (1938), *Storm over Bengal* (1938) and *Gunga Din* (1939).[2] Why was Hollywood so supportive cinematically of an empire from which the USA had seceded in 1776? Britain was the biggest market for Hollywood films outside America, the two countries shared a cultural commitment to the values of chivalry, service and *noblesse oblige*, and the myth of the North-West Frontier functioned as the British equivalent of the American western. In the 1930s, few major westerns were made and imperial epics served as surrogates, dramatising the same subjects: white settlement, tribal uprisings, the exploitation of natural resources.[3] It is no coincidence that three of the great 1930s imperial adventures were remade subsequently as westerns: *The Lives of a Bengal Lancer* as *Geronimo*, *Four Men and a Prayer* as *Fury at Furnace Creek* and *Gunga Din* as *Sergeants Three*. But the original 1930s imperial epics had a new lease of life in the 1950s and 1960s when the Hollywood studios sold their film libraries to television, thus exposing a whole new generation to these favourable images of the Empire.

The outbreak of the Second World War put an end to the 1930s cycle of imperial films. The final two Hollywood contributions were *The Sun Never Sets* (1939) and the prophetically titled *Sundown* (1941), in both of which heroic British district commissioners in Africa fight fascist villains who are stirring up the tribes to revolt against the essentially benign rule of the British. The two films clearly contrasted a benevolent British paternalism with totalitarian tyranny. But it soon became clear that the war was promoting a new ethic which rendered the old-style imperial epics out of date. The war was promoted as a crusade for democracy, racial equality, self-determination and freedom. Its enemies were the cruel and racist tyrannies of the Third Reich and the Italian and Japanese Empires. The war aims of the Allies, as embodied in the Atlantic Charter, included self-determination for all nations. As the US Under-Secretary of State, Sumner Welles, declared in 1942: 'The age of imperialism is dead. The right of people to their freedom must be recognised. The principles of the Atlantic Charter must be guaranteed.'[4]

While it would obviously be wrong to equate the British Empire with the Axis powers, they did share a fundamental belief in a racial hierarchy, an idea at odds with the Allies' principles of the brotherhood of Man and democratic government. This became an embarrassment when expressed in Hollywood films at a time when for instance India's role as a bulwark against Japanese aggression in Asia was vital. Consequently the American Office of War Information scotched MGM's plans for a film version of Kipling's *Kim* and banned a planned reissue of the pre-war film *Gunga Din* which on its initial release had been banned in India, Japan and Malaya for 'offending against racial and religious susceptibilities'.[5]

The British Colonial Office had come to terms with the new imperative and by mid-1942 had evolved the concept of 'partnership' to replace the old 'trusteeship', equality rather than dependence, and in July 1943 Colonial Secretary Oliver Stanley made a statement of colonial war aims in the House of Commons containing a specific pledge 'to guide colonial peoples along the road to self-government within the framework of the British Empire'.[6] Aware of the need for positive propaganda to promote its new commitment, the Colonial Office and the Ministry of Information commissioned a feature film, *Men of Two Worlds*, which featured the struggle by a British district officer and an African concert pianist to break the power of a local witch doctor and facilitate the removal of a tribe from its tsetse fly infested homeland to a new settlement area as part of a government programme to eliminate sleeping sickness. Although partnership was the ostensible theme, it was the British district officer, wise, understanding and experienced, who emerged as the stronger character of the two. When it was released in 1946, the critics were unanimous in dismissing it as a well-meaning bore.[7]

After the war, the retreat from empire began. India was granted independence in 1947, Britain withdrew from Palestine, uprisings convulsed Kenya, Malaya and Cyprus, and the so-called 'wind of change' swept away Britain's African colonies, beginning with the Gold Coast in 1957. Nigeria, Somaliland, Sierra Leone, Tanganyika, Uganda, Kenya and the Gambia rapidly followed. The final major imperial withdrawal would come in 1997 when Hong Kong was handed back to China. In 1944 the British ruled an empire whose world-wide population approached 800 million souls. After the hand-over of Hong Kong, the population of the scattered handful of islands which was all that remained of that empire was 168,075.

The end of the war and the period of post-war austerity witnessed an increase in emigration to the so-called 'white Dominions' (Australia, Canada, New Zealand and South Africa) and this was reflected in a cycle of what were in effect Dominion westerns featuring the exploits of settlers, explorers and fortune hunters in Australia, New Zealand and South Africa. They highlight the romance and adventure associated with white settlement. Ealing Studios produced on location in Australia a trio of Australian westerns, all three starring Chips Rafferty, who was seen as the Australian Gary Cooper. *The Overlanders* (1946) was the story of an epic cattle drive across Australia during the war. *Bitter Springs* (1950), set in 1900, is the classic settler movie, with an Australian family, together with a newly arrived Englishman and Scotsman, undertaking a 600-mile trek, settling on Aboriginal land, and, after a violent clash with the natives, achieving a rapprochement. The best of the three, *Eureka Stockade* (1949), was also the most political. The story is set carefully in the context of the growth of democracy and compares the Eureka Stockade episode to England's Magna Carta and America's Declaration of Independence. Police ill-treatment and government oppression of the goldminers in 1850 leads the miners to demand full citizenship rights, to rise in rebellion, to set up the Eureka Stockade and to resist the authorities, under the heroic leadership of Peter Lalor. But it is stressed that the rebellion is against oppressive officials rather than against the Queen. 'She is our Queen as much as yours', declares Lalor when told he is rebelling against his sovereign. The stockade is stormed and the rebels dispersed. But their stand arouses the conscience of Australia and reforms are initiated which lead to justice for all. The three films all show Australians, Englishmen and Scots working and fighting side by side and the clear idea that these are 'our kith and kin' is conveyed by *The Listener*'s review of *The Overlanders*. It proclaimed it to be 'a grand tribute to the stubborn valour of people of our own blood on the other side of the world'.[8]

South Africa was the setting for two British adventure films. *Diamond City* (1949), set in the 1870s, is a 'law and order' African western. It centres on ex-naval captain Stafford Parker (David Farrar), who imposes order on the disorderly society of the Griqualand diamond diggings. In order to end the disorder Parker proclaims a Diggers' Republic, but after he defeats and drives out the criminal and disruptive elements, the British Government annex the territory to the Empire, and Parker, described as 'more a pioneer than a settler', moves on to fresh frontiers. *The Adventurers* (1950) is a South African version of the Hollywood classic *The Treasure of the Sierra Madre*. An oddly assorted group of treasure hunters – two ex-Boer commandos, a cashiered British officer and a shifty bar-owner – join forces to hunt for diamonds in 1902. But a watchful eye is kept on proceedings by a canny policeman, born in South Africa, the son of Irish immigrants, who predicts a bright future for his country.

The Seekers (1954) is a flaccid and studio-bound saga of the trials and tribulations of English settlers in early nineteenth-century New Zealand. It ends unusually with hero and heroine (Jack Hawkins and Glynis Johns) burned to death when a hostile Maori tribe attacks their settlement. But it offers hope for the future when their child is saved by a friendly Maori chief and the film ends with new settlers landing. All these films stress the role of settlers in bringing order and civilisation but also seek to indicate that they achieve peaceful co-existence with the native peoples.

There were still in the 1950s films which celebrated a life of imperial service and dedication. *Where No Vultures Fly* (1951) and *West of Zanzibar* (1954) were in effect updated district officer films with the last of the British imperial actors, Anthony Steel, as a British game warden protecting both animals and Africans from exploitation by the Arabs. *Pacific Destiny* (1956), based on Sir Arthur Grimble's reminiscences, affectionately recounts the experiences of a fledgling district officer in the Pacific where he teaches the natives cricket as an acceptable substitute for inter-tribal warfare.

There was a group of films set in India which centre on a battle of wits between a British officer and a tribal chieftain, highlighting the mutual respect that develops between them and illustrating Kipling's dictum: 'There is neither East nor West, Border, nor Breed, nor Birth, when two strong men stand face to face, though they come from the ends of the earth'.

Zarak (1956) and *The Bandit of Zhobe* (1958) tell virtually the same story, with tribal chieftains (Victor Mature in both cases) initially fighting against the British but in the end fighting with them against the invading Afghans. Mutual respect is the theme and British rule is not seen as heinous. But in 1966 when the theme was reworked in the *The Long Duel*, which featured a similar battle between British officer Trevor Howard and tribal chieftain Yul Brynner, the background was the definite oppression of the tribe by the British, who – with the single exception of Howard – are all seen as prejudiced, stubborn, stupid or nasty. This reflects a decisive change in cinematic attitudes to the Empire from the 1960s on.

The 1950s had actually witnessed some affirmative throwbacks to the full-blown glories of the 1930s. Alexander Korda remade his splendid 1939 epic *The Four Feathers*, featuring Kitchener's campaign to retake the Sudan, as *Storm over the Nile* (1955). But it was a sign of the cutprice times that the remake incorporated all of the battle footage from the previous version, stretched to accommodate the Cinemascope format. *North-West Frontier* (1959 – US title *Flame over India*) was a classic train thriller in which assorted Britons led by the Anglo-American alliance of Kenneth More as a dedicated British officer and Lauren Bacall as a spirited American governess helped a Hindu prince escape from an uprising of Moslem rebels. But such celebrations of imperial triumphs had been overtaken by imperial humiliation in the form of the 1956 Suez crisis – a real-life storm over the Nile.

The real counterpart of the celebrations of the white settlers were denunciations of nationalist rebels. During the 1950s and early 1960s, the nationalist uprisings against colonial rule inspired a series of films in which heroic white settlers and gallant British officers resisted the insurgents who are depicted throughout as ruthless terrorists. *The Planter's Wife* (1952 – US title *Outpost in Malaya*) is actually dedicated to the Malayan rubber planters 'daily defending their rubber trees with their lives'. It features rubber planter Jack Hawkins defending his plantation against Communist rebels, who are referred to throughout as 'bandits'. These ruthless terrorists shoot their own people in cold blood, use children to carry weapons and intimidate ordinary decent Malays, who would, it is suggested, otherwise be loyal to the British. The film culminates in a lengthy and heroic defence of the plantation by Hawkins and his improbably glamorous wife, played by imported Hollywood star Claudette Colbert. The unrest in Malaya made it necessary to shoot the film in Ceylon.

Simba (1955) and *Safari* (1956) were set against the background of the Mau Mau uprising in Kenya, an uprising viewed entirely from the British perspective. *Simba* attempted to put all the points of view. There are enlightened Britons who seek to understand the Africans (Dirk Bogarde and Virginia McKenna) and blinkered, old-fashioned white settlers who want punitive action (Basil Sydney). But the Mau Mau are seen as cruel and ruthless, directing their violence against whites sympathetic to Africans and against blacks sympathetic to whites. It is this which in the end leads the enlightened black doctor Peter Karanja (Earl Cameron) to denounce his own father as the mysterious Mau Mau leader Simba. Karanja dies for his pains but the Mau Mau are driven off and enlightened white settlers Dirk Bogarde and Virginia McKenna symbolically adopt a black boy whose parents have been killed by the Mau Mau, suggesting an alliance of decent whites and decent blacks against terrorist violence.

Safari centres on the murder of white hunter Victor Mature's son by the Mau Mau and his quest to track down the Mau Mau leader responsible, Jeroge (Earl Cameron). This is eventually successful when the Mau Mau attack the safari being led by Mature. The police are alerted by a faithful black boy (Juma) and arrive in the nick of time, and Jeroge is killed by Mature. Interestingly both films feature a black boy, symbol of youth and hope, siding with the whites, just as both films denounce the Mau Mau.

The High Bright Sun (1965) is set in Cyprus in 1957 during the EOKA campaign against British rule. It features decent if disenchanted British officers (Dirk Bogarde and Denholm Elliot), who, although fashionably weary, are fair-minded, resourceful and carrying out the duty of maintaining order. They are pitted against ruthless EOKA terrorists (George Chakiris, Gregoire Aslan). Caught in the middle is an American archaeologist of Greek descent (Susan Strasberg) who can see both sides of the argument and agonises lengthily and tediously but eventually settles for the British hero.

Tony Shaw sees these supportive British films as a defence of the imperial achievement in the context of the Cold War and in the light of continual Soviet denunciations of 'reactionary imperialism'. This interpretation is given substance by the comments of John Stafford, producer of *The Planter's Wife*, at the time of the film's release. Stafford hoped the picture 'would help make American people as a whole more aware of the part Britain is playing against Communism in the Far East'.[9]

The onset of the Cold War meant that for Hollywood, subject to the McCarthy purge and anxious to demonstrate its anti-Communist credentials, nineteenth-century British India provided a useful warning lesson about the dangers of Russian infiltration. When MGM finally made its long-planned film *Kim* (1950), this and subsequent Hollywood British India films like *Rogues March* (1952) and *Khyber Patrol* (1954) centre squarely on attempts by Russian agents to stir up the Afghan tribes against the British. But *Kim* also highlighted an identity crisis; an Irish boy raised as an Indian is torn between two different futures, Indian and British. This focused attention on the question of race which had largely been avoided in the 1930s imperial epics where the natives invariably figured as gallant allies, faithful servants or ruthless enemies. The dilemma of a mixed-race figure caught between two cultures featured in *King of the Khyber Rifles* (1954), set at the time of the Mutiny, and *Bhowani Junction* (1956), set in the run-up to Independence. However, in the former, mixed-race Captain King (Tyrone Power) successfully overcomes both racial prejudice and a rebel uprising, and in the latter the Communists and not the British are the real villains. In *Bhowani Junction* the Anglo-Indian Victoria Jones (Ava Gardner), having failed to live as English and as Indian, decides to stay on in India as an Anglo-Indian. But of all her suitors, she settles for British officer Stewart Granger who will stay on with her. None of these films were unequivocally anti-British and it was still possible even in the early 1960s to celebrate imperial heroism in the heyday of the Empire, as long as it was clearly historical and there was an ostensible justification.

The Boxer Uprising and the siege of the foreign legations in Peking in 1900 was memorably recreated in *55 Days at Peking* (1963). Ostensibly it is about the outnumbered representatives of the western imperial powers defying the military might of imperial China, but by extension this could be seen in 1963 as the United Nations versus Communist China. In fact it emerges far more as a tribute to the British imperial spirit. For when the crisis comes, the foreign envoys agree to evacuate Peking, all that is apart from the British minister, Sir Arthur Robertson (David Niven). He announces that whatever the other nations decide, Great Britain will stay. So the others also have to stay for fear of losing face. They then manage to hold out until relieved by an allied army fifty-five days after the siege begins. The film implies that the siege provided a blueprint for UN co-operation.

The humiliating débâcle of Suez caused the resignation of Prime Minister Sir Anthony Eden. But the ruling Conservative Party was re-elected in 1959 with a substantial majority over Labour, whose vote actually fell. Rising domestic prosperity assuaged discontent and Prime Minister Harold Macmillan, reassuringly patrician but shrewdly pragmatic, realising that the country could no longer afford to sustain its world-wide imperial role, managed to disengage from empire while suggesting that independence for the colonies was the fulfilment of the imperial mission, and that the Commonwealth, with the Queen as its head, was the natural successor to the Empire. In this context up until the 1960s both Hollywood and British films for the most part demonstrated a sympathy with and even support for the British Empire and its ideals. This stance changed dramatically from the 1960s on. Between the 1960s and the 1990s, there was a massive shift of attitudes due in part to structural changes in the film industry and in part to wider social and cultural changes in the western world.

During the 1960s the old Hollywood studio system, already weakened by the court decision which forced studios to divest themselves of their cinema chains and further undermined by the rise of television, began to break up and instead a wider range of independent producers emerged. At the same time the nature of the audience changed. Increasingly from the 1960s the core audience for films was perceived to be largely under thirty. This had far-reaching ideological consequences. The old studio system had by and large aimed at a cross-class, mixed-gender, all-age audience from six to sixty and had demonstrated in its films a commitment to the political, social and cultural status quo, dramatising what it perceived to be widely held common values and seeking to avoid controversy. The new youthful audience was assumed to be on the whole anti-establishment and unsympathetic to the values and beliefs of the older generation. The British Empire symbolised everything that members of the young audience were deemed to be against, and their hostility was reinforced by changing political and social values, where a new commitment to gender and racial equality went hand-in-hand with the idea that imperialism was now and had always been unequivocally wrong and indefensible. The Empire had also largely ceased to exist, so like the Third Reich could safely be invoked as a timeless and stereotyped villain.

Britain had traditionally been the biggest foreign market for US films and one of the reasons Hollywood had produced pro-British and pro-empire films in the 1930s and 1950s was to keep British audiences happy. By the 1960s, mass cinema closures in Britain and a general decline in cinema-going meant that Britain was no longer the lucrative market it had once been for American films. Since then Hollywood has no longer cared what British audiences think or feel and the British Empire has become a convenient all-purpose villain, the antithesis of the democratic, multi-ethnic, equal opportunities culture that is Hollywood's ideal. The Empire, which in Hollywood's heyday had been seen very largely as benevolent, wise and well-intentioned, is now seen exclusively as racist, snobbish, cruel and exploitative.

Hollywood now pours its resources into making films celebrating the heroism of leaders of the resistance to what is often seen as specifically English colonial oppression. This can be seen in *Braveheart* (1995), Mel Gibson's ludicrous travesty of the events in the career of William Wallace, hero of the thirteenth-century struggle to free Scotland from English occupation, and *Michael Collins*, Neil Jordan's 1996 tribute to the IRA leader who fought the British to a standstill and secured the independence of Southern Ireland in 1921.[10] And when in need of a sneering, supercilious and sadistic villain, Hollywood now turns largely to British, or more specifically English, actors. There was a long tradition of casting British actors as Roman emperors and Egyptian pharaohs, on the assumption that the representatives of a modern empire would do just as well as the representatives of ancient empires. But now they are more likely to be found as international terrorists, murderers and torturers.

The single exception to this trend has been the continuing popularity of the James Bond films. As James Chapman has persuasively argued, the Bond novels and films at one level 'represent a nationalist fantasy, in which Britain's decline as a world power did not really take place. One of the ideological functions of the Bond narrative is to construct an imaginary world in which the *Pax Britannica* still operates. Thus Britain is presented as being in the front line of the conspiracies directed against western civilization.'[11] In the film series, which began in 1962 and continues to the present day, MI5 agent James Bond and CIA agent Felix Leiter function as partners in a special relationship but in a reversal of political reality, with the American as the junior partner. Bond is permanently on 'Her Majesty's Secret Service' and as late as *Tomorrow Never Dies* (1997) the Prime Minister is able to order the British battle fleet to the China Seas in a confrontation with Red China. 'What British battle fleet?', the informed observer might ask.

Raymond Durgnat, describing Bond as 'the last man in of the British

Empire's Superman XI', placed the first film in the sequence, *Doctor No*, squarely in an imperial context:

> Whatever Brand X critics may have written, Bond isn't just an Organization Man, but a rigid jingoist, almost lovably archaic. If you have forelocks, prepare to touch them now, in fond farewell to the Edwardiana in modern drag lovingly panoplied forth in the first half of *Doctor No* (1962) as Bond glides along the Establishment's Old Boy Net. The British Raj, reduced to its Caribbean enclave, lords it benevolently over jovial and trusting West Indians and faithful coloured police-sergeants, Uncle Toms of Dock Green ... Meanwhile out in Crab Key lurks Dr. No, last of the war lords, whose 'chigro' minions ... blend of the Yellow Peril and the Mau Mau, battle it out with his English co-anachronism.[12]

But it should be pointed out that the three most successful James Bond actors have been Scottish (Sean Connery), Irish (Pierce Brosnan) and self-parodying upper-class English (Roger Moore). The one authentically English unparodied stiff-upper-lip Bond (Timothy Dalton) was unsuccessful and rapidly replaced. The attitude of Hollywood is significant as Hollywood films provide the staple viewing of British cinema-goers and during the 1960s at least the bulk of British film-making was funded by Hollywood companies.

Britain too in the 1960s underwent a profound and far-reaching social and cultural revolution. The background to this revolution was the affluence, full-employment and materialism of the 1950s which released people from the immediate disciplines of survival and turned their attention to their 'expressive' needs – self-discovery, self-assertion, sensation. In a delirious upsurge of Romanticism similar to that which overtook early nineteenth-century culture, the rebel and the deviant became heroes, the self was exalted, spontaneity was encouraged and rules, restrictions, conventions and traditions in both life and art were ditched. The old structures, old values and old certainties which for over a century had made Britain a disciplined, deferential society, were increasingly derided and rejected. Violence, profanity and sexuality, hitherto rigorously suppressed by puritanical social and legal codes, were unleashed and became prominent in both high culture and low. Personal style, cool, chic, cynical and consumerist, became the ideal – self rather than service, immediate gratification rather than long-term spiritual or intellectual development.

In the 1960s it became fashionable for the first time in British history to be young and working-class. This emphasis on youth with its desire to be free and on the working-class of the 'rough' rather than the 'respectable' variety, plus the promotion of the philosophy of the self, completely undermined the two shaping creeds behind the British national identity, both of them based on the idea of the subordination of the self for the greater good: evangelicalism and chivalry. The fact that both of these ideologies also underpinned the doctrine of altruistic imperialism meant that a belief in imperialism was rejected along with the belief in such values as duty, honour, service, decency and respectability. They were regarded and depicted as either outdated bourgeois conceits or as oppressive patriarchal constructs. Symptomatically the 1959 film of the epoch-making John Osborne play *Look Back in Anger* has its hero, Jimmy Porter, in a cinema mocking the 1939 imperial epic *Gunga Din*.[13]

This development had profound consequences for popular culture. For over a century the idea of chivalry had been embodied in the notion of the gentleman. This was not, Sir Ernest Barker argued, a class idea. 'It is the idea of a type of character ... a mixture of stoicism with medieval lay chivalry, and of both with unconscious national ideals, half Puritan and half secular.'[14] Bernard Crick saw the idea of the gentleman as an integrative image for the ruling elites of Great Britain, an idea which transcended the boundaries between England, Scotland and Wales, and percolated down from the elite to the rest of the population through popular culture.[15]

Of the utmost cultural significance was the fact that the idea of the gentleman as the dominant image of masculinity was shared by Britain and America. As John Fraser has written: 'The family of chivalric heroes has been by far the largest and most popular one in twentieth century American culture and its members have entered into virtually everyone's consciousness'.[16] The figures Fraser cites, celebrated in books, plays, comic strips, radio, television and films on both sides of the Atlantic up to the 1960s, include the Virginian, Robin Hood, Prince Valiant, the Scarlet Pimpernel, Zorro, Philip Marlowe, Superman, Tarzan, the Saint, Bulldog Drummond and many more, a gallery of immortals committed to a code of values which included stoicism, selflessness, duty, service and honour.

That officer and gentleman hero found himself eclipsed during the 1960s and replaced by the working-class individualist, rebellious, non-conformist, self-centred and devoted to immediate gratification, or the classless meritocratic professional, dedicated to modernity and the conscious rejection of the past in all its forms.[17] The gentleman increasingly became imbued with the negative values retrospectively associated with the Empire: snobbery, arrogance, racism and irrelevance.

This clash of archetypes surfaced in one of the key 1960s films of empire, *Zulu* (1963). The Empire still had some good stories to tell but they had to be rewritten to fit them for a post-imperial age. *Zulu*, directed by Cy Endfield and written by him and John Prebble, recreated the defence of the mission station at Rorke's Drift in 1879 where one hundred and five men of the South Wales Borderers held out against four thousand Zulus in an action which resulted in the award of eleven Victoria Crosses. But this was no straightforward triumphalist paean to the British Empire such as might have been seen in a version of the story made in the 1930s. The action itself is stripped of any imperial significance. When the terrified Private Cole asks 'Why us?', Colour Sergeant Bourne replies: 'Because we're here lad, and nobody else'. The regiment is Welsh rather than English, the local missionary is drunken and ineffectual, the regimental surgeon denounces the butchery and at the end the two leading officers proclaim themselves disgusted by the slaughter. As a sign of the changed times, a continuing theme of the film is the class tension between the two senior officers, the languid, drawling aristocratic Lieutenant Gonville Bromhead (Michael Caine), the old-style officer and gentleman, and the classless engineer and bridgebuilder Lieutenant John Chard (Stanley Baker), the new-style meritocrat. Although they develop a mutual respect during the course of the action, it is significantly Chard who takes command and secures the victory. The main theme of the film, however, is the mutual respect between the two fighting forces, with the Borderers answering the Zulu war chants with a rousing chorus of *Men of Harlech*, and in a final chivalric gesture the Zulus returning to salute the Welsh soldiers as gallant warriors.

Director David Lean explored the nature of Britain's last imperial hero in *Lawrence of Arabia* (1962), scripted by Robert Bolt. The myth of T. E. Lawrence was created in the aftermath of the First World War and he was presented straightforwardly as a romantic desert warrior, who understood the Arabs and led them in a successful guerrilla campaign against the corrupt and oppressive Turkish Empire. Lean's Lawrence, memorably played by Peter O'Toole, was an imperial hero for a post-imperial age, a heroic individualist who loves Arabia but a strange mixture of idealist, exhibitionist and masochist, with a view of himself as a man of destiny. The dramatic hinge of the film is the Deraa scene where, after his savage flogging by the Turks, a substitute for the rape which is actually believed to have taken place, Lawrence's view of his invulnerability is destroyed. He gives way to ferocious bloodlust and alienates his former friends. Not only is he therefore a flawed hero, but the film also presents him ahistorically as an Arab nationalist, desiring freedom and self-government for the Arabs, a plan which breaks down, leaving the scheming Allied politicians to carve up the liberated lands. In fact Lawrence was no nationalist but envisaged the liberated lands as the British Empire's 'first brown dominion'.[18]

It was undoubtedly the world-wide box-office success of *Lawrence of Arabia* that inspired the making of *Khartoum* (1966), in which director Basil Dearden and writer Robert Ardrey recreated the last stand of General Gordon in 1885. Charlton Heston gives a convincing performance as Gordon, the mystical patriot, Christian idealist, and heroic individualist who knows no fear and acts strictly according to his own notions of duty. The film does not attribute imperial ambitions to Gordon. Instead it stresses his devotion to the Sudan and its people; his opposition to slavery and oppression; his sense of stoicism and service. Nor does the film attribute imperial ambitions to the British Prime Minister W. E. Gladstone (Ralph Richardson), who declares roundly: 'I will not undertake a British obligation to police the world'.

The film simplifies the Sudanese political situation. In reality Egypt was the colonial power in Sudan, Khartoum an alien settlement and the Mahdi was backed by slave-trading tribes and was seeking to free the Sudan from Egyptian interference in the slave trade. None of this is discussed. Instead the film universalises, suggesting the similarity of Gordon and the Mahdi as visionaries, mystics and military geniuses, each with a sense of mission, each loving the land and the people. This is brought out clearly in the ahistorical face-to-face confrontation of the two protagonists. It is Gordon's death, contrary to the Mahdi's orders, that leads directly to the British occupation of the Sudan and prompts Gladstone to observe with heavy irony: 'When I think how history will record some day that the decisions of an empire were made by greedy businessmen, scheming generals and conniving politicians'.[19]

Although imperialism is played down in all three films, it is impossible to remove the sense of admiration for the leading figures: the handful of red-coated Welsh soldiers who successfully face down an entire army, and the lone heroism of Lawrence and Gordon on their respective missions against overwhelming odds. For all the changed times, there is still something here of the Victorian notions of glory captured in Lady Butler's famous painting of the stand at Rorke's Drift, and G. W. Joy's equally celebrated canvas of the death of Gordon, both of which are effectively recreated in the films.

The shift of sympathies in the cinema has taken place in a comparatively short time. Symbolic of this is the filming of *Gandhi*. In 1972 Richard Attenborough directed *Young Winston*, a lavish and large-scale celebration of Britain's unrepentantly imperialist wartime Prime Minister, featuring the heroic charge of the 21st Lancers at the Battle of Omdurman during Kitchener's campaign in the Sudan and Churchill's adventures as a war correspondent during the Boer War. Yet within ten years Attenborough was directing his inspiring if wholly uncritical tribute to the Mahatma and his non-violent campaign to get the British out of India.

A similar shift of sympathies can be seen to have taken place between 1963 when *Zulu* was released and 1979 when *Zulu Dawn* appeared. The former was a celebration of the courage of both sides in the stand at Rorke's Drift in 1879 but it lacked any sense of historical context. That was abundantly present in its prequel, *Zulu Dawn*, a spectacular recreation of the Battle of Isandlwana, one of the heaviest military defeats in British history. The film begins with Lord Chelmsford (Peter O'Toole) and

Sir Bartle Frere (John Mills) conspiring to provoke the Zulus into war, with Frere aiming at what he calls 'a final solution' to the Zulu problem, a phrase which carries with it all the genocidal overtones of the Nazi Holocaust of the Jews. It is made clear that the British Government favours a peaceful solution and that the war is the result of free enterprise imperialism by the men on the spot. Nevertheless it is undoubtedly a ruthless and cynical policy of imperial expansion, with both British soldiers and Zulu warriors seen as its victims. One of the principal opponents of the policy is an irregular colonel, Anthony Durnford (Burt Lancaster), who loves the country and admires the Zulus, and is significantly Irish. The Irish are now invariably used in films as the spokesmen of truth and justice and the arch-opponents of imperialism.

Further evidence of the shift of sympathies can be seen in the transformation in depictions of white settlers in Kenya and army officers in British India. During the 1950s, both groups were seen as gallant, upright and honourable. By the 1970s and 1980s, with *Conduct Unbecoming* (1979), the British regiment in India is so hidebound by tradition and blinkered in its notions of honour that it is willing to cover up a series of vicious assaults on women by one of its officers. And in the BBC film *Happy Valley* (1985) and the cinema feature *White Mischief* (1986), the white settler community in Kenya is depicted as a hot bed of promiscuity, drug-taking, voyeurism, sadism and murder. Australia too as part of a process of cultural and emotional emancipation from 'the old country' has joined in with films about the exploitation and ill-treatment of Australian soldiers by snobbish and racist British officers in the imperial wars: the Boer War in *Breaker Morant* (1980) and the Great War in *Gallipoli* (1981). Morant was in fact a ruthless murderer who shot down blacks for pleasure but the effluction of time has made him a national hero. Historians have expended much ink and fury in cataloguing the factual errors, distortions and misrepresentations in such films, to no avail. For of course what is being depicted in such films is not history but mythology, just as what was being depicted in the pro-imperial films of the 1930s was not history but mythology. Complex issues are simplified and individualised, events telescoped, significant figures omitted and confrontations invented to highlight themes. Most seriously, history is recast to emphasise present-day attitudes, approaches and preoccupations.

In a similar fashion, the great literary works of imperial fiction have been adapted to the changing needs of a modern cinema-going public. The classics of imperial adventure, despite the fact that they embody values and attitudes that are anathema to present-day Hollywood, have been steadily remade by film-makers aware of the recognition value of familiar titles. But they are invariably rewritten to give them an anti-imperial slant and in effect reversing the value systems on which they were predicated.

Kipling is probably still spinning in his grave at the memory of the 1994 film of *The Jungle Book*, in which, apart from the spirited heroine, the British are depicted as either comic idiots or brutal thugs, and the subtle allegory of the original is ditched in favour of an inter-racial love affair and Indiana Jones style adventures in a temple of doom. Similarly Rider Haggard's *King Solomon's Mines* was remade in 1985 with Richard Chamberlain as Allan Quatermain. This was effectively turned into *Indiana Quatermain and the Mines of Doom* with dialogue of unremitting banality, an infuriatingly stupid heroine and non-stop serial-style action bearing little resemblance to Haggard's magnificent original.

Greystoke (1984) was touted as the first authentic version of Edgar Rice Burroughs's *Tarzan of the Apes*, the classic novel about the abandoned child raised by African apes, who eventually takes his place in the House of Lords as Lord Greystoke. But actually it was no more authentic than any of the previous versions and was tricked out with fashionable attacks on a snobbish English aristocratic establishment, nineteenth-century science and big game hunting. *The Last of the Mohicans* (1992), dealing with the colonial wars in North America, wholly subverts Fenimore Cooper's original novel. It turns Hawkeye from a wizened old Indian-hating scout into a handsome child of nature, living with the Indians, and preaching a doctrine of ecological balance. It foists anti-Indian atrocities on the British that Cooper never envisaged and injects a strongly anti-British story-line wholly absent from the novel. So the wheel comes full circle and a cinema which during the Empire's heyday produced film versions of *The Jungle Book* (1942), *The Last of the Mohicans* (1920), *King Solomon's Mines* (1938) and *Tarzan of the Apes* (1932) uncritical of the Empire now turns out versions totally critical of the same Empire.

Only one film has bucked the trend, John Huston's superb *The Man Who Would Be King* (1975), in which Sean Connery and Michael Caine as a pair of Indian Army veterans take over an Afghan kingdom but are finally brought to death and ruin. *The Man Who Would Be King* was marketed as a straightforward action film with the slogan 'Long live adventure – and adventurers'. But it is much more than this. It is cinema at its best, cinema as allegory, myth and history lesson. Kipling's short story, inventively expanded and embellished in the masterly script by John Huston and Gladys Hill, explores the nature of the imperial illusion. The two veterans gain control of Kafiristan by their military skill, courage and determination and maintain it by a combination of sublime self-confidence, superior technology and a godlike mystique. Although Peachy Carnehan (Caine) declares 'Not gods but Englishmen – which is the next best thing', his companion Daniel Dravot (Connery) comes to share the natives' belief in his own divinity and invulnerability. When the more pragmatic Carnehan wants to leave with the wealth they have plundered from the kingdom, Dravot decides to stay on as King. But the spell of the Englishman is broken when Dravot proves all too human – by yielding to sexual desire and losing blood when he is bitten by the woman he wants and who is terrified of mating with a god. Dravot is killed, Carnehan is mutilated and the imperial adventure ends in disaster. With its flawed heroes and pervading sense of irony balancing the excitement, action and salty humour of the classic adventure format, *The Man Who Would Be King* is perhaps the most convincing presentation of imperial heroes for a post-imperial age that cinema has yet produced.

The predominant view of the Empire since the 1960s on films and television has been hostile and critical. But – and this does suggest an interesting sidelight on the effects of the media – the *Daily Telegraph* poll with which I began asked: 'Do you take pride in the fact that Britain had an empire?' Seventy per cent said yes. 'Do you regret Britain no longer has an empire?' Sixty per cent said yes. 'Did Britain do more good than harm in her colonies?' Fifty-eight per cent said yes (as opposed to thirty-one per cent saying more harm than good). This went along with the striking ignorance about the facts of the Empire which the survey also revealed.

How is it that after thirty years of exposure to largely hostile depictions of the Empire and in the light of a demonstrated and colossal factual ignorance about it, the public are still proud of their vanished Empire? That shrewd populist, Tony Blair, acknowledged this curious state of affairs when he wrote in a newspaper article: 'We can be justly proud of many of the achievements of the British Empire'.[20] I suspect this relates to the widely acknowledged crisis of English identity, which contrasts with the confident assertions of national identity by Wales, Ireland and Scotland. The problem for England is that it became interchangeable with Britain for a century. The British Empire has gone, the United Kingdom is facing transformation into the Federal Kingdom with devolution in Scotland, Wales and Ireland, and the English stubbornly refuse to commit themselves to Europe. Indeed if anything they would rather be American than European, and Harold Wilson's political secretary recently revealed that he considered petitioning to join the USA when frustrated by de Gaulle's constant opposition to Britain's entry into the Common Market. And so the English retreat into nostalgia for an empire which they barely remember and of which they know almost nothing.

Notes

1 *Daily Telegraph*, 26 August 1997.
2 Jeffrey Richards, *Visions of Yesterday* (London, Routledge, 1973), pp. 2–220.
3 Richard Slotkin, *Gunfighter Nation* (New York, Harper Perennial, 1993), pp. 266–7.
4 J. M. Lee and Martin Petter, *The Colonial Office, War and Development Policy*

(London, Institute of Commonwealth Studies, 1982), p. 122.

5   Clayton Koppes and Gregory D. Black, *Hollywood Goes to War* (London: I. B. Tauris, 1988), p. 225.

6   Lee and Petter, *Colonial Office*, p. 244.

7   Jeffrey Richards, *Thorold Dickinson and the British Cinema* (Lanham, MD, Scarecrow Press, 1997), pp. 97–121.

8   *The Listener*, 10 October 1946.

9   Tony Shaw, *British Cinema and the Cold War: The State, Propaganda and Consensus* (London, I. B. Tauris, 2001); Susan Carruthers, *Winning Hearts and Minds: British Governments, the Media and Colonial Counter-Insurgency 1944–1960* (Leicester, Leicester University Press, 1995), p. 112; Susan Carruthers, 'Two Faces of 1950s Terrorism: The Film Presentation of Mau Mau and the Malayan Emergency', *Small Wars and Insurgencies*, 6 (1995), pp. 17–43.

10 On the 'Braveheart Phenomenon' see Colin McArthur, '*Braveheart* and the Scottish Aesthetic Dementia', in Tony Barta (ed.), *Screening the Past* (London, Praeger, 1998), pp.167–87, and Fintan O'Toole, 'Imagining Scotland', *Granta*, 56 (Winter 1996), pp. 60–76.

11 James Chapman, *License to Thrill* (London, I. B. Tauris, 1999), pp. 38–9.

12 Raymond Durgnat, *A Mirror for England* (London, Faber, 1970), p. 151.

13 Jeffrey Richards, *Films and British National Identity* (Manchester, Manchester University Press, 1997), pp. 1–28; Bernice Martin, *A Sociology of Contemporary Cultural Change* (Oxford, Blackwell, 1981).

14 Ernest Barker (ed.), *The Character of England* (Oxford, Oxford University Press, 1947), pp. 566–7.

15 Bernard Crick, *National Identities* (Oxford, Blackwell, 1991), pp. 94–5.

16 John Fraser, *America and the Patterns of Chivalry* (Cambridge, Cambridge University Press, 1981), pp. 12, 16.

17 Hugh David, *Heroes, Mavericks and Bounders* (London, Michael Joseph, 1991).

18 John M. MacKenzie, 'T. E. Lawrence: The Myth and the Message', in Robert Giddings (ed.), *Literature and Imperialism* (London, Macmillan, 1991), pp. 150–81.

19 Gerald Herman, 'For God and Country: Khartoum (1966) as History and "Object Lesson" for Global Policemen', *Film and History*, 9 (February 1979), pp. 1–15.

20 *Daily Telegraph*, 25 November 1999.

CHAPTER EIGHT

Imperial legacies, new frontiers: children's popular literature and the demise of empire

Kathryn Castle

Enough scholarly attention has now been paid to children's literature to establish that it played an important role in transmitting the imperial ethos to generations of children from the 1890s through the inter-war period. Particularly in the popular press, boys' and girls' papers brought home to the youth of empire the positive benefits of belonging to a 'Greater Britain'. These publications encouraged the young to assume ownership of Britain's imperial identity as a counterpart to the transition to adulthood, and consistently used the imperial setting both to entertain and to instruct their audience. Studies have shown that these papers were responsive to the dynamics of the Empire, the lessons of its history and its current value. Children's magazines and annuals offered a very positive view of colonial rule, which included the opportunity for adventure, supremacy, conflict, riches and service.[1] This was what made Britain 'great' and empowered the individuals who lived within it. Having aligned themselves so closely with the attractions of the imperial world, how would these publications adjust their content to the contraction of British power?

The popular press had been in the process of modernisation well before the end of the Second World War. Children's papers, a highly competitive market, had responded to the changing needs and tastes of youth in the inter-war years.[2] Entertainment increasingly displaced a concern for educational or improving features as a primary selling point. Competition for leisure time from the radio and the cinema in the 1920s and 1930s increased the pressure to appear 'up to date', while the stresses of the economic depression and the looming clouds of war in Europe also encouraged a flight from excessive realism. Arguably the sacrifices of the First World War had also brought questions about the value of patriotism and nationalist propaganda, particularly in materials for a new generation. Two of the most jingoistic of the boys' papers, the *Captain* and *Chums*, stopped publishing in 1925 and 1933 respectively, while the old favourite, the *Boy's Own Paper*, struggled to survive. The *Girl's Own Paper*, the last

[145]

of the traditional girls' titles, folded in the 1940s.

Paper shortages during the war didn't help to keep the old titles afloat. The *Boy's Own* coped with falling revenue and war restrictions by reducing its format and lowering the price from 1s to 6d. Serial stories, which had previously extended across months of weekly instalments, were now concluded in two or three weeks. This partly reflects the decreasing popularity of fiction with the boy readership, and also the declining number of children who could afford or were willing to subscribe to the magazine. In March 1954, Jack Cox, the editor of the *Boy's Own Paper* until its final demise in 1967, celebrated the paper's seventy-fifth anniversary with 'The Story of the Boy's Own Paper'. While he blamed the decline of the paper on inflation, new management, and loss of advertising revenue, he acknowledged that the *Boy's Own Paper* was proudly old-fashioned, holding 'steadfast' to its principles in a world of changing values.[3] A strong part of its identity had been the imperial ethos, scouting, the family and Christian values, all of which seemed increasingly out of touch with the world of post-war children.

It was in part the vitality of the post-war popular press which squeezed out publications rooted in the past. One of the major areas of growth was girls' magazines. Whereas before the war crossover reading from girls' to boys' papers was common, increasingly girls demanded their own titles like *Girl, Schoolfriend* and *Girls' Crystal.* Class was less of a factor now than gender in the pattern of children's reading, particularly for girls. Boys' publications demonstrated the successful formula of weekly penny papers and comics, although the success of the *Eagle* (1950–73) showed that there was still room for a well-produced middle-class paper.

The juvenile press was also in the national spotlight in the 1950s. A crusade for decency echoed the concerns of the late nineteenth century over the pernicious influence of 'penny dreadfuls' and the 'gutter press'. Sections of the public, publishers and Parliament became agitated over the invasion of American horror comics into the UK market. These had first arrived with GIs during the war, and the move to ban them betrays anxieties both about their excessive violence and about US influence in Europe after 1945. The Children's and Young Persons' Act of 1954 banned the comics in England as they had previously been excluded in Italy and France.[4] While never completely successful in keeping out the horrors, the legislation did assist the launch of one of the most successful decent alternatives of the era, the *Eagle.* Like the *Boy's Own Paper* of eighty years earlier, it capitalised on the call for respectable magazines in the market. The success of the *Eagle* was that it managed to provide an alternative to the horror comic without losing its appeal to the reader. Visually it was very well produced: the bright colours and excellent graphics of Dan Dare, racing cars, planes and space ships, the comic strips and the adventure stories made a winning combination.

It quickly becomes apparent when reading these magazines that certain aspects of the colonial relationship were no longer of interest to publishers or audience. Even in the *Eagle*, edited by the Reverend Marcus Morris, where the Christian imprint was felt most, there was little sermonising. There were few mentions of the advantages of British administration, the achievements of the British armed forces, nor any attempt to explain the reasons for changing relations between Britain and her former colonies. This does not, however, necessarily indicate that children's papers easily gave up imperial themes and preoccupations. The idea that the Empire passed away with little public concern, or that new venues and updated characters dropped the mantle of imperial consciousness from children's shoulders, should be more closely considered.[5] By isolating some persistent and popular themes, ideas and assumptions of the papers during the imperial era and investigating whether they continue into the post-war years, and if so in what shape or form, one can consider how these materials adapted to imperial decline and transition. Would this new generation of British youth, reading the *Eagle* or *Schoolfriend* or the *Lion*, have encountered a different story of Britain's presence in the wider world, of new post-imperial relations? Would the colonial world be regarded as less appropriate for the narrative of adventure? Would the racial supremacy implicit in the colonial relationship give way to a more complex negotiation?

The empire of nature

One of the most characteristic images of the children's papers before the Second World War was the hunter in the wild. He appeared on the covers of many papers and annuals in the act of repelling the advance of dangerous beasts or enraged tribesmen. Dominance of the colonial landscape and its inhabitants through physical force was a central theme of adventure stories and children's experience of the colonial encounter. The natural world also offered a meeting point for the European and subject peoples. In India the imperial administrators joined the local rulers in displays of power over the beasts of the jungle. In Africa the native guide was crucial in facilitating western access to the untamed areas of the continent. The hunter might also be explorer or scientist, and all of these activities opened the imperial world to the audience of children's papers. Women and girls also interacted with the natural world, but in a manner which betrayed the gender conventions of the era. Their appreciation was of the novel, the romantic and the picturesque, not of nature's savagery, but of its beauty.[6]

The post-war papers did not abandon such a successful setting for children's stories, but do show new relations with the savage world and its inhabitants. The killing of game for sport was now seen to be less acceptable. The indiscriminate slaughter of wildlife became subject to refinements in the drama of dominance. Hunters now moved through the landscape in search of animals for capture and transport to European zoos. Poachers became villains in stories set in Africa or the East, opposed by British game wardens. Elephants, in particular, featured as heroes of adventure in their own right, defeating the rogue in their midst and working as allies of local commissioners and business interests. English visitors replaced their weapons with the modern equivalent, cameras and recorders, which would 'capture' and preserve the experience of travel abroad. Film companies and their employees, as in 'Jungle Joe Foils the Film-wreckers', were presented as benign influences. As Joe says 'it's time to preserve wild life ... not the old stuff of hunting and killing'.[7]

The introduction of modern technology into the natural world took a variety of forms. British characters now tended to move through uncharted territory in planes or helicopters, trucks and jeeps. This changed the encounter from a character-building test of individual strength to a demonstration of the hardware of advanced societies. There was as much interest in the speed, strength and agility of the machine as there had been in the prowess of the pre-war hero.[8] While the outcome of an encounter between the West and the primitive world remained predictable, the agency for securing success served to distance the British character from a direct contest. Perhaps the best example of this trend was Archie the Robot, who roamed the world with his controllers, Ted and Ken. While exploring in Central Africa, Archie becomes 'Pal o' the Pygmies' – indeed by the end of the story they proclaim him their 'God'. This is an interesting modernisation of the Livingstone story, a popular reference point in imperial fiction. Archie can wrestle elephants, rebuild whole villages and uproot forests. He is portrayed as a positive force in relations with local people, but he also displaces the need for negotiations or British heroics. The introduction of a mechanical adventure hero who possesses selected characteristics of the imperial character is an interesting aspect of changing dynamics in the colonial world. Just as television or the documentary film presents the natural world at second hand, so Archie makes the British influence one of remote control.

The appeal of technology and futuristic stories was balanced by the continuing attraction of the remote and exotic island. The sovereignty of these areas was made deliberately vague, and they appeared open to castaways, traders and travellers. Here was the most lush and romantic of natural settings, offering escape from the drab reality of post-war recovery. The sensuality of the encounter with uninhibited dusky maidens marked a definite change from the earlier papers. Adolescents of the 1950s and 1960s, certainly in the girls' papers, demanded more romance, and the South Seas was an ideal setting. During the days of empire this was a taboo subject, and even after the war there was no evidence of boys and girls of England entertaining such encounters in India or Africa. However, the lifting of the serious imperatives of empire building could allow more relaxed relations in an area of the world which seemed to offer an uncritical welcome to British travellers. In 'Lola of the Blue Lagoon', a friendship grows between Lola, 'who had always longed to have a white friend', and Denise, who is entranced by 'a pretty golden brown face'. In 'Karrini's Charm; A Romantic Story of the South Sea Islands', Philip Neale is a young English trader who finds it hard to leave. He tells Karrini, 'I'd like to live here always, it is so peaceful. No talk of war, no noise of big city.' The limits of these friendships can be seen in 'Sumuna's South Sea Isle', where Tim, the hero, wants Sumuna, who has saved his life, to return to England with him. She replies, 'No Tim, Sumuna belongs on her island and you to the big world beyond the horizon. Let us each stay where we truly belong.' Even in this most idyllic of settings, permanent relationships which crossed racial boundaries remained forbidden. Sovereignty may not have been an issue in the South Pacific, but the time had not yet come when Englishmen could return home with the trophies of exotic brides.[9]

There are a number of crosscurrents here in the experience of nature which reflect both continuity and change in the face of a declining imperial power. While children's papers continued to employ the conflict with the wild to enhance the excitement of adventure fiction, there were signs that the confines of the imperial mentality were out of date. No longer could young Englishmen roam the world to ruthlessly dominate the environment, either man or beast. The emphasis now was on a protective role, both for the interests of commercial advantage and to demonstrate a positive legacy of imperial responsibility. Supremacy was no longer about force, but rested on an evolved spirit of paternalism and persuasion. Nature, both man and beast, became dissociated from the imperial project although not from the control of advanced societies. In a sense nature became less threatening, the encounter less adversarial, when released from the paradigm of imperial relations. The unpredictable and strange could be tolerated, even enjoyed, as diversity became more valued, and suppressing the environment less desirable than exploiting its attractions.

Progress and the primitive

Fiction set in the pre-war period which involved the travel of young Britons into the colonial world had often shown conflict between progress and the primitive: the rational and irrational. Africa in particular had provided a setting for the agents of Christianity and civilisation to expose and overcome the powers of native superstitions, although high priests in India and China had also been portrayed as controlling the peasantry with demonstrations of magical powers. While in the post-war fiction the Christian dimension was largely absent, there remains the question of whether the acceptance of developing independence and withdrawal of western power was accompanied by a recasting of the old polarity between the enlightened and the backward nations. Would the rapidly developing technology of the western world, the interest in space travel and the marvels of science diminish the popularity of the witch doctor and his black magic as a feature of children's adventure? Rather surprisingly, it seems not. The continued fascination with supernatural powers and the persons who claimed or believed in them was marked. While the popularity of serials like Dan Dare extended the arena to outer space and new alien belief systems, the struggle for the mind of the 'native' between the westernised hero and the forces of superstition continued to be replayed in papers through the 1960s.[10]

Although the formal Empire was in its declining days, the British abroad continued to work their own white magic in the far-flung reaches of the globe. Non-fiction features in the annuals offered the reader an introduction to tribal fetishes in 'The Weird Ways of Witch Doctors' and 'Witches and Spirits Beware'. In 'The Real Mysteries of the East', the 'hippie' interest in India seems imminent, for it recasts the unknowable mysteries of India into a discussion of 'mind training' and expansion of consciousness.[11] Generally the papers preferred to keep black magic as part of the action narrative, operating in opposition to the figure of a westernised hero, occasionally allied with a reform-minded local leader. The witch doctor had changed little from his predecessors in the world of imperial fiction. In the 'Haunted Lagoon' from the *Lion* in 1956, the witch doctor Nurd is described as wearing a 'huge and hideous mask painted in vivid colours ... a master of evil magic'. Sarja, in 'Buzz's Whirlybird Outwits the Witch Doctor', performs a 'whirling dance outside the chief's hut'. Buzz, the young Englishman, observes that 'the new ideas we're bringing are making him a back number'. The friendly chief concurs: 'the days of superstition are past ... I do what is best for my people. The gods do not speak to Sarja.' Buzz of course has his helicopter to impress the tribe with a display of alternative wondrous powers. In 'Pal o' the Pygmies' it is Archie the robot who defeats the witch doctor's ju ju and becomes the god of the little men.[12] While the power of the witch doctor can still exert a strong influence on his people, the encounter with him now more often ends through the rising of his own people, a negotiated settlement, or if he is particularly evil, imprisonment. White men's magic, to counter entrenched superstitions, has progressed from magic tricks, in pre-war stories, to the skills of the helicopter pilot.

The post-war papers continue to show people living in the developing world whose lives are susceptible to, if not ruled by, superstitious fears. British characters are constantly hardening the resolve of even the most faithful of servants in the face of irrational terrors. While stories often display contempt for the ignorance which produces such behaviour, or humour when a tribal chief is terrorised by a radio, there are signs of a changing perspective. The *Eagle* in 1963 ran a story called 'African Terror, the Day White Magic Failed'. The main character is George Alakwe, a British-trained local working for a locust control programme in a newly independent African state. He is overseen by Johnson, the white boss. The local chief calls George an 'imitation white man' and continues to rely on the advice of the witch doctor when soldier ants march on the village. As the witch doctor 'mumbled and chanted, hopped and chattered, danced and sweated, made clicking and grunting noises' the ants turn away. George feels he has lost face and asks for a transfer. Johnson gives him some advice:

> They wanted to teach you a lesson. Do I have to tell you that there are things in Africa that can't be explained away by science? If they can't understand our magic insect killers why shouldn't they have something we can't understand? Your primitive brothers have pride, just as you have! They'll co-operate now they feel they've had their own back ... keep it up George, you're doing well.

The traditional paternalism of this story is enhanced by Johnson's role as mediator between the forces of old and new on the continent. George is impatient in his conversion to science, but Britain has the greater wisdom and maturity. Independence may have come, but the kindly intervention of Johnson represents a continuing need for British advice and mentoring in the post-colonial relationship.[13]

For girls, as was often the case in imperial fiction, 'service' and the challenge to old ways meet in the practice of medicine. 'Jean of the Jungle Hospital' was a long-running serial story in the *Schoolfriend* of 1960. She works with her father, who is a 'doctor in deepest Africa', and Olaka, an African nurse. Each week they turn back the obstacles to western medicine and treat the local tribes. Witch doctors are particularly hostile. Only when Jean is bitten by a snake whilst rescuing the witch doctor's son does he relent and allow the 'magic needles' to be used for his own tribe. In subsequent stories Jean introduces glasses so locals 'can really see', shows native mothers how to boil milk to produce 'big and strong' babies, and shows men how to use safety pins. This new generation of British workers in Africa, however, knows better than openly to defy local custom. Jean is prepared to use local wisdom when necessary, and explains to a new doctor that she works with superstition to combine 'ancient tradition with modern medicine'. Olaka, the nurse, and George, the trained scientist, are two examples of British success in bringing the benefits of science to bear on the harsh unpredictability of tribal life. This theme is a popular one in the papers. The *Eagle's* gallery of real-life 'heroes' – Albert Einstein, Albert Schweitzer, John Flynn and Sir Ronald Ross – all appeared as champions in the victory of medicine over tropical disease.[14]

There is also evidence in the papers of a sense that the duties of empire could be safely abandoned. Tribal societies, which had often been portrayed as hostile to the British imperialist, now were shown as having benefited from the experience. The Zulu, proud warrior in the imperial mythology, evolved into a telephone salesman in 'Kulu the Zulu'. Kulu has learned to apply his natural skills to the maintenance of the telephone wires, and shares with his supervisor Marchbanks the problem of a 'backward' tribe who steal the wire for bangles. Other signs that the British presence has advanced primitive societies can be seen in 'Beware Harpoons', where a local chief's son discovers the value of conserving turtle eggs. In stories set in Australia, the papers often included Aboriginal tribes in adventure stories. Along with pygmies, the most undeveloped of societies by imperial standards, here they were shown helping the police to track criminals, or co-operating with officials to remove their fellow tribespeople from weapons testing areas. While these characters were still treated as objects of curiosity and seldom released from stereotypical characterisations, they were generally viewed as assisting the agents of civilisation. The reader would, arguably, have been left with the impression that British withdrawal was leaving behind a sound foundation for change and development.[15]

Within both the realm of nature and the traditional opposition between rational and irrational forces one can sense the writers, editors and publishers of children's papers in transition from the old world of imperial fiction to a more modern view of relations with developing nations. There are still dangerous beasts to be subdued or neutralised, but it is often by capture for zoos, containment by game wardens, or the persuasive skills of jungle boys and girls. Young travellers are more likely to be photographing than killing the great creatures of jungle or plain, and fighting the poachers or ivory sellers. With the exception of 'rogue' elephants, who are often opposed by their own kind, brute strength has been harnessed for British interests or can be controlled through peaceful means. The magic and mystery of the colonial encounter can also be contained, if not understood. Witch doctors can be won over, or if really dangerous, subjected to imprisonment by their own people. As Britain hands back control to local peoples, the young reader encounters positive post-imperial roles for the

British abroad in working to protect wildlife, and improving the life of ordinary people by bringing the advances of science and technology. The desire to end the chapter of empire on a positive note also evokes a greater optimism about the potential for progress in former colonial areas, introducing British-trained scientists and nurses as the vanguard of change.

The state of the nation

In post-war Britain as the Empire contracted there was great concern over the economic state of the nation and its relegation to a second-rate power. In stories published during this period of readjustment one can consider whether these anxieties found their way into the publications. There are signs that wealth and the health of British commercial ventures were of interest to the publishers and editors of the papers. Stories set within Britain illustrated some of the economic changes which were occurring after the war. 'Connie and the Crocodile' in the *Girl Annual* of 1959 makes some interesting connections between economic change and the imperial legacy. Connie is trying to save her family business from the 'bright, gaudy new self service store' which has opened nearby. She has an idea that the famous explorer Professor Packer can help her with a publicity stunt to help sell crocodile skin articles she has found in the storeroom. He finally agrees, and in the window appears a jungle scene, complete with stuffed animals, and Hector the live pet crocodile who 'tied in splendidly with the display of crocodile skin articles that Connie had arranged in one corner'. A television crew shows up to film the spectacle, and business booms again. So the exotic allure of empire can still produce wealth for Britain, but here used as a marketing gimmick. This is the 'up-to-date' role for the Professor and his menagerie, who come out of retirement to help Connie defend family fortunes and a service ethos against a harsh profit and loss economy. The imperial legacy may appear to be redundant to the economy of contemporary Britain, but this story illustrates that it is still there to be exploited by enterprising young people, and put to the service of traditional values.[16]

Stories of empire migration evinced a greater tendency to emphasise the material benefits to the characters. While this might involve benefits to the wider British economy, or bolster the fortunes of economically undeveloped regions, the stories usually stressed the gains for individuals or their families. The British who emigrated to Commonwealth areas, like Australia or New Zealand, were in search of a better life which clearly implied an improved standard of living. In 'Adventure in the Outback', a *Girl* story, English siblings go to join their parents newly settled in Australia. Dad greets them with a surprise, 'I've struck it rich ... richer than I could imagine'. As a result of finding oil on his land the family can now move to Sydney. Bunty exclaims, 'Bondi Beach, surf riding, sailing, sunny beaches ... won't life be exciting!' Another story of 1957, 'Gold in the Mountains', provides Paul, an English visitor, with the possibility of staying in the country and making a fortune unimaginable at home. There were many stories in the juvenile press which stressed the attraction of leaving Britain for greater economic opportunity abroad, mainly to the white settlement areas where the myth of a 'greater Britain' still retained considerable potency in the post-war years.[17] These stories projected an assumption that for the young, living in post-imperial Britain, getting ahead often meant getting out. Here was the confident imperial spirit, not discarded, but re-deployed in individual initiatives.[18]

While striking it rich was a possibility on the Commonwealth frontier, British characters were also showing their financial and commercial acumen in other parts of the world. 'Karrini's Charm' shows the young reader how maintaining Britain's global position can be satisfied without disadvantaging local peoples. Philip Neale, a young English trader, tries to persuade Karrini and her people to lower the price of their sponges, as the market is fluctuating. This makes them very unhappy, but because Karrini likes him she gives him a 'magic charm'. Philip returns with a geologist from England and Karrini, despite her fears, leads them to the Forbidden City where she found the magic rocks. The rocks are uranium, 'the finest deposit anyone will ever see', and a stake is claimed for Britain. The islanders stand to make a lot of money out of the arrangement, and it will greatly help Britain to hold her own in the atomic age. This is not presented as exploitation, but a 'partnership' for mutual advantage. W. E. Johns has Biggles engaged in a similar quest in 'The Adventures of the Luminous Clay'. As the British hero proclaims, 'we are in a race, a race to be first in world markets with a practical atomic power unit!'. The blue clay essential to the project can only be found on a remote island in the Pacific. The Air Commodore admits 'there is a problem of sovereignty ... several countries lay claim to this island ... we don't want an international rumpus, this must be top secret'. This is the modern scramble for riches in the post-imperial world, with Britain playing a new role of wealth by stealth, justified if it means winning the race for atomic advantage. Biggles, however, shows little concern for the locals. He represents a harsher reality of protecting British interests in a world where nations compete for advantage without the protection of the flag. In both stories the use of uranium as the 'treasure' of post-war adventure quests shows the sensitivity of authors to Britain's search for atomic capability, reflecting a new post-war balance of power, where access to nuclear arms went hand-in-hand with colonial possessions as a means of securing British prestige.[19]

The importance of oil to post-war Britain is also apparent in the children's press. Non-fiction articles showed oil rigs, tankers, the history of oil, the uses of oil, all highlighting its place in the wealth of developed nations. Oil workers became romanticised 'roughnecks', tough physical specimens who risked their lives on the rigs. Adventure stories were now set in the oil fields of the Middle East, in which young British employees of Anglo-Iranian companies or local rulers either make exciting finds or become involved in protecting oil interests against saboteurs. In 'The Tower of the Dead', Sam and Bill get 'more excitement than they bargained for' when they find themselves kidnapped by Kurds while prospecting in North Persia. Storm Nelson, ex-navy man and gun for hire, is called in to help a sultan in the Persian Gulf defend his pearl beds from interlopers. The 'Mystery of the Purple Patch' turns out to be oil, and Storm not only solves a mystery but also delivers immense wealth to a British ally. Bill and Mike in 'Skyway Police for the Desert Sheikh' serve as Sheikh Suliman's desert patrol. By unmasking the evil intent of El Keba, a 'crook', to trick their employer into selling oil-bearing land for a fraction of its worth, the oil concession is signed over to an Englishman, who comments, 'this means a fortune for all of us, including Bill and Mike'. By 1963 the oil fields of Arabia are the setting for a 'Desert Escape', which features British employees of the Tehrain Oil Company defending their interests against Herr Schmidt of the Schweiner Company, a German enterprise based in Muscat.[20]

Economic competition and conflict over the oil resources of the Near East became a more popular feature in the adventure format after the war, and the stakes were presented as high. Immense wealth and power flow from the success of the British 'hero' who finds or defends oil, whether as an employee of a joint venture, or as the private troubleshooter for a local ruler. There was opposition to British interests maintaining their presence in the Middle East, but the children's papers presented a view of their countrymen holding their own in the struggle to maximise profits in the region. Arguably there were signs in the juvenile papers of the 1950s and early 1960s that wealth was an important part of both individual and national well-being. Access to oil was a major determinant of British status in the post-war world. Children's papers show a race for accumulating such advantage on all levels, and a sense that material reward was equally if not more important than other types of achievement. This was more true for the boys' papers than the girls' in relation to the outside world, but at home girls could equally be concerned about financial independence or the family business.

In the areas of former colonial control Britain's continued presence was often based on the economic stake white settlers had established there. A number of stories based the conflict in the narrative between the success of a British venture threatened by local or international competition. In India 'Chalu the Elephant Boy' defends the interests of a British teak plantation. In 'Rogue Stampede' and 'Return to India', the main characters are pictured fighting off the commercial sabotage of western competitors. Stories set in Africa featured British traders and farmers struggling to maintain viable operations against hostile local interests and natural disasters or predators. Pirates still sailed Chinese waters impeding the operation of legitimate trade and threatening the commercial operations of Hong Kong. There are many more examples in the Pacific and South America of adventure stories which feature the defence of economic interests, trade, shipping, mining or farming.[21]

The threat to Britain's economic security which accompanied the loss of colonial power can be detected in the papers, although it is usually presented as challenges met and overcome. It is interesting to note that children's periodicals in the imperial era paid little attention to the extraction of wealth from areas under imperial control. This was seen as secondary to the military encounters, diplomatic intrigue, or 'Boy's Own' adventures in the wild. In this later period, those who remained abroad in the era of decolonisation did so without the protection of British official power, and were consequently more reliant on their own skills and initiative. If a spirit of empire remained, it was represented by the continued commitment of individuals to overseas ventures. While the papers pictured the difficult life of those who worked within newly independent states, they also presented the economic possibilities of seeking a fresh start within the white Commonwealth.

Empire into Commonwealth

If anxiety about British wealth, power and prestige can be seen in the papers, can the same be said about the transition from Empire into Commonwealth? Do the contents show signs of the changing power relations, the local insurgencies, or the transition from colony to independent nation? In some areas of the world and in some variations of the adventure story political change was taken for granted. In India there is little sense that the Empire of official control ever existed – what remains is the economic and to some degree the cultural links. It is true that the *Eagle* featured Robert Clive in its story strips of 'heroes' in 1961, and Cecil Rhodes the year before, respectively the architects of British success on the subcontinent and sub-Saharan Africa.[22] With the end of empire the two men have become symbols of Britain's historic achievement, whose legacy can be seen in the advancement of India and the city of Salisbury, 'a perpetual memorial to one of Britain's greatest sons'. Few papers, however, replayed the past glories of the British Empire. Arguably they sensed children were no longer interested, or it was a painful reminder of what was slipping away.

There were stories which featured the contemporary deployment of British troops abroad, for example in the insurgency in Malaya. The *Eagle* in 1961 featured 'The Mystery of the Buried Boxes', in which Jim and his Malay friend Ahmad foil the gun-smuggling of a group described as 'bandits' and 'terrorists', and turn them in to the local police. In another story Bob, 'The Jungle Vet', is employed by the government in Malaya and captured by a 'Chinese gang of terrorists' whose leader had been educated in the United States. Intervention by young Britons in the internal politics of sovereign states could also save the throne of a rajah, or prince or mandarin, faced with local rebellion.[23] This alliance between British protagonists and the forces of progress or the upper classes abroad was a familiar pattern from imperial children's fiction, but whereas English youth might in earlier days have consciously acted for British interests, in these post-war stories their presence abroad was in an unofficial capacity. Their intervention was based on personal friendship, payment, or unexpected events. It heightened the tension of the story to include mutineers or rebels, and placed the English characters on the side of pro-western locals, but there was little sense of Britain's national power or prestige at stake. There was a reward for the assistance, but it was very much rooted in the individual dynamics of the story.

One interesting story called 'The Sons of Simba' brought the political issues of post-war South Africa to London. The story revolves around a revolutionary group whose slogan was 'Africa for the Blackmen', and who planned operations in the metropolis. Brian Collins has come from South Africa to join the London police force and is assigned to 'track' the conspirators. He expresses sympathy for their aims, but is intent on stopping their plan to kill Sir Hugh Stebbing, an exploitative mine owner who lives in Hampstead. Brian sees 'a perplexing problem, some of the finer races, like the Zulus, may be fit to govern themselves, other tribes, less advanced, are not. A question bristling with difficulties.' The conspirators laugh at him when he suggests that propaganda is the solution; they insist only fear works. When the assassins are caught at Sir Hugh's house, all are returned to South Africa. The government department wants it hushed up, afraid of stirring up worse trouble. Brian admits that, in their own way, the men were 'patriots', but both he and the Commissioner are pleased to be able to send the problem back to Africa. This is a problem of the post-imperial world London authorities do not have to shoulder. While expressing to the reader liberal sentiments over the exploitation of blacks, the police are clearly relieved to get them out of England, abrogating responsibility for the resolution of racial tension in the Republic.[24]

While there were other stories which involved the Royal Navy on good-will missions, or aligned the plots of saboteurs with hostility toward colonial powers, there was little sign that Britain wished to overcommit itself abroad. One senses in these stories a certain feeling of relief that the imperial burden of political responsibility has been lifted, and that for the future issues of sovereignty and legitimacy have been handed back to local figures. British characters continue to have adventures with political overtones, or may get caught up in local power struggles, but the limits of their responsibility show that 'the white man's burden' has been considerably lightened. The heroes are no longer imperial youth, even if they carry with them as a legacy of empire local knowledge, class allegiances, contempt for rebellion, or impulses to protect a local population from exploitation.

Two stories from the early 1960s serve to illustrate the new attitudes in the juvenile popular press: 'Biff Bailey, Fighting Fury' and 'Miss Fix-it of TV'. Biff is a British heavyweight boxer who sets off to West Africa for a bout with 'Dark Dynamite', the heavyweight champion of Kiman. 'Kiman was a go ahead country which had recently gained independence. It had a dazzling modern capital of white skyscraper buildings, flanking wide streets teeming with traffic, where a half century ago there had been nothing but jungle.' Biff is overwhelmed by his reception, for sport was a crucial part of the new relationship with the former colony. Dark Dynamite was 'obviously no thug from the jungle, but an educated and exceptionally intelligent sportsman'. Despite attempts to fix the fight with 'African black magic', Biff refuses to be deterred by the 'Kiman Dream Demon'. On the day of the fight his opponent shows his African heritage, 'the menace of a black panther … the speed of a striking viper … good enough to hold his own anywhere'. Although Dark Dynamite loses the contest, he behaves in a sportsmanlike manner, defusing the hostility of the crowd, and showing that the ethos of 'playing the game' was now a part of his own code of conduct. While there are echoes here of the noble adversary of the imperial ethos, and the traditional role of sport uplifting the savage, the author is quite explicit that this is a post-imperial encounter. The message to the reader was that after independence one can see the positive legacy of empire in the new setting and a new relationship, if not based on equality, then on respect for individual ability. In a shining white city, black and white boxers fight under traditional British rules of engagement. The sporting arena replaces the battlefield. The British win, but the Africans have shown themselves to be on the path of modernisation.[25]

'Miss Fix-it of TV' is set in London and features the heroine Meg, who works for a television company. Her assignment, on which promotion depends, is to persuade five African girls to take part in a documentary on West Africa. The producer wants 'Ghanaians, wonderful singers and dancers, a smash hit acting this old custom'. Problems occur, however, when

Princess Tamaloe, daughter of an Ashanti chief, refuses to dance to music from the tribal area of the other girls. It is Meg who gives her advice: 'It's absolutely wonderful when people are willing to co-operate and pull together for the sake of what they are all doing. I expect that's one of the things your country will be discovering since it got its freedom.' The Princess replies thoughtfully, 'yes, in Ghana we do not all work together or pull together as we should'. Meg reminds her that this was once true of England and Scotland, and that music can bring people together. The Princess explains to Meg how tribal custom has separated rather than united her country, and listens carefully to Meg's suggestion that this will change 'when a country grows up'. The Princess replies, 'I see what you mean Meg. I and my people, we must grow up and learn to work with each other, just as you have done in Britain.' She agrees to dance to other tribal music. Meg has saved the documentary and earned the approval of Barton, the director: 'without her there would probably have been no dusky beauties and no drums!'. This story brings together the exciting new world of television and the Commonwealth spirit in documentary programming. While the participants are presented as highly educated westernised young women studying in England, the spectacle of Africa, which has a long history of appearing on the British stage, is revived and modernised. Meg, the 'go ahead' young production assistant, suggests a way forward for the Princess's dilemma, projecting a mutually beneficial relationship with a young country three years into independence. At the same time, some concern is expressed that emergent nationalism may be derailed by the divisions of tribal conflict.[26]

Biff Bailey and Meg represent a new era of connections with the former colonial world. While their activities may be updated versions of traditional contacts, sport and the staging of ethnic performance, they project the attitudes of modern youth. Biff is engaged in sanctioned violence in the ring, and transposes the older imperial relationship into a contest of individual sportsmen. Sport divested of political overtones may be an ideal that has not always characterised relations with former colonial areas, but that is the spirit of this story. While British youth meet the Commonwealth on the sports field, Meg meets independent Ghana in the television studio, and shows her skills at both production and diplomacy. In the early 1960s, while the end of empire is clearly accepted, the tone of these stories suggests less certainty about how well these new nations will fare without British influence. In both, it is the British characters who confidently steer the narrative to a successful conclusion, while Africa is portrayed as still susceptible to superstition and tribal divisions. The stories reflect the atmosphere of the early 1960s, of a rapidly dissolving empire, with attendant anxiety over the consequences of premature withdrawal. Children's papers had traditionally projected the strongest case for the benefits of

British intervention in Africa. Here again, the strongest case was made against the image of abandonment, and the positive projection of an empire 'growing up', rather than 'breaking up'.

As one might expect in children's literature, nowhere was there an explicit admission that Britain was in decline or that the loss of the Empire represented a serious problem for the nation. Papers continued to exploit the imperial legacy and highlight the fun and adventure for young English men and women travelling abroad. Stereotypical images of foreigners, whether in newly independent states, colonial dependencies or Europe, remained the norm. Outsiders in England continued to operate within rather narrow confines – royalty, the occasional criminal in docklands or the performers in travelling shows. There was no sign here of the realities of Commonwealth immigration into England.

Nonetheless, publishers, editors and writers needed to strike a balance between tapping into the old formulae and updating their content for a new post-war audience. Competition in the market was fierce, with comics and television attractive alternatives for leisure time. By the late 1950s stories set in the developing world show clear evidence of adaptation and change in narratives which signal the transition from empire to a Commonwealth spirit. Power relations and conflict are downplayed or relocated into other venues. This may mean battling elephants, intergalactic clashes, a recycling of the Second World War, or confronting international crime. The popular press was reflecting the realities of the post-Suez world. By the early 1960s children's papers were in step with official British policy in accepting new relations with the colonial world. Independence was to be celebrated in the knowledge that the British Empire had achieved its ambitions, raising colonies to the threshold of nation-states and offering advice when needed.

The formal study of decolonisation was left to the classroom, where new maps reflected the shrinking number of colonial territories. In the children's popular press, Britain's global role took on new meanings and a changed emphasis. Influence in the remaining empire, although clearly paternalistic, more often meant partnership than control. Boundaries or sovereignty were irrelevant to spies, secret service agents, or space heroes. The wonders of technology and the atomic age generated a modern spirit of adventure. The search for wealth and the good life, an uncomfortable theme in the era of the 'white man's burden', now seemed a natural part of British ventures abroad. There were still touchstones of the imperial past. The reader could feel the imperative of the 'civilising mission', the spirit of progress meeting primitive terrors, and the positive impact of the caring professions. Fiction still transported one to exotic places, and introduced pygmies and witch doctors, Chinese pirates and dusky maidens. The door had not closed on the excitement of travel or the opportunities of finding a new life abroad in the Commonwealth. Magazines and annuals in the post-war period claimed the legacy of empire while they redirected youth to new frontiers. While the boys and girls, young men and women, who appeared in the popular press made every claim to be modern, and would have dismissed the serious, constricted lives of their predecessors, one should also note that Dan Dare sang his spaceman's lament to the tune of 'Home on the Range'.[27]

Notes

1 Kathryn Castle, *Britannia's Children* (Manchester, Manchester University Press, 1996); Martin Green, *Dreams of Adventure, Deeds of Empire* (London, Routledge & Kegan Paul, 1980); Jeffrey Richards (ed.), *Imperialism and Juvenile Literature* (Manchester, Manchester University Press, 1989).

2 Kirsten Drotner, *English Children and their Magazines, 1751–1945* (New Haven, Yale University Press, 1988), pp. 239–43.

3 Jack Cox, *Take a Cold Tub, Sir: The Story of the Boy's Own Paper* (Guildford, Lutterworth, 1982), pp. 121–2.

4 R. Dixon, *Catching them Young* (London, Pluto Press, 1977), pp. 42–3; Drotner, *English Children and their Magazines*, p. 243; M. Pickford, *I Could a Tale Unfold* (London, Tavistock Press, 1961), pp. 111–19, A. Orde, *The Eclipse of Great Britain* (London, Macmillan, 1996), pp. 7–8.

5 See the discussion of the allegedly 'minimal impact' of the end of empire on British culture and society in Stuart Ward's introduction to this volume.

6 John M. MacKenzie, *The Empire of Nature: Hunting, Conservation and British Imperialism* (Manchester, Manchester University Press, 1988), p. 169.

7 'Zoos Bringing Them Back Alive', *Girl Annual* (1952), pp. 53–5; 'A Lion's Roar to the Rescue', *Schoolfriend* (1960), pp. 5–6; 'Her Mystery Pen Friend in Africa', *Girls' Crystal* (1955), pp. 63–4; 'Women of Action', *Girl Annual* (1959), p. 80; 'Mabu Saves the Herd', *Lion Annual* (1956), p. 82; 'African Drums', *Eagle Annual* (1953), pp. 70–4; 'Jungle Joe Foils the Filmwreckers', *Lion Annual* (1957), pp. 122–3.

8 'Pal o' the Pygmies', *Lion Annual* (1954), pp. 108–17; 'Robot Archie's Quest for the Stolen Juju', *Lion Annual* (1960), p. 51, see also 'Robots on the March', *Eagle Annual* (1953), p. 144; 'The Iron Man', *Boys' World Annual* (1965), p. 106.

9 'Lola of the Blue Lagoon', *Girls' Crystal Annual* (1952), pp. 133–43; 'Karrini's Charm', *Girl Annual* (1952), pp. 117–22; 'Sumuna's South Sea Isle', *Girl Annual* (1952), pp. 25–32.

10 Castle, *Britannia's Children*, pp. 50, 107–8; 'Booboo Drums', *Eagle Annual* (1963), pp. 95–9; 'The Witch Doctor of Taloofa', *Lion Annual* (1960), pp. 144–9; 'Secret of Juju Island', *Lion Annual* (1954), pp. 97–104; 'The Fires of Vishna', *Boys' World Annual* (1965), pp. 93–6; 'Lucy's Lucky Locket', *Girls' Crystal*, 2 March 1963, pp. 5–6; 'The Girl who Lived in the Treetops', *Girls' Crystal Annual* (1955), pp. 185–91; on Dan Dare see 'He Who Dares', *New Statesman*, 1 May 2000, pp. 43–4.

11 'The Weird Ways of Witch Doctors', *Lion Annual* (1954), pp. 46–7; 'Witches and Spirits Beware', *Girl Annual* (1959), pp. 154–5; 'The Real Mysteries of the East', *Eagle Annual* (1963), pp. 12–14.

12 'Haunted Lagoon', *Lion Annual* (1956), pp. 136–40; 'Buzz's Whirlybird Outwits the Witch Doctor', *Lion Annual* (1957), pp. 78–83; 'Pal o' the Pygmies', *Lion Annual* (1954), pp. 108–17. See also 'The Isle of Missing Men', *Eagle Annual* (1960), pp. 8–11; 'Trooper Tom in Operation Rocket Shell', *Lion Annual* (1957), pp. 32–46.

13 'African Terror, the Day White Magic Failed', *Eagle Annual* (1963), pp. 126–30.

14 'Jean of the Jungle Hospital', *Schoolfriend*, 2 January 1960, p. 16; 9 January 1960, pp. 16–17; *Eagle* (1952), p. 149; (1955), p. 176; (1956), p. 171; (1960), p. 93.

15 'Kulu the Zulu', *Lion Annual* (1957), pp. 11–15; 'Beware Harpoons', *Eagle Annual* (1954), pp. 76–80; 'The Croc Shooters', *Eagle Annual* (1957), pp. 126–8; 'The Blacktrackers', *Eagle Annual* (1963), pp. 59–62; 'The Bush Bandit Meets his Match', *Lion Annual* (1960), pp. 122–3; 'The Unknown Quantity', *Daily Mail Annual* (1963), pp. 177–84.

16 'Connie and the Crocodile', *Girl Annual* (1959), pp. 8–11. See also 'Julie's Corner Shop', *Girls' Crystal Annual* (1960), pp. 16–17, 'Miss Pemberton's Puncture', *Girl Annual* (1952), pp. 81–85.

17 See Kathleen Paul's contribution to this volume.

18 'Adventure in the Outback', *Girl Annual* (1965), pp. 45–7; 'Gold in the Mountains', *Eagle Annual* (1957), pp. 37–40; see also 'Shark Island', *Eagle Annual* (1960), pp. 89–92; 'The Road from Gundagai', *Eagle Annual* (1965), pp. 70-1; 'Anne Arnold; Flying Nurse', *Girls' Crystal*, 2 February 1963, pp. 4–5; 9 February 1963, pp. 8–9.

19 'Karrini's Charm', *Girl Annual* (1953), pp. 117–22; 'The Adventures of the Luminous Clay', *Eagle Annual* (1955), pp. 17–19; see also 'Jon of the Jungle', *Schoolfriend*, 22 December 1951, pp. 2–4; 29 December 1951, pp. 2–4; 'Demon of Darra River', *Lion Annual* (1957), pp. 43–8; 'The Sign of Three', *Eagle Annual* (1952), p. 158; 'Atomic Power for Peace and Industry', *Eagle Annual* (1955), p. 172.

20 'Oil Treasure in the Earth', *Eagle Annual* (1952), p. 90; 'Oil', *Boys' World Annual* (1965), pp. 40-1; 'The Tower of the Dead', *Ideal Book for Boys* (1952), pp. 84–90; 'The Mystery of the Purple Patch', *Eagle Annual* (1957), pp. 164–7; 'Skyway Police for the Desert Sheik', *Lion Annual* (1956), pp. 146–53; 'Desert Escape', *Daily Mail Annual* (1963), p. 105.

21 'Chalu the Elephant Boy', *Lion Annual* (1954), pp. 48–55; 'Rogue Stampede', *Daily Mail Annual* (1963), pp. 36–42; 'Return to India', *Schoolfriend*, 2 January 1965, pp. 21–3; 29 April 1965, pp. 17–18; see also 'The Grey Peril', *Eagle Annual* (1962), pp. 156–60; 'Great Plane Wrecking Plot', *Lion Annual* (1960), pp. 136–41; 'River of Stars', *Ideal Book for Boys* (1949), pp. 65–7; 'The Tree that Stopped a Rebellion', *Lion Annual* (1954), pp. 12–16.

22 'Robert Clive', *Eagle Annual* (1961), pp. 65–8; 'Cecil Rhodes', *Eagle Annual* (1960), pp. 93–7.

23 'The Mystery of the Buried Boxes', *Eagle Annual* (1961), pp. 106–8; 'The Jungle Vet', *Ideal Book for Boys* (1952), pp. 44–54; 'The Jewelled Elephant Talisman', *Daily Mail Annual* (1963), pp. 85–96; 'Vicky and the Feast of Ramadan', *Girl Annual* (1959), pp. 89–92; 'The Purple Pagoda', *Girl Annual* (1954), pp. 25–32.

24 'The Sons of Simba', *Ideal Book for Boys* (1949), pp. 106–16.

25 'Biff Bailey, Fighting Fury', *Tiger Annual* (1960), pp. 19–24.

26 'Miss Fix-it of TV', *The Bunty Book* (1960), pp. 49–52.

27 'Dan Dare', *Eagle Annual* (1957), p. 25.

CHAPTER NINE

Wandering in the wake of empire: British travel and tourism in the post-imperial world

Hsu-Ming Teo

In 1945 Evelyn Waugh penned the following words in the preface to one of his last travel books, *When the Going was Good*:

> My own travelling days are over and I do not expect to see many travel books in the near future ... There is no room for tourists in a world of 'displaced persons'. Never again, I suppose, shall we land on foreign soil with letter of credit and passport ... and feel the world wide open before us ...
>
> Perhaps it is a good thing for English literature. In two generations the air will be fresher and we may again breed great travellers like Burton and Doughty. I never aspired to being a great traveller. I was simply a young man of my age; we travelled as a matter of course. I rejoice that I went when the going was good.[1]

He was, of course, writing in the aftermath of the atrocities, deaths and massive destruction of the Second World War, his tone of melancholic reflection and dismal pessimism befitting a farewell to a halcyon age of civilised British life that, for the middle and upper classes, included travel abroad. Waugh had travelled during an age when Britain's scattered colonies and global dominance meant that every continent was open to the British traveller. In various parts of the world, existing colonial administration and transport infrastructure acted as a springboard to more distant, remote, largely untravelled places. British travellers had confidently made their way from Angora to Afghanistan, from the Cape to Cairo, from Nepal to New Zealand; their journeys were written up in the books that Waugh reviewed. The world had indeed been wide open before this privileged group of travellers who took travel abroad as 'a matter of course'.

Waugh's gloomy prediction was notably incorrect. There was in fact room for tourists in a world of 'displaced persons'; indeed, tourism would take off spectacularly as an industry in the decades that followed. In the post-war years, however, the closure of many former colonies to travel because of the internecine warfare that accompanied decolonisation, and the inundation of the world with other tourists, meant that the British travel experience changed dramatically and has often been characterised by a sense of mourning for the lost opportunities of 'real' travel. This was an understanding of travel which was refracted through the lens of nineteenth-century British imperial culture, and it looked back nostalgically to the colonial past as a 'golden age' of travel.

The association of exploration and travel with subsequent mercantile imperialism and colonisation has been well documented.[2] In Africa, for example, British explorers travelling through the continent – Mungo Park, Richard Burton, James Speke, Frederick Selous and, of course, David Livingstone – surveyed, mapped and documented the regions through which they travelled, opening new parts of the African continent to be carved up and subsequently colonised by European imperial nations during the 1870s and 1880s. Travel and travel writing played an important role in creating imperial consciousness among those Britons who stayed at home, acquainting them with the non-western world. Recent scholars of British travel writing have created a greater awareness of the persistent ideological tropes through which westerners have imagined and represented non-western cultures both visually and verbally, demonstrating how 'the vestiges of imperialism continue to linger: less in the narrow sense of militant jingoism or explicit advocacy for annexing new territory than in a more ingrained and nebulous confidence about being culturally and racially superior'.[3] Mary Louise Pratt, in particular, has examined how panoramic descriptions of non-western landscapes in travel writing position the narrator – and subsequently, the reader – as the 'monarch of all I survey', presenting the territory spread before the victorious traveller as a lush, unpopulated territory, ripe with natural resources for western appropriation. A relationship of mastery is predicated between the seer and the seen. The western imperial traveller possesses the power and aesthetic taste to evaluate the landscape for readers and officials back home, presenting it as a challenging new frontier to be penetrated, explored, made known, and possibly colonised.[4]

Travel books were in fact sometimes written with the aim of encouraging other travellers and settlers to visit the Empire's new dominions and colonies. Charlotte Mansfield's 1911 travel book *Via Rhodesia* was written with the express purpose of urging 'the possibility of Rhodesia as a good settling-ground for women'.[5] The role of travel in building imperial consciousness among the British was recognised by the imperialist Lord Curzon, who argued 'the case of travel as one of the supreme duties of an Imperial race':

> It seems to me that no man has any right to be a citizen of this great Empire unless he knows something about it, and the only way to know it is to take advantage of the opportunities for travel, which, formerly the monopoly of the rich, are now brought within the reach of the relatively poor.[6]

The rise of British tourism abroad rode on the coat-tails of colonisation. In this process Thomas Cook's company played a significant role. Throughout the nineteenth century and in the pre-war years of the twentieth, Thomas Cook & Son had gradually become synonymous with the tourist experience, and the company had taken care to foster its imperial connections. In the 1870s and 1880s, under the guidance of John Cook, the firm laid the foundations of tourism throughout India, Egypt, Australia and New Zealand. The journal of Cook's company, *The Excursionist*, was full of proud references to the Queen and the 'Empire on which the sun never sets'. By the turn of the century, Cook's firm had earned the title: 'Booking Clerk to the Empire'. At the silver jubilee celebrations of Cook's firm, peers, politicians and journalists publicly 'acknowledged the imperial, as well as the international, role of an organisation embracing what Joseph Chamberlain called "Greater Britain beyond the seas"'.[7] The association of the firm with imperial tourism was such that, in 1924 and 1925, the firm acted as chief passenger agents and guides to the British Empire exhibition at Wembley, which attracted 17 million visitors in the first year alone.

Travel and tourism throughout the colonies allowed Britons a glimpse of modernisation under British or European administration, and to make comparisons between British colonial rule and that of other imperial nations. Many late nineteenth- and early twentieth-century travel books combine a report of modernisation and westernisation along with their travel narrative. The traveller and Orientalist Gertrude Bell informed her readers that

> all over Syria and even in the desert, whenever a man is ground down by injustice or mastered by his own incompetence, he wishes that he were under the rule that has given wealth to Egypt, and our occupation of that country, which did so much to alienate from us the sympathies of Mohammedans, has proved the finest advertisement of English methods of government.[8]

India, in particular, was promoted as a site of imperial tourism for those who wished to witness the effects of British rule. Patriotic Britons who wished to visit the scene of the British victory over Tipu Sultan went to Mysore. After 1857, Britons went to Lucknow, Kanpur, and the Kashmiri Gate in Delhi to pay homage at memorials to the 'mutiny'. In the last quarter of the nineteenth century, visitors to India expressed in their writings their pride in the glory of the British Empire and their admiration for the great port cities of Bombay, Calcutta and Madras which had been built up by the British. They toured Agra and Delhi, describing 'the glory of the Mughal predecessors whose accomplishments they thought the British Empire expanded and integrated with modern social responsibilities'. Inter-war travellers such as Robert Byron devoted space in travel books to describing British colonial administration and to discussing the pros and cons of Indian demands for self-governance.[9]

In Britain, then, travel abroad and the production of travel books were inextricably linked with the expansion and consolidation of empire. From descriptions of new and fabulous lands for colonisation and imperial appropriation, the cataloguing of strange flora, fauna and the quaint or crude customs of the 'natives', to ambivalent descriptions of the often traumatic and culturally destructive modernising processes that British administration brought, the content of travel books informed those Britons who stayed at home of the extent and diversity of their Empire. If travel had been shaped to such a degree by the imperial experience, then to what extent did the consciousness of empire and imperialism impinge on and structure the travel experience of Britons in the decades of decolonisation that followed the Second World War?

There were greater opportunities and enthusiasm for travel after the Second World War than there had ever been in British history. Stanley Adams told *The Times* in April 1946 that 'the urge to travel is sweeping the people of this land and other war-weary lands like an epidemic'.[10] In 1947 Clement Attlee's Government imposed a ban on foreign holidays after a quarter of a million Britons tried to escape the country during the winter, although this ban was lifted in early 1948. After 1950 a million Britons were travelling abroad each year. The international growth of the tourist trade throughout the 1960s was such a remarkable phenomenon that the United Nations General Assembly declared 1967 the International Year of the Tourist. In 1970 British travel-allowance restrictions were removed, and by 1988 20 million Britons journeyed abroad each year, out of a global total of 355 million tourists.[11]

Undoubtedly, 'abroad' had changed in significant ways since the supposedly halcyon days of British travel during the late nineteenth and early twentieth centuries. Post-war travellers felt that the automatic prestige and respect accorded their predecessors had been eroded. Gone were the esteem and admiration for white skin wrought by the civilising influences of British colonialism and Christian missionary work. Well-established tourist sites suddenly became less safe. In Egypt, for example, anti-colonial protest erupted into violence against British institutions in January 1952 when British tourist buildings – the Turf Club, Shepheard's Hotel, and Cook's Cairo office – were set on fire. At times, the internecine warfare which often followed decolonisation made travel in certain former colonies difficult, if not impossible.

In many post-colonial nations, however, the tourist economy was dependent upon the legacy of imperialism both for its organisational infrastructure and for the promulgation of cultural fantasies of exotic travel. For example, visitors to Kenya in the 1970s and 1980s might have given less thought to the country's colonial past than to wildlife safaris; nevertheless there could be no better example of the imperial legacy in post-imperial tourism than the African safari which was often run by old colonialist proprietors – former 'great white hunters' and soldiers.[12] Big game hunting had of course featured prominently in many Victorian imperial adventure stories and travel narratives. As Kathryn Castle demonstrates in the previous chapter, the British hunter in Africa continued to appear in post-war juvenile literature which no doubt fed the fantasies of future travellers. The difference now was that in African travel, the new great white hunters of big game were armed with expensive photographic equipment rather than with rifles, and in place of black porters and servants, they were shepherded around by black drivers and guides.[13]

The imperial legacy was an ambiguous one for many post-imperial British travellers. British authors of travel guides to Africa often displayed a personal distaste for imperialism. Indeed, by the time British traveller Geoff Crowther produced his travel guide *Africa on the Cheap* for the Lonely Planet series in 1977, many African countries were being framed within an anti-colonialist historiography which was itself a legacy of imperialism. Potted histories of Angola, Botswana, Ghana, Kenya, and so forth, which introduced each country to the prospective traveller were generally progressivist narratives with a teleology of triumphant nationalism. 'History' more often than not began with the European encounter, the establishment of trade ties, followed by colonisation, anti-colonial movements, and the victorious establishment of a new African republic that had thrown off the shackles of colonial rule. Yet little mention was made of the huge, controlling economic interests that the former colonialists still had in the country; little awareness was shown of the uneasy possibilities of affluent western tourism as a new form of imperial intervention, of the commodification of non-western culture for leisurely western consumption. Furthermore, travel guides continued to emphasise the 'call of the wild' and the possibilities of adventures 'off the beaten track' – images of African travel that had been inherited from Victorian imperial travel tales.

The experience of travel and tourism in post-colonial nations was thus refracted through the prism of British imperialism. Yet it would be misleading to argue that post-war travellers and tourists exercised the same hegemony over the cultures they visited as did their nineteenth-century counterparts, unilaterally producing and sustaining fantasies of backward though exotic 'others' in order to dominate them economically and culturally. The governments of post-colonial nations often colluded in maintaining such ideas in order to attract tourist dollars. For example, the international tourist brochures, posters and magazines put out by South-East Asian tour operators and official tourist boards continue to give a prominent place to images of people and cultural activities that are rooted in the colonial era, and that are part of the European discourse on exoticism based on theories of biological and social evolution which assumed the superiority of western civilisation. The two images that feature heavily in various ASEAN tourist advertising campaigns – the richly adorned, exotic dancer and the 'traditional' craftsman surrounded by ancient tools – can be traced back to the colonial period but are still used to promote the 'Far East' as 'exotic' and 'oriental'.[14] Furthermore, as Victor T. King argues, in order to present Malaysia as an attractive site for 'historical tourism' (along with 'ethnic' and 'cultural tourism'), the country's colonial experience and the remains of colonial architecture have been refurbished and repackaged as 'heritage'.[15] Similarly, in its official brochure, the Tourist Promotion Board of Singapore hawks a romanticised, sanitised colonial past as part of the country's tourist attractions, inviting visitors to sit 'on the verandah of a stately colonial mansion, sipping a refreshingly chilled cocktail as the tropical sun paints the sky crimson as it sets'.[16] Travellers to these post-colonial countries are thus encouraged to indulge in nostalgic colonial role-playing, and it is no surprise to find that many British travel agents emphasise that 'the feel of a British colonial past lives on' in places like Sri Lanka.[17] The countries of South-East Asia are ironic examples of nations which have expelled their imperial masters only to exploit their colonial past.

Yet if, for most Britons who travel abroad, the nostalgic colonial experience is but one of many different modes of tourism available – the 'colonial heritage' tour juxtaposed with a shopping trip, for example – there is nevertheless a significant number of travellers who go abroad specifically in search of the imperial experience. Already by the 1950s the former colonies were becoming commodified as touristic sites, while the former routes of imperial travellers in the nineteenth and early twentieth centuries were becoming packaged into theme tours for modern-day travellers. The Thomas Cook Group, in particular, took advantage of what one chief executive called its 'Kipling image of pith helmets and paddles up the river' to organise cruises, tours and journeys that duplicated *en masse* the Victorian and Edwardian routes of exploration throughout the world. In 1955 the travel firm conducted the first world tour party ever to enter Nepal, and the following year saw three Cape to Cairo safaris, 'offering tourists the opportunity to meet both pygmies and the giant warriors of the Watusi tribe, all for £980'. Throughout the 1960s, there were 'luxury adventure holidays on the Golden Road to Samarkand, to the Mountains of the Moon, to Ayers Rock in central Australia, round Cape Horn in a square rigger', and a 'tribal tour' of Papua New Guinea, in which tourists, for a fee of £800, could pretend to be explorers who trudged 'a hundred miles through the jungle during the rainy season, encountering crocodiles, pythons and reformed Biami cannibals'. Cook exploited its distinctive links with empire in 1984 when it organised the Gordon Centenary Nile Cruise celebrating the firm's role in the attempt to relieve Khartoum, and again in 1987 when it ran a special tour to commemorate the firm's part in celebrating Queen Victoria's Golden Jubilee during the days of the Raj a century before.[18]

Travel to India often provoked nostalgia for the 'palmy days' of the Raj. This is certainly demonstrated in Stephen Weeks's *Decaying Splendours* (1979), an unusual book published by the BBC, in which the author, a film-maker by profession, travels to India to find an image of the stranded empire: 'some place in India where homesick colonials would have built an England-forever-England: an Anne Hathaway type of place with roses growing over cottage doorways and strawberries and cream for tea'.[19] Weeks was trying to escape from a modern England which he felt was no longer 'English'; an ugly England – demoralised by the strikes and power failures of the sordid 1970s – in which 'talentless artisans struggled to erect nihilist structures'; a cowed and pusillanimous England which demonstrated 'a sinister, paranoid desire to hide the most confident elements of the nineteenth century' and had consequently demolished its triumphs of imperial architecture – Euston Arch or the Imperial Institute at South Kensington, for example. In India Weeks headed for the famous colonial hill station Ootacamund, and stayed at Fernhill Palace until he himself began 'to feel a *pukka sahib*'. The architecture and furniture were grandly Victorian, the palace staff servile and deferential ('In Ooty', claims Weeks, 'the servants had gone on strike in 1947 in an effort to keep the British'[20]), and the English garden at dusk was a conducive place for lingering to think melancholy thoughts and contemplate 'the sunset of an era'. In Ootacamund Weeks witnessed

> everywhere the remains of the Palmy Days, almost intact. Not only buildings but whole atmospheres remained, and it seemed such a short step, especially for someone like myself, so used to peopling film-sets at the drop of a hat with handfuls of fake Dukes or ballrooms of Edwardian ladies, to restore, perhaps, and certainly to regret the loss of, the British Empire.[21]

Dislocated and alienated from his homeland, Weeks went in search of and found in India a remnant of the British imperial past that was to him a lost, perfect England, 'trapped and preserved like a fly in amber'. Yet he recognised that it would not last: 'Slowly everything that is British and that made it important will disappear' – but at least he had visited India while it was still recognisably British.[22]

This was 'wandering in the wake of empire' indeed, a nostalgic and melancholy tour of Britain's former colonies which enabled the traveller to relive the glory days of the empire while simultaneously mourning their demise. As a mode of travel it is perhaps epitomised by Anthony Powell's book *The Empire Revisited* (1985), which tells of a journey he made around the world in 1982–83. It is perhaps no coincidence that Powell made his visit to the former colonies and dominions of the British Empire at a time when, in Britain, a conservative government under Thatcher looked nostalgically back to the glories of empire and made a stand in the Falklands, and when, in literature and films such as *Out of Africa*, *A Passage to India*, *Heat and Dust*, *The Far Pavilions* and *The Jewel in the Crown*, a resurgence of interest in colonial matters led Salman Rushdie to comment on the 'Raj revival' in popular culture.[23] Powell consciously and deliberately set out, not only to trace the footsteps of imperialists before, but to mimic the dress style of the early twentieth-century traveller. When he arrived in India, he gleefully reported: 'To all these people I seemed to conjure up surprise, for to them I was like an apparition from the days of the Raj: my light suits, straw hat and walking cane only adding to the illusion'.[24] His trip to India saw him treated like a sahib by servile, smelly Indians, and goggled at by stupid Americans who exclaimed, 'Gee, these eggs are just like ours', or 'Elmer, I can't get over that our English friend is from England'. He was marvelled at by uncouth Australians 'who found it bewildering that I actually wore a jacket and tie for dinner', chattered at by Italians 'who talked so fast and loud that the Indians just looked on blankly', contemptuously amused by 'some French who insisted on a special menu', and mistaken for Prince Charles in a Bombay restaurant. On a train from Bombay to Delhi, he was gratified to hear some Hindus speaking of England and the English 'in very endearing terms', telling him that 'The English are a great nation' which has 'produced many truly great men'. Nearly forty years had elapsed since India gained its independence, reflected Powell.

> Long gone are the British of the Raj; even those who 'stayed on' are now old and small in numbers, and so for the Indians of today to meet someone they imagine to be 'truly English' (rather than the student-types who maintain no national identity) it comes as a delightful flashback. For underneath all the hostilities that developed during the latter days of the Raj there is a sense of unity between the English and the Indians.[25]

This is 'Raj revival' stuff indeed, a sentimental belief that Indian nationalism was espoused by a small, probably unrepresentative section of the population. Most Indians, Powell believed, were grateful for British colonial intervention and remain so to this day.

Leaving India, he reached Australia – 'England's most distant Dominion' – and was quietly amused at the locals. South Africa brought more annoying encounters with stereotyped American tourists who pointed, stared, and continually made remarks such as 'Gee honey', 'Is that really true?' and 'We've got a bigger one of those'. Cape Town irresistibly gave rise to reflections on South Africa's role in the British Empire. He happily remembered that, during the two world wars, 'the fact that British ships could call at her ports helped us to ensure that Britannia did rule the waves'.[26] Everywhere Powell went, he determined to explore 'off the normal tourist track' like the travellers of yore, and he refused to be ripped off by the locals as though he were no better than what he called a 'checker-trousered tourist'. So what had his nostalgic trip around the world, in the wake of empire, achieved? His six-month trip had been inspiring, confirming the beliefs drummed into him by his conservative public schooling and Thatcherite political convictions. As he stood on the deck of the ship to catch a first glimpse of England, he reflected sentimentally:

> It is an emotional moment to arrive back home, and as I stood that night on the boat deck … I was full of pride. England has had a glorious past and over the last three hundred years she has played a dominant role in the world's affairs. She lost an empire in America and immediately replaced it with the expansion of her trading posts in the East, then later she became the victor in the scramble for Africa, taking all the prizes that were worth winning; she was pre-eminent in the hinterland and she controlled the Suez and the Cape. Her ships became seen throughout the globe and her pioneers explored every corner of the earth. She found wealth and poverty; she found life and death; she found friends and foes; she found alien cultures and she found strange gods, but whatever she encountered she enabled the varying peoples that she came across to thrive and to live more happily together. For whoever was bounded by her yoke became ultimately more prosperous and more secure.[27]

Here is unashamed and unapologetic imperialist history: a journey motivated by a curiosity about the former colonies of the British Empire that filtered each country and its inhabitants through the paternalistic eyes of a nostalgic, latter-day imperialist who had arrived too late on the scene to participate in the glories of empire building, and who could only marvel at what had gone before. It is, perhaps, the most blatant and obvious example of how the Empire and imperialism continue to shape the experience of travel long after decolonisation.

One of the most notable features of Powell's book is his phobia about being thought a common tourist by the locals, and his profound dislike of other tourists. There is in British literature a long tradition of self-styled 'travellers' who construct themselves as such against the universally despised 'tourist'. As James Buzard points out, the traveller/tourist dichotomy, especially as it functions in British culture, is implicated in class hierarchies that enable members of the affluent, educated, culturally enriched classes to travel independently and sneer at the tourist masses who lack access to such financial and cultural capital.[28] The animosity of the self-appointed British traveller – the sensitive, thoughtful, intelligent, aesthetically superior, culturally aware individual – towards other tourists spread into much English-language travel writing of this century and is indeed one of the lasting legacies of British travel writing. Grievance over encroaching tourists who made it increasingly impossible for the 'real' traveller to experience the exotic 'otherness' of foreign lands and cultures spilled over into the twentieth century and has been adopted by modern Anglo-American travel writers such as Paul Theroux, who writes scornfully of the masses of 'mock travellers'.

Indeed, the clamour against mass tourism and the lament over the lost opportunity for travel has increased throughout the twentieth century. After constructing a chronology of travel that divides western history into the respective ages of exploration, travel, and then the degraded tourism of our time, the travel critic Paul Fussell wrote in 1980: 'I am assuming that travel is now impossible and that tourism is all we have left'. John Julius Norwich, too, deplores the difficulty of having a 'real' travel experience. 'The easier it becomes to travel', he laments, 'the harder it is to be a traveller.' Norwich looks back nostalgically to an imaginary 'golden age' of travel, before the world became modernised and Coca-Colonised, and when the archetypal traveller had been the lone Englishman, scion of a wealthy family:

> Half a century ago, any young Englishman prepared to venture beyond the shores of Western Europe could lay claim to the title; patience, resourcefulness and robustness of digestion were the only qualities he needed. A year or two later he could return, the pride of his family, the envy of his friends: a trail-blazer, a hero. Alas, those days are over. Everybody goes everywhere – or nearly everywhere – buying their air tickets with their credit cards and being met by airport buses, secure in the knowledge that their hotel reservations have been confirmed, that the rent-a-car firm is expecting them, and that it will be perfectly safe to drink the Coca-Cola.[29]

Towards the end of the twentieth century, in the decades after decolonisation, an astonishing number of travel writers express a nostalgic sense of loss, not just of the Empire, but of the possibilities of 'real' travel and exploration that British imperial dominance over the world had made possible in the nineteenth century: when the archetypal traveller in the non-western world was likely to be British; when 'real' travellers could expect deference and servility from the colonised natives, and support and hospitality from colonial officials in remote places in India, Africa, Australia, South-East Asia, and the Pacific islands; when it was imaginatively possible to escape from the ubiquitous and monotonous culture of western modernity that was even then spreading to exotic locations in the non-western world through imperialism's civilising mission; when it was still possible to enact those adventure narratives with which, as Martin Green has argued, English boys put themselves to sleep and dreamt about each night.[30]

Yet although Fussell may have declared the end of travel, in a manner reflective of what Frank Kermode would call our 'hunger for ends and for crisis', many contemporary British travel writers still assert staunchly the possibilities of 'real' travel in remote, exotic, unmodernised locations: Eric Newby in the Hindu Kush, Redmond O'Hanlon in Borneo, on the Amazon, and through the Congo, Christina Dodwell in Papua New Guinea, and many others. For self-styled travellers, 'real' travel involved getting off the beaten track of the tourist. The term 'traveller' connoted the intrepid, lone adventurer who went where none, or few, had gone before. Travel was a vocation, not a vacation; a hardship to be endured, not a holiday to be enjoyed. It was, above all, a restless impulse deep in the hearts of the English. In 1907 Beatrice Grimshaw – journalist, travel writer, coffee planter and diamond prospector in New Guinea – wrote that over the centuries many Englishmen had heard the call to leave their settled life and loves in order to travel. 'Not one in a hundred may answer that call', she observed, 'yet never think ... that scores out of every hundred Englishmen have not heard it, all the same.' For 'in the heart of almost every Briton a wanderer once has lived. If this were not so, the greatest empire of the world had never been.'[31]

Nearly eighty years later, Eric Newby too pondered the question of why the British travel. 'To escape their creditors', he wrote wryly. 'To find a warmer or cooler clime. To sell Coca-Cola to the Chinese. To find out what is over the seas, over the hills and far away, round the corner, over the garden wall ...' – the answers that range from the touristic to the impulse of the 'real' traveller. Turning the question on himself, 'Why have I travelled?', he reflected:

> Partly ... for amusement and sheer curiosity and partly, as Evelyn Waugh wrote in the preface to a book I wrote which described a journey through the Hindu Kush, to satisfy 'the longing, romantic, reasonless, which lies deep in the hearts of most Englishmen, to shun the celebrated spectacle of the tourist and, without any concern with science or politics or commerce, simply to set their feet where few civilized feet have trod'.[32]

The quote from Waugh substantiates Newby's reputation as a 'real' traveller in the style of those who had journeyed during the golden age of travel, while Newby refers again to the perhaps unconscious feeling of many British travellers that a fundamental part of being a 'real' traveller is his or her Britishness – even Englishness.

Gavin Young, who journeyed on boats all over the world, lived among the Marsh Arabs in the Euphrates valley, and travelled extensively in South-East Asia, also mused over the travel impulse so many British people possessed. (Indeed, one might argue that the need to ponder this question of why the British travel is a characteristic of the British travel book.) 'Why do so many of us in the West go on travelling?', Young wondered. 'Why do hordes of Britons seem to welcome the least opportunity to be jostled about in airports, to endure inexplicable delays corralled in departure lounges redolent of *1984*?' For him, the answer was to encounter foreignness and, in doing so, to lose himself in anonymity. 'Abroad, our upbringing, class, education, even our financial condition, go for nothing. We start again with a clean slate.'[33] Yet if travel abroad sometimes allows the traveller to escape the social and economic markers of his or her identity back in England, self-conscious literary travel simultaneously confirms a particular social and educational status. The mediation of the literary text – the apposite quote from Conrad or Stanley – 'invests their travels not only with meaning but with status; it distinguishes them as gentlemen, the possessors of a certain kind of education'.[34] It is, perhaps, Britons of a certain social class – those who had often undergone a classical public school and Oxbridge education, who were steeped in the history of Victorian imperialism and exploration – who seek to reconstruct the adventure narratives of past imperial days: travellers such as Philip Glazebrook, Tim Severin, Eric Newby, Gavin Young and Redmond O'Hanlon, who familiarised themselves with the fiction and travel writings of the imperial travellers before venturing forth themselves.

These modern British travellers often look back to travel writings and adventure stories of the imperial age to frame the stories of their own journeys, and to create a density of meaning in their text. If, as Martin Green has argued, the adventure narrative is 'the energising myth of empire', it is just as much the energising myth of a certain type of modern nostalgic travel. The same characteristics of the imperial explorer are aspired to by modern travellers who seek to journey to remote spots of the world; to struggle to Lake Télé in the heart of the Congo, for example, because as Redmond O'Hanlon says: 'This is the most difficult equatorial African country to get into, the least visited, the least explored', and hence, 'the most interesting'.[35] These travel texts conform to the generic requirements of the adventure story. 'Adventure,' observes Green,

> seems to mean a series of events, partly but not wholly accidental, in settings remote from the domestic and probably from the civilised … which constitute a challenge to the central character. In meeting this challenge, he performs a series of exploits which make him a hero, eminent in virtues such as courage, fortitude, cunning, strength, leadership and persistence.[36]

Imperial adventure stories in the form of travel writing or the novels of Henry Rider Haggard, Rudyard Kipling, Joseph Conrad and John Buchan, among others, provide the models – ironic or otherwise – utilised by these travel writers. Often, the imperial text becomes a pretext for travel: following in the footsteps of Stanley, tracing the journey of Conrad's heroes.

Philip Glazebrook's *Journey to Kars* is framed by the mid-nineteenth-century travel accounts of Alexander Kinglake's *Eothen* (1844) and Eliot Warburton's *The Crescent and the Cross* (1845). Glazebrook suggests that while tourists view the present, 'real' travellers search for a glimpse of the past. 'The truth is that few individuals have ever travelled, in modern times, to see what other countries are like nowadays', writes Glazebrook, 'in general people travel in search of traces of past eras.'[37] He delights in travelling 'in the company of ghosts' – those intrepid Victorians who shape and give meaning to his journey[38] – for 'real' travel is, above all, associated firmly and nostalgically with the age of imperialism.

In 'Amazonian Adventure', Redmond O'Hanlon claims that before leaving for his four-month journey to Venezuela and Brazil, he had to 're-read my nineteenth century heroes', consisting of all the major travel writers on that region.[39] O'Hanlon, the Oxford-educated writer and naturalist, self-mockingly acknowledges his own obsession with nineteenth-century travel. In *Congo Journey*, his American travel partner Lary Shaffer accuses him of wanting to travel in the mode of the nineteenth century. 'You love all that, don't you? You should have been born 150 years ago', Shaffer tells him. Back in the days of 'Bearers and paddlers and those white Brit hats like a bra-cup stuck on your head. I know. And a sedan-chair or whatever you call them with punkah-wallahs and tiffin boys and under-pig-stickers and things.'[40]

The Victorian adventure text mediates the late twentieth-century traveller's present experience. Nicholas Rankin's literary wanderings in the Pacific were written up in his book *Dead Man's Chest: Travels After Robert Louis Stevenson* (1987). Gavin Young went to South-East Asia 'in search of Conrad'. His eponymous travel book 'is a pilgrimage – a search for scenes and ghosts' known to and created by Conrad. Young wrote enthusiastically:

> I hope I can attract others to his world, to entice others to venture among the echoes and flickering shadows of the past, and among the swashbuckling ghosts, some evil, some noble, of strong men Conrad knew and made as familiar to us as if we had encountered them in real life. Eager to meet them, I packed my old metal suitcase with the works of Joseph Conrad, and set off to the East.[41]

As Heather Henderson contends:

> these literary pilgrimages are examples of mediated desire: the value of a scene, landscape, or monument lies not so much in its own intrinsic qualities as in the pleasure of seeing for ourselves what someone else has seen and described before us. The observer's relationship to the scene is indirect, filtered through the literary representation by which he first came to know it.[42]

[175]

But as Mary Louise Pratt points out, many of those original observers viewed the non-western world through 'imperial eyes' that surveyed, aestheticised, catalogued and colonised the landscape.[43] To travel in the literary wake of empire was thus to position oneself with the imperial gaze, colonising the non-western world with the phantoms and fantasies of western literary heritage.

It is almost as if, given the perceived difficulties of 'real' travel in the post-imperial world, nostalgic travellers seek to authenticate their wanderings, to give them meaning and substance, by focusing them around the journeys – whether real or fictional – of travellers of a more heroic age. The ubiquitous culture of modernity is carefully filtered out and an imaginary, pre-modern landscape superimposed over the contemporary scene. The non-western world once again becomes the backdrop to bygone imperial adventures. From his ship steaming towards Singapore harbour, Gavin Young wrote with disappointment that:

> The view from the water is memorable; but from the office towers on the reclaimed land in the area of Shenton Way and Collyer Quay round to the massive, unimaginative, neo-Babylonian shapes of the ultra-smart hotels near the confluence of venerable Beach Road and upstart Raffles Avenue there's nothing – no domed mosque, no pagoda, no palm tree – to tell you that you are in the East. You must strain your eyes … to make out odd bits of the city Conrad knew – the formal colonial front of the City Hall behind the leafy avenues of Esplanade Park, the stately wedding-cake façade of Parliament House, or the regal mass of Victoria Memorial Hall. The elegant white spires of St Andrew's Cathedral is today crudely dwarfed by a huge hotel and a shopping complex called Raffles Plaza.
>
> So coming back to look for Conrad's world I wondered: 'Have I come ghost-hunting too late?'[44]

With a bit of effort, however, and regular immersion in Conrad's novels *Lord Jim*, *Victory* and *Falk*, Young was soon able to repopulate the streets of Singapore with the fictional characters of bygone colonial days. The more he thought about them, 'the more characters like William Lingard, Jim, Schomberg the innkeeper, the miserable Almayer and the rest of them seemed to be there, lounging in wait for me under a seafront awning or in the porticoed doorway of Emerson's tiffin room. They became as real as actual Singaporeans or Thais passing me in the street.'[45]

The landscape of the decolonised world is haunted by the ghosts of British adventurers past. Eric Newby tries to spot in Jordan's arid landscape the landmarks of Charles Doughty's explorations and the vestiges of T. E. Lawrence's adventures in the desert: the wreck of a Turkish locomotive, the remains of twisted, rusting tracks that had been blown up, telegraph poles along the new railway line that 'were the same sort

Lawrence's Beduin had so much enjoyed pulling down'. Various routes and desert towns brought reminiscences from *The Seven Pillars of Wisdom*. Following a camel track from Guweira to Mudawwara, Newby recollected:

> This was the route that Lawrence had taken, riding out of Wadi Rumm with the mutually hostile tribes which he held together, for their first successful attack on a train ... This same track was also used by a battalion of the British Imperial Camel Corps when they attacked and took the station in August 1918, having crossed the desert from Egypt to Aqaba. We were only just in time to travel on this track and see it much as it had always been. Even then the Jordanians, with American aid, were making a motor-road out to the foot of Wadi Rumm, where a tourist rest-house was to be built ... I felt that I was lucky to be where I was before these changes took place.[46]

The sense of belatedness in Young's and Newby's travel books, the futile efforts to recapture the imperial past, the longing for a 'golden age' of travel, are in fact some of the recurring motifs of modern travel literature by self-appointed travellers who feel the frustration of not being the 'first' to set foot in exotic places; of not getting there before modern western culture had destroyed an imaginary, idealistic and unchanging non-western world. Conversely, it could also add cachet to the traveller as one who had experienced a mode of travel and seen a world that no longer existed; who went when the going was good. It was a rather self-congratulatory sense of *après moi, le déluge*, of making it there just in time, before the Americans – synonymous with the promotion of the touristic experience – modernised and sanitised remote places, made them accessible, and brought in the tourist masses.

This melancholy nostalgia for a bygone era is more characteristic of twentieth-century British travel texts than their nineteenth-century counterparts. In his book *Orientalism*, Edward Said claims that there was an imaginative distinction between 'British realities and French fantasies' in respective travellers' visual and verbal representations of the Orient. For the British, Said argues, 'the room available for imaginative play was limited by the realities of administration, territorial legality, and executive power', while 'the French pilgrim was imbued with a sense of acute loss in the Orient'[47] – an idea that has been explored by Ali Behdad in his examination of the travel writings of Gustave Flaubert, Gérard de Nerval and Isabelle Eberhardt.[48] The Orient might figure as an ancient unchanging biblical or sybaritic landscape, according to the individual author's proclivities, but there were many British travellers in India who also reported enthusiastically on the positive modernising influences of British colonial rule. This is not to say, of course, that nineteenth-century travellers did not bemoan the importation of modern culture to the East. British travellers roundly condemned the destructive effects of British imperial commerce on local trade and merchandise, decrying the corrupting ugliness of new buildings and construction work in the exotic landscape and mourning the spread of cheap tourist trinkets and cloth imports from Britain in bazaars which used to sell traditional crafts. But that sense of melancholy and loss, of arriving too late on the scene, as experienced by nineteenth-century French literary travellers such as Flaubert and Nerval, is largely missing from nineteenth-century British travel writing. Then, it was still possible to be a 'real' traveller and explorer. Not so after the post-Second World War era of decolonisation.

The modern self-appointed traveller joins in Claude Lévi-Strauss's lament of belatedness in *Tristes Tropiques* (1955): 'I wish I had lived in the days of real journeys, when it was still possible to see the full splendour of a spectacle that had not been blighted, polluted and spoilt'.[49] Few pristine worlds remain to be discovered, many of the old exotic ones have long since been modernised and westernised, leading certain travel writers to deplore such aesthetically unpleasing changes in scathing terms, dissociating themselves from this process entirely, as if there were no history of western imperialism intervening in these cultures and bringing about these changes. But for most travellers and tourists, modern urban infrastructure and amenities are greatly appreciated. For those literary adventurers intent on wandering in the wake of empire, however, the modern by-products of western imperialism are greatly deplored. How they must have wished that, like Evelyn Waugh, they had gone when the going was good: during the age of empire, but before the modernising tendencies of western imperial cultures had brought uniform cityscapes and other 'vulgar tourists' to all parts of the well-travelled world.

Notes

1   Evelyn Waugh, *When the Going was Good* (Harmondsworth, Penguin, 1951; first published 1946), pp. 9–10.
2   See, for example, Edward Said, *Orientalism* (New York, Vintage, 1979); Sara Mills, *Discourses of Difference: An Analysis of Women's Travel Writing and Colonialism* (London, Routledge, 1991); David Spurr, *The Rhetoric of Empire: Colonial Discourse in Journalism, Travel Writing, and Imperial Administration* (Durham, Duke University Press, 1993); Tim Youngs, *Travellers in Africa: British Travelogues, 1850–1900* (Manchester, Manchester University Press, 1994).
3   Michael Kowalewski, 'Introduction: The Modern Literature of Travel', in M. Kowalewski (ed.), *Temperamental Journeys: Essays on the Modern Literature of Travel* (Athens, GA, University of Georgia Press, 1992), p. 11.
4   Mary Louise Pratt, *Imperial Eyes: Travel Writing and Transculturation* (London, Routledge, 1992).
5   Charlotte Mansfield, *Via Rhodesia: A Journey Through Southern Africa* (London, Stanley Paul & Co, 1911), pp. 7, 8.
6   Cited in Piers Brendon, *Thomas Cook: 150 Years of Popular Tourism* (London, Secker & Warburg, 1991), pp. 212–13.
7   Brendon, *Thomas Cook*, pp. 212–13, 221.

8   Gertrude Bell, *The Desert and the Sown* (London, William Heinemann, 1907), p. 58.
9   Barbara N. Ramusack, 'The Indian Princes as Fantasy: Palace Hotels, Palace Museums, and Palace on Wheels', in Carol A. Breckenridge (ed.), *Consuming Modernity: Public Culture in a South Asian World* (Minneapolis, University of Minnesota Press, 1995), pp. 72, 82–3.
10 Quoted in Brendon, *Thomas Cook*, p. 281.
11 Brendon, *Thomas Cook*, p. 311.
12 For the link between imperialism and game hunting and preservation, see John M. MacKenzie, *The Empire of Nature: Hunting, Conservation and British Imperialism* (Manchester, Manchester University Press, 1988).
13 Maxine Feifer, *Tourism in History: From Imperial Rome to the Present* (New York, Stein & Day, 1985), p. 231.
14 Michael Hitchcock, Victor T. King and Michael J. G. Parnwell (eds), *Tourism in South-East Asia* (London, Routledge, 1993), pp. 12–13.
15 Victor T. King, 'Tourism and Culture in Malaysia', in Hitchcock *et al.* (eds), *Tourism in South-East Asia*, pp. 101–2.
16 Quoted in Tom Selwyn, 'Peter Pan in South-East Asia: Views from the Brochures', in Hitchcock *et al.* (eds), *Tourism in South-East Asia*, p. 135.
17 Ibid., pp. 123–4.
18 Brendan, *Thomas Cook*, pp. 285, 288, 290, 311.
19 Stephen Weeks, *Decaying Splendours: Two Palaces. Reflections in an Indian Mirror* (London, British Broadcasting Corporation, 1979), p. 13.
20 Ibid., p. 35.
21 Ibid., p. 68.
22 Ibid., pp. 21, 52.
23 Salman Rushdie, 'The Raj Revival', *Observer*, 1 April 1984.
24 Anthony Powell, *The Empire Revisited* (London, Cleveland Press, 1985).
25 Ibid., p. 107.
26 Ibid., p. 209.
27 Ibid., p. 236.
28 James Buzard, *The Beaten Track: European Tourism, Literature, and the Ways to 'Culture', 1800–1918* (Oxford, Clarendon Press, 1993), p 5
29 Quoted in Kowalewski, 'Introduction: The Modern Literature of Travel', p. 4.
30 Martin Green, *Dreams of Adventure – Deeds of Empire* (London, Routledge & Kegan Paul, 1980).
31 Beatrice Grimshaw, *In the Strange South Seas* (London, Hutchinson, 1907), pp. 1–2.
32 Eric Newby, *A Traveller's Life* (Boston, Little Brown, 1982), p. 10.
33 Gavin Young, *Worlds Apart: Travels in War and Peace* (London, Penguin, 1987), p. 1.
34 Heather Henderson, 'The Travel Writer and the Text. "My Giant Goes With Me Wherever I Go"', in Kowalewski (ed.), *Temperamental Journeys*, p. 239.
35 Redmond O'Hanlon, *Congo Journey* (London, Penguin Books, 1997), p. 12.
36 Green, *Dreams of Adventure*, p. xi.
37 Henderson, 'The Travel Writer and the Text', p. 232.
38 Ibid., p. 239.
39 Redmond O'Hanlon, 'Amazonian Adventure', in B. Buford (ed.), *In Trouble Again: A Special Issue of Travel Writing*, Granta 20 (Harmondsworth, Penguin, 1986), p. 17.
40 O'Hanlon, *Congo Journey*, p. 32.
41 Gavin Young, *In Search of Conrad* (London, Hutchinson, 1991), p. 3.
42 Henderson, 'The Travel Writer and the Text', p. 232.
43 Pratt, *Imperial Eyes*.
44 Young, *In Search of Conrad*, p. 47.
45 Ibid., p. 2.
46 Newby, *A Traveller's Life*, p. 242.
47 Said, *Orientalism*, pp. 169–70.
48 Ali Behdad, *Belated Travelers: Orientalism in the Age of Colonial Dissolution* (Durham, Duke University Press, 1994).
49 Quoted in Henderson, 'The Travel Writer and the Text', p. 233.

CHAPTER TEN

Communities of Britishness:
migration in the last gasp of empire

Kathleen Paul

One of the markers by which the 1997 Blair administration may come to be known is that it witnessed the search for a new British identity. Politicians and journalists alike appear to be in the midst of a debate about how the inhabitants of the various nations which constitute the United Kingdom should define themselves in the light of devolution and the subsequent openings of a parliament in Scotland, an assembly in Wales, and a power-sharing executive in Northern Ireland.[1] The essential question appears to be whether there is a place for a universal and singular British identity in the face of increasingly assertive Scottish, Welsh and Irish national identities. The essential answer is less easy to find. On the right, there are those such as former Conservative Party leader William Hague who lament the fragmentation of Britishness into its Celtic fringes but who at the same time call for the birth of a new identity, one which, wrapped around the flag of St George, will boost English pride in the notion and nation of England.[2] Thus for William Hague, and others on the right, while they would prefer the continuing existence of a single British national identity, they will mark its passing by creating a new English identity to take its place. By contrast, those on the left such as Prime Minister Tony Blair proclaim not only that Britishness is alive and well, but that it is strengthened not weakened by the presence of Scottish, Welsh and Irish nationalism.[3] For Tony Blair, all inhabitants of the United Kingdom, from whatever nation they hail, may still take pride in the notion of *civis Brittanicus sum*. While, as these different responses suggest, left and right may disagree on the future of Britishness, what both have in common is the assumption that Britishness was real in the past: that is, that at least up until the advent of devolution there was a singular and universal British national identity which covered all inhabitants not only of the United Kingdom but of the whole British Empire.

But in reality, the great British national identity which spanned continents and won world wars has always been fractured, and has always consisted of narrowly defined exclusive identities at the inner core, which for political reasons were wrapped in an inclusive, broadly defined Union Jack flag. All that has happened in recent years is that the fracturing has become more visible. Even this trend, however, did not begin with the opening of the Scottish Parliament but can be traced back to the early post-war period – a period when, for political and economic reasons, Britain was battling to retain at least the shadow of the British Empire while coming to terms with the fact that the substance was on the brink of disappearing. At that time, British policy-makers sought to use the myth of a single, universal Britishness as one means of holding on to the international power and prestige associated with Britain's position at the centre of an empire. Unfortunately for those same policy-makers, however, this task became more difficult with the advent of independent migration to the United Kingdom from Britain's colonial territories. Indeed, it was this migration of British subjects of colour, and the concurrent existence of three other migrant groups in post-war Britain, which revealed more clearly than ever before the fact that behind the façade of a universal British national identity lay competing communities of Britishness, reflective of separate spheres of nationality. This chapter explores these different communities and suggests that their coming to the surface was a direct consequence of the end of empire.

In June 1948, Clement Attlee's Labour Government passed a British Nationality Act which provided for an extremely generous definition of Britishness. According to the Act, all residents of the British Empire and Commonwealth were to be known as British subjects and all enjoyed equal rights and privileges. Thus, whether born in England, Australia or the West Indies, all British subjects were equal and all had the right to live and work in Britain. Passed just a year after Indian independence and the declaration of an Irish Republic, the Act appeared to be a public profession of faith for the continuing future of the ideal and reality of the British Empire. For in its assertion of common citizenship rights throughout the Empire, the Act proclaimed the continuing existence of a singular and universal British nationality, a nationality which remained in place despite the ravages wrought by the Second World War, and despite the increasingly strident voices for independence which could be heard throughout the Empire/Commonwealth. The Act appeared to suggest that no matter what the children of the Empire might do, the mother country would always know her own children, and know them as British. Such was the image propagated by the 1948 Nationality Act. In reality, the Act was little more than a façade. Its generous grant of common citizenship and assertion of a single nationality were little more than political ploys designed to shore up Britain's position as a great power. In fact, as the discussions surrounding the formation of the Act reveal, rather than perceiving a common nationality throughout the Empire, the British policy-making elite perceived the residents of the Empire to belong to different communities of Britishness, and thus to inhabit separate spheres of nationality.

The reality of these separate spheres was evident in the earliest committee debates surrounding the Nationality Act. The mechanics of the Act compelled Britain to create a new area of national citizenship, membership of which would in theory confer the right of belonging, as well as provide the pathway to British subjecthood.[4] In deciding which area of the British Empire to carve out as Britain's own, policy-makers ran through a number of options. Significantly, the option which was eventually adopted, the creation of a single citizenship covering the 'United Kingdom and Colonies' (UKC), was initially rejected out of hand by all but the Colonial Office. Home Office representatives, for example, considered the idea of a combined United Kingdom and colonial citizenship as 'too artificial an entity for citizenship purposes' since to confer 'UK citizenship upon the inhabitants of a remote island thousands of miles away seemed to be a violation of geography and common sense'.[5] Officials' perception that a common citizenship was in some way unnatural was echoed in Parliament. Opposition members rejected the new citizenship as 'not real, because the peoples of the Colonial Empire, are not united with us, or with each other, by the ties of which true national citizenship is made'.[6] They defined these ties as 'some homogeneity and some true community of interest and status'.[7] Furthermore, this new citizenship, by trying to link 'what is geographically, socially, and politically a most heterogeneous community at many different stages of development' did not bind 'like to like', was 'not a recognition of reality' but rather 'a departure into complete and utter unreality'. Passionately declaring that 'the title of British is ours by every right of blood and soil', Conservative peers decried the bill for allowing residents of the colonies 'however primitive of mind' who were not 'racially British' to assume equal rights with the residents of the United Kingdom.[8] In response, the Government defended its bill, but in so doing merely reinforced the idea that there was something unusual about the coupling of the United Kingdom and colonies. Thus Lord Tweedsmuir referred to the residents of the colonies as 'our wards', who were 'dependent' on Britain for their 'guidance, security, and future'. This suggestion of inferiority was taken further by the Lord Chancellor when he asked the House whether it would be right that Britain, 'responsible for [the] peace, order and good government of our colonial territories ... should differentiate between our own people and the people for whom we are trustees'.[9] With these words, the Lord Chancellor made clear that his Government did not see a natural equality between the residents of the United Kingdom and the residents of the colonies but rather recognised an obligation to take care of them, much as one would take care of children.

In addition to pointing out Britain's responsibility for the colonies, the Labour Government tried to defend its new citizenship area by pointing out that the new entity mattered hardly at all since all rights pertaining to UKC citizens would also be available for all British subjects.[10] In this generous distribution of its citizenship rights, Britain was unique. No other member of the Commonwealth recognised all residents of the Empire as equal but rather privileged their own citizens above other British subjects. Thus in both its generosity and its inclusiveness, the Attlee Government appeared to be confirming the existence of a singular British national identity which spanned the Empire. In reality, the decision to link the United Kingdom with the colonies and the decision to treat all British subjects equally stemmed less from a belief in a universal nationality and much more from pragmatic politics. For as the Colonial Office warned other committee members in 1946, not to link the colonies with the United Kingdom in a single citizenship would be akin to promoting colonial independence since it would provide ammunition for colonial nationalist extremists.[11] Thus to avoid independence, and to maintain the unity of the Empire, it was best that the colonies be linked in a single citizenship with the United Kingdom. Likewise, all British subjects retained the right to live and work in Britain on the grounds that allowing 'free right of entry into this country to all British subjects from whatever part of the Empire they come' would contribute 'to the loyalty and solidarity of the Empire'.[12] The intent behind the bill was made clear by Attorney-General Sir Hartley Shawcross, who, noting Britain's 'special responsibility' as the 'historical motherland', explained that 'the bill's whole purpose is to maintain the common status [of British nationality] and with it the metropolitan tradition that this country is the homeland of the Commonwealth'.[13] Thus the Act, and the generosity within it, was a political endeavour designed to maintain Britain's unique position as a metropolitan motherland and to demonstrate to the world that the United Kingdom was still the centre of a great Commonwealth of nations even as certain parts of the Commonwealth began to assert their independence. From this perspective it may be suggested that the declaration of a universal nationality contained within the 1948 Act was less a profession of faith in the enduring ideals of empire and more a desperate last stand against encroaching colonial independence and imperial disintegration. Indeed, it was the very vulnerability of the Empire and Britain's own position in international affairs in the immediate post-war years which made a formal statement of universal Britishness all the more imperative. Policy-makers hoped that by asserting a common nationality and professing a commitment to a singular national identity of Britishness, they could stave off colonial and dominion nationalism while at the same time bolstering Britain's claims to be treated as a great power.

A similar reasoning lay behind the Government's use of migration policy. Post-war Britain witnessed the migration of four major population groups: residents of the United Kingdom encouraged to emigrate to the Dominions, continental refugees and aliens imported to work in Britain's essential industries; Irish citizens facilitated in their movement to Britain; and residents of the colonies and former colonies who sought to act upon their common nationality by coming to live and work in Britain at a time of great labour shortage in the mother country. The treatment received by each group, both in the initial stages of their migration and over the ensuing decades, clearly reveals that the policy-making elite believed that each group could be categorised according to a hierarchical understanding of the world's population, an understanding based on a racialised conception of humanity.[14] This division of British nationality into separate spheres placed each group into a different community of Britishness, which in turn resulted in each group experiencing Britishness in a very different way. Manifest in the official discussions surrounding the 1948 Act, these competing communities of Britishness began to assume a more public face as the post-war period progressed, until by the early 1960s, a period which one might describe as post-imperial, they were fully visible in both political and daily life.

The theory of a common citizenship first became an applied practice with the Labour Government's decision in 1946 to participate in joint schemes with Dominion governments whereby selected UK residents were encouraged to emigrate to the 'old' Dominions, primarily but not exclusively through the provision of free or assisted passages. The schemes were sufficiently successful that the period between 1945 and 1960 witnessed an annual average imperial emigration rate of 125,000.[15]

The relationship between this movement of people and the separation of British nationality into distinct spheres becomes apparent when one examines the language in which the flow was described. Replete with references to 'kith and kin', 'blood', 'British stock' and 'family', both committee discussions and parliamentary debates suggest that emigrating UK residents, and the Dominion residents whom they would soon join, were considered to be part of a single family, and were thus perceived to inhabit the same sphere of nationality. Thus, emphasising the anticipated role of the emigrants, a Ministry of Labour official explained that it was the United Kingdom's responsibility to despatch 'men and women who will carry to these Commonwealth countries our own particular traditions', that is 'British traditions and British ways of life'.[16] Only through such migration could the 'British stock' of the Dominions be 'replenished and fortified'.[17] The Conservative Commonwealth Relations Secretary, Lord Salisbury, referred to the effect of imperial migration upon the Commonwealth as 'a transfusion of blood which strengthens the whole', while Prime Minister Harold Macmillan in 1958 proclaimed his commitment to helping Australia 'remain British in blood and tradition'.[18] That British in this case meant white was made plain enough by a number of MPs who justified imperial migration as a 'duty of the White Race as a whole and particularly the British community of nations to make the best use of the areas of the world that we control'. MPs were particularly fearful of the 'Asiatics' who would surely take over the Dominions if the 'whites and Europeans' did not populate them themselves.[19]

This focus upon a white skin as a prerequisite for both imperial migration and membership in the real British family was also evident in the eligibility criteria for the various Dominion schemes. When the New Zealand Government, for example, wanted its application form to specify that only persons 'wholly of European race' need apply, the British Government suggested that such an 'official recognition of a colour bar might be embarrassing' and persuaded Wellington to exchange such open discrimination for a more subtle form, commenting that 'the rejection of a coloured applicant after interview without any reason being given was not open to the same objections'.[20] The British Government likewise co-operated with Australia so that although technically open to all, the Australian Free Passage scheme would in reality be available only to 'white British servicemen'.[21] Southern Rhodesia, meanwhile, made plain to UK officials that it sought migrants who could help 'build up a large white population', while Canada sought migrants who would augment the nation's 'fundamental character'.[22] The Dominions refused to relax their white-only rule even when the number of emigrants, as in the case of child emigrants, fell far below expectations.[23] Thus despite the use of language common to all members of the Empire, the public record makes clear that both the UK and Dominion political elites understood the migration of 'British stock' to be the migration of white residents of the United Kingdom.

If UK residents were perceived to be the children of the Empire, sent out to perform the job of empire for the good of whites everywhere, the second group of migrants in post-war Britain might well be categorised as the in-laws of the Empire, that is as individuals who though themselves not British would marry real Britons and whose children would be British. Constituting this group were 345,000 European aliens from various parts of the continent who, recruited for life and work in Britain, were intended to help fill some of the gap created by a domestic labour shortage estimated variously at between 600,000 and 1.3 million.[24] According to the Cabinet, filling this gap and restoring Britain's economic strength was an imperative if Britain was to maintain its position as a great power, an imperative made all the more urgent by strains elsewhere in Britain's imperial and international status.

So important were these aliens to Britain that the Government went to a great deal of trouble to ensure their happiness. Thus, not only was their transport to Britain provided, but upon arrival they were housed in government hostels, given jobs which paid the same wages as were available to British workers, and, perhaps most significantly, protected from any possible show of hostility on the part of the UK population. Fearing, for example, that the UK public might not understand the technical significance of the United Nations label for the refugees – 'displaced persons' – the British Government decided that a better label would be 'European volunteer workers'. Such a change would prevent 'any misconception which might arise among ordinary British workers and the public generally' as to the origins of the immigrants.[25] Likewise, wherever possible, policy-makers replaced the use of the word '"foreign" which was repugnant to the British' with 'European' when describing the new immigrants. In addition to these linguistic changes, the Government undertook an extensive public relations campaign designed to ensure that the receiving British public saw the immigrants in the best possible light. Thus, as a central part of 'shaping public opinion', women's magazines and local newspapers were 'continuously fed with good information' and the BBC agreed to broadcast programmes likely to cast the immigrants in a favourable light.[26]

This level of concern on the part of the Government for continental aliens would appear odd were it not for the fact that in recruiting the refugees for short-term labour, the Government was also recruiting a demographic increase for the long term. Making this demographic recruitment possible was the fact that policy-makers perceived the aliens, though not yet British, to have the potential to become British. This perception of demographic acceptability was manifest in policy-makers' language, which, as in the case of imperial migration, was replete with metaphors of blood, family and stock. Thus government representatives referred to the 'benefits that come from the assimilation of virile, active and industrious people into our stock' while MPs applauded the 'immigrants' infusion of vigorous new blood'. MPs believed that the immigrants would 'absorb the British way of life and become one of us' and thereby help produce a 'refreshed, enriched and strengthened' British population.[27] Quite simply the European aliens were recruited for 'permanent settlement here with a view to their intermarrying and complete absorption into our own population'.[28] Evident in these debates is the view, held by members of both the Government and the wider policy-making circle, that although the aliens were not yet British, they could become so, that they were, in short, full of 'the spirit and stuff of which we can make Britons'.[29] It was as a result of this potential Britishness, based on perceived blood and racial compatibility, that the 345,000 continental immigrants received such a favourable reception from the UK Government, a reception which created a community of Britishness for their use and which ensured a relatively smooth transition into an alien land.

Also recipients of a special category of Britishness were the 50,000–60,000 Irish men and women who each year in the post-war era entered the British labour force.[30] As in the case of imperial emigrants and continental aliens, the language employed by policy-makers to describe the Irish demonstrates where they were perceived to fit within the hierarchy of Britishness. The confines of the distinct Irish community of Britishness first assumed concrete form in the negotiations surrounding Ireland's imminent declaration of a republic. Upon that occasion representatives from Ireland, Britain and the Dominions worked hard to find a means by which Ireland, though leaving the Commonwealth, could continue to enjoy the rights of membership. After much discussion, a mechanism was found which by its very nature emphasised the perception of a familial link between Eire and Great Britain. Thus, the mechanism of association rested on 'ties of kinship, ties of blood, history and intermingling of peoples which bound Eire to the older countries of the Commonwealth', as well as 'historical, racial and geographical links'.[31]

As a result of this 'specially close relationship', Irish people migrating to Britain in the post-war era received all the privileges of British subjecthood without having actually to be British subjects. The importance of the perceived familial link between Eire and Britain was made clear by policy-makers' assurance to Attlee that India and Pakistan, being 'Asiatic', could not claim association on the same basis.[32] The slightly separate status of the Irish may have placed them outside the inner circle of pure domestic Britishness, and may have exposed them to some local instances of prejudice such as the persistence of 'No Irish Need Apply' notices, but their inclusion in all the privileges of subjecthood, including unfettered access to the United Kingdom, confirmed that to the governing elite, which ultimately helped shape public opinion, they, like the continental aliens, were racially and demographically acceptable and thus eligible for their own community of Britishness.

Also constituting their own community of Britishness, but with less happy results, were the 492 British subjects who arrived in Britain on board the *Empire Windrush* in June 1948. Given their status as British subjects, and in light of the labour shortage in Britain, it was perhaps not so naive of the would-be workers to think that their arrival would be welcomed by the mother country.[33] In reality, because the migrants were black, the arrival of the *Empire Windrush*, and the ships which followed, sparked a crisis within the Labour Government which, once again, highlighted the existence of competing communities of Britishness and revealed the ideal of a single universal British national identity to be nothing more than a façade.

Immediately upon hearing of the ship's impending arrival, policy-makers made it explicit to each other, and implicit to Parliament, that although they recognised the passengers' legal right to travel to Britain, they did not think it right that they should have done so. This dual approach of recognising the migrants' legal claim to Britishness while at the same time placing a barrier between them and the residents of the United Kingdom both helped create, and was reflective of, the clash between an inclusive formal nationality policy (the legal definition of who had the right to live and work in Britain) and an exclusive constructed national identity (the informal notion of who really did or could belong). Thus, ministers referred to the migrants' arrival as an 'incursion', lamented that it could not be prevented, and took steps to ensure that similar 'influxes' did not occur in the future.[34] In Parliament, the Government upheld West Indians' right to come to Britain, but hoped that 'no encouragement will be given to others to follow their example'. Even more specifically, the Parliamentary Under-Secretary for Labour, Ness Edwards, proclaimed that while the Government would do all that it could for the travellers, 'it could do no more for these men than we do for our own men'.[35] With this, Edwards made clear that the migrants, though British subjects, though possessed of the legal right to live and work in Britain, were not really British, were not really 'our own men'. It was exactly the same type of comment which had been made during the discussions surrounding the creation of the 'United Kingdom and Colonies' as an area of citizenship. In both cases, it became clear that policy-makers perceived there to be a distinction between residents of the colonies who were British in law only, and residents of the United Kingdom who were British in reality. This perception that apparent cultural and racial differences were more important than a common legal nationality was a consistent facet of policy-makers' subsequent deliberations. Thus, according to senior Ministry of Labour official Sir Harold Wiles, 'whatever may be the policy about British citizenship ... [no] scheme for the importation of coloured colonials for permanent settlement here should be embarked upon without full understanding that this means that a coloured element will be brought in for permanent absorption into our own population'.[36] Just as Ness Edwards had done in Parliament, Wiles proclaimed a distinction between colonials and 'our own' people. In this case the distinction was heightened by the assumption that 'our own population' and a 'coloured element' were two separate entities. If the civil servant's 'own population' was British, then by implication the 'coloured element' could not be. Startling about both Edwards's and Wiles's observation is their willingness to admit the reality of a common legal nationality, while at the same time alluding to a more important blood Britishness from which the migrants were excluded.

British subjects of colour continued to migrate to the United Kingdom throughout the 1950s. The annual averages remained in the low thousands until 1954, when most likely in response to the 1952 US McCarren–Walter Immigration Act, which limited West Indian migration to the United States, the annual intake jumped to 10,000. From 1955 to 1957 just over 40,000 entered each year, and although numbers dropped to 30,000 and 22,000 in 1958 and 1959, they climbed to 58,000 in 1960 and 136,000 in 1961.[37] In addition to continuing migration from the West Indies, the numbers by the 1960s included a significant representation from India and Pakistan, whose citizens, though not citizens of the United Kingdom and colonies, were, like Australian and Canadian citizens, British subjects still, and thus, under the terms of the 1948 Act, entitled to all the privileges of a singular and universal nationality.

This migrant flow terrified British policy-makers, who sought throughout the decade to stop it. They were hampered in their efforts, however, by the existence of the inclusive legal nationality policy which gave all British subjects, of whatever colour, the right to enter Britain freely. Given policy-makers' hostility to black Britons availing themselves of this right, it might seem that the most logical course would have been to bring this right to an end. Policy-makers were hampered again, however, by their continuing desire to maintain Britain's position as a world power, a position which they believed could only be maintained through the maintenance of a strong British Empire and Commonwealth. Legislating that all British subjects could no longer enter Britain freely would have been akin to admitting that there was no common British nationality. Admitting this, it was feared, particularly in the light of an Empire/Commonwealth already clearly vulnerable by the mid-1950s, would be but the first step to admitting that the Empire itself was no more. Indeed, as Churchill's Private Secretary put it, 'the minute we said, we've got to keep these black chaps out, the whole Commonwealth lark would have blown up'.[38]

Policy-makers could have avoided the stigma of racial discrimination by controlling the flow of all non-resident British subjects, black and white alike. Doing so carried risks of its own, however, since it would have had the unfortunate effect of keeping out migrants 'of good type from the "old" Dominions ... who come here, with no clear plans, in order to try their luck'.[39] Officials feared that restricting the rights of these people to return to 'the land which they still regard as home' threatened to undermine Britain's position as a metropolitan motherland around which the Empire rotated.[40] The Commonwealth Relations Office, in particular, argued against a universal bill, contending that British subjects' right to enter freely played an ever-increasing role in binding the Empire together and countering 'centrifugal tendencies within the Commonwealth'.[41] The last alternative, however, was perhaps the most frightening of all, since to do nothing and allow colonial migration to continue would be to 'produce a significant change in the racial character of the English people'.[42] Alarming on its own account, this 'large coloured community' was 'certainly no part of the concept of England or Britain to which people of British stock throughout the Commonwealth are attached' and might well 'weaken the sentimental attachment of the older self-governing countries to the United Kingdom'.[43] In light of these constraints, policy-makers attempted to design a bill which would allow for the informal control of black migration while allowing migrants from the 'old' Dominions, assumed to be white, to pass freely. Such a bill, by controlling black migration secretly, would not damage Britain's position 'as the Motherland, or at least the hub, of the Commonwealth'.[44] Clearly, white migrants, the children of the Empire, were truly Britons, to be admitted freely to 'the land which they still regard as home'. By contrast, British subjects of colour, though they too had been educated to regard Britain as 'the Motherland', were perceived not as children of the Empire but as mere acquaintances.

Also excluded from any likely control, and on the same familial basis, were Irish citizens, even though policy-makers noted that many of the complaints levied against the colonials could also be levied against the Irish – alleged domestic overcrowding, poor standards of hygiene, and outbreaks of anti-social behaviour. The 'outstanding difference' between the two groups, however, was that the Irish 'whether they liked it or not were not a different race from the ordinary inhabitants of the United Kingdom'. Thus although policy-makers admitted that it would often 'be difficult to find any difference between a Jamaican and a New Zealander and an Irishman except for the colour of their skins', this single difference was enough to make the one unwelcome and the other two regarded as part of the family.[45]

In addition to fearing for the effect upon the Empire/Commonwealth of controlling legislation, policy-makers were also inhibited in their actions by the perception that such legislation would be unpopular with the UK public. Specifically, ministers feared that any attempt to control the inward migration of British subjects of colour would be condemned as 'illiberal' by the 'more vocal elements' of public opinion.[46] Given the editorials running in journals such as *The Economist* and even popular newspapers such as the *Daily Sketch*, these fears were not unreasonable. *The Economist*, for example, suggested that any refusal to accept West Indians into Britain would be a 'moral defeat' since 'if their skins were white there would be no problem'. Condemning the operation of an informal colour bar, both publications called on the Government 'to receive these men and women on equal terms' and thereby 'live up to this country's profession of political aims'. Failing to do so, warned journalists, could cause irreparable damage to the Commonwealth.[47] These comments suggest that among the educated circles of public opinion, there remained still in the 1950s a great deal of respect for the ideals of equality allegedly manifest in the British Empire and Commonwealth. Acknowledging this continuing belief in the liberal imperial ideal, policy-makers hesitated to act in advance of UK public opinion.[48] Instead, they sought to bring public opinion around to their point of view. To this end, ministers wondered whether to appoint a committee of investigation which 'would serve to focus public opinion on this question and would help to gain public support for legislation to deal with it'.[49] Rejected in 1954, the idea reappeared in 1955 when officials made clear that the purpose of an investigative committee 'would not be to find a solution (for it is obvious what form control must take) but to enlist a sufficient body of public support for the legislation that would be needed'. Cabinet members agreed, noting that 'the first purpose of an enquiry should be to ensure that the public throughout the country were made aware of the nature and extent of the problem; until this was more widely appreciated the need for restrictive legislation would not be recognised'. As a result, the Government established yet another official investigation into the issue of colonial migration and thereby hoped to gather evidence sufficient 'to rally public opinion in support of restrictive legislation'.[50]

Suggested in these comments is the role played by the policy-making elite in shaping the reaction of residents of the United Kingdom to the presence of British subjects of colour. Traditional historiography has tended to blame the general public, especially the working class, for the racism which greeted many colonial migrants, suggesting that the Government would have preferred to continue a policy of free entry.[51] As this account makes clear, this was not the case. Indeed, as we have seen, successive governments of both major parties expended a great deal of energy trying to devise a means by which black Britons could be kept out. This argument does not deny the reality that many colonials faced discrimination and racism on a daily basis from ordinary UK residents – there are too many documented instances of racism to suggest that.[52] It does, however, suggest that just as the policy-making elite helped shape the public response to UK emigrants, European aliens and Irish citizens by way of parliamentary speeches, media reports, publicity campaigns and indeed legislation, so too they shaped the response given to migrating British subjects of colour. Thus, for example, it was the Government which first began referring to British subjects of colour as Commonwealth immigrants. This linguistic shift, which might at first glance appear of little import, was in fact quite significant since in the transformation from British to Commonwealth the migrants lost their most immediate connection with residents of the United Kingdom, and in the switch from subject to immigrant they lost their right to be in Britain.

In assessing responsibility for the colonials' treatment, however, this clever use of language, and indeed the general role of the policy-making elite, has generally received less attention than the much louder and thus much more noticeable popular expression of hostility which occurred in the disturbances in Nottingham and Notting Hill in August 1958. These 'riots' between black and white British subjects have traditionally been regarded both as the moment when the ordinary residents of Britain suddenly realised that they had acquired a black component to their population, and as the cause of the controlling legislation which followed four years later. In fact, as we have seen, the suggestion of controlling legislation had been on the table since the arrival of the *Empire Windrush* in 1948. Thus, what brought about legislation in 1962 was not the 'riots' of 1958, but the culmination of a whole decade of official anxiety, together with some much more recent realisations about the continuing prospects for the British Empire.

In the years immediately following the disturbances, colonial migration reached new levels with 58,000 new colonial migrants of colour entering Britain in 1960 alone, for example, and a projected figure of over 100,000 for 1961.[53] In light of the 'startling increase' in numbers, the Cabinet established a new series of investigative committees which, as before, reported that the migrants posed no immediate economic, health or employment threat and that the only tangible area of difficulty was housing. More important according to the committees, however, and the Cabinet to which they reported, was the intangible 'dangers of social tension inherent in the existence of large unassimilated coloured communities'.[54] As in the preceding twelve years, ministers weighed up their fear of developing a US-style 'colour problem' against the potential dangers to the Commonwealth and Empire that would surely result from the introduction of migration control.[55] As the Home Secretary saw it, removing some British subjects' right of access to the United Kingdom 'would remove one of the bonds which help to unite the Commonwealth, and might also seem to cast doubt on the idea of the Commonwealth as a multi-racial society'.[56] As the numbers continued to rise, however, the image of 'unassimilated coloured communities' spreading through Britain appeared almost to mesmerise policy-makers and gradually came to overshadow the potential dangers to the Commonwealth. Thus, by the end of July 1961, ministers concluded that 'it was more important to contain this danger ... of social tension ... than to avoid unfavourable reactions to control in coloured Commonwealth countries and elsewhere'.[57] It was this conviction that Britain 'could not assimilate coloured immigrants on the current scale' which ultimately led Harold Macmillan's Conservative Government to announce legislation to control 'Commonwealth immigration' in October 1961.[58]

[192]

The fear of potential damage to the 'old' Commonwealth remained at the forefront of policy-makers' thinking, however, and the method of control chosen was specifically designed to allow maximum flexibility towards the 'old' Dominions. Indeed as the Home Secretary explained, 'although the scheme [of migration control] purports to relate solely to employment and to be non-discriminatory, its aim is primarily social and its restrictive effect is intended to, and would in fact, operate on coloured people almost exclusively'.[59] Thus, although all British subjects resident outside the United Kingdom would have to apply for an employment permit to live in Britain, ministers believed that residents of the old Dominions would most likely apply for the permits for which there was no numerical cap. Only colonial migrants, it was presumed, would be applying for the limited unskilled labour permits. With this mechanism, policy-makers hoped finally to have discovered a solution to their problem of how to welcome those they considered family while keeping out mere acquaintances.

However flexible its implementation was intended to be, the 1962 Commonwealth Immigrants Act nonetheless marked a decisive break with the expansive declarations of the 1948 Nationality Act. What had been a singular and universal national identity in 1948 was now a fractured and insular vision of Britishness. One may speculate that in allowing this fractured identity to surface, policy-makers were influenced not only by the rising numbers of British subjects of colour coming to Britain but also by the diminishing possibilities for the imperial project. In 1948, Clement Attlee's Labour Government could perhaps be forgiven for thinking that the Empire could still be a useful tool of British foreign policy, that its very existence could help buttress British claims to be taken seriously as a third great power. By 1961, however, following the ANZUS pact, by which the United States effectively replaced Britain as the primary protector of Australian and New Zealand waters; the fiasco of Suez, which proved to both Britain and the world that Britain was no longer capable of mounting an independent international operation without US approval; and the 'wind of change' in Africa, by which Britain formally recognised the reality and righteousness of independence movements on the continent, Macmillan's Conservative Government could no longer pretend that the Empire was as significant as it had once been, nor hope that it offered a route to British greatness. In light of the declining importance attached to the Empire abroad, the growth of the Empire at home assumed ever-increasing importance. So much so that by 1961 policy-makers were ready to sacrifice whatever might be remaining of the former in order to deal with the problems they were sure would come from the latter. Thus, although conscious of the damage likely to be inflicted upon the imperial ideal, they nevertheless went ahead and introduced migration control because the dangers of a growing black population within Britain were considered to be of greater importance than the benefits of continuing harmonious relations within the Commonwealth.

This philosophy remained true throughout the ensuing decade, even as large numbers of Australians voiced disquiet at their apparent exclusion from the United Kingdom. Australians felt excluded, or at least unwanted, because under the terms of the 1962 Act, they, as other non-resident British subjects, were subject to questioning upon their arrival in the UK, and those suspected of wishing to reside in the UK permanently, but not possessing the necessary employment voucher, could technically be refused entry. In actuality, the number of Australians refused entry was tiny – in 1966 of over 79,000 Australians who sought admission without an employment voucher of any kind, only 72 were refused.[60] This generosity stemmed not only from the goodwill of immigration officers on the spot, but from an official policy which allowed 'working holidaymakers' from the 'old' Dominions the informal right to stay in Britain for anything up to three years.[61] Despite such generosity, however, Australians continued to argue that to be subject even to notional questioning was to question their Britishness. The dispute continued for several years with its significance lying less in the numbers involved than in UK policy-makers' steadfast refusal to discriminate openly in Australians' favour, even when threatened with the accusation that their failure to do so was leading to a weakening of Anglo-Australian ties.[62] Repeatedly throughout the correspondence, UK officials made it clear to Australia House that while they already discriminated in practice in favour of the 'old' Dominions they could not do so more openly for fear of being found guilty of racial discrimination, a charge they were already combating thanks to the original 1962 Act. Significantly, it was not the act of racial discrimination itself which worried officials, but rather the fear of being caught. Thus, UK officials made clear that they were ultimately ready to sacrifice Australian friendship, and by extension the exterior communities of Britishness and the wider boundaries of empire, in order to preserve both the appearance of liberalism and the reality of the domestic community located within the narrowly defined geographical territory of the United Kingdom.

This willingness received ever more concrete form in 1968 with the introduction of a second Commonwealth Immigrants Act. This Act was passed solely to exclude the 'large numbers of United Kingdom and Colonial citizens who have no connection with the United Kingdom' save their passports, but who, subject to Africanisation campaigns in their countries of residence in East Africa, had begun to migrate in significant numbers to their country of citizenship, the United Kingdom.[63] That their passports alone might have been thought to have been a sufficient link with the United Kingdom was dismissed by ministers who in internal discussions emphasised that the individuals involved 'did not belong in this country in the sense of having any direct family connection with it'.[64] In re-defining the rights of citizenship in this way, so as to exclude one group of citizens from the national territory, ministers recognised that they opened themselves to charges of racial discrimination, moral approbation and possible legal challenges. For some, such as Commonwealth Relations Secretary George Thomson, these difficulties were sufficiently great as to prohibit the imposition of control. Indeed, according to Thomson, such controls as were envisaged by the Cabinet were 'wrong in principle, clearly discriminatory on grounds of colour, and contrary to everything that we stood for ... our whole tradition in this field'.[65] While the Attorney-General agreed with Thomson that the controls would be difficult to justify to the international community, he assured the Cabinet that such extraordinary action as denying the entry of one's own citizens could be justified on the grounds that 'the persons to be dealt with, although technically our nationals, are not so closely connected with this country that they can be said to "belong" to it'.[66] In the end, the Cabinet followed the will of the Home Secretary, Attorney-General and Prime Minister, accepting that the moral and legal objections, together with the incumbent practical difficulties, were far outweighed by the potential dangers of a 'flood' of 'immigrants' and the consequent pressure this would place upon the social services and domestic race relations, the latter being of significance since the individuals in question were entirely of so-called 'Asian descent'.

The importance of the potential migrants' 'racial' status cannot be overemphasised. Policy-makers repeatedly referred to the migrants as Asian even though according to their passports they were British. In this way, and in their willingness to reconstruct the legal nationality to suit the constructed national identity, ministers followed an earlier tradition of reclassifying Britons as immigrants in order to facilitate their eventual exclusion from the territory. Thus the 1968 Act once again re-defined the notion of who was British, and did so in a manner which further narrowed the concept and practice of Britishness down from an expansive imperial ideal to a much more narrowly conceived geographic practice. Significantly, in carrying out this process, ministers were willing to endure the anger of other Commonwealth governments such as Uganda and India which made clear that they perceived the Act to be driven by notions of race. Thus, even at the expense of good relations with the wider imperial political community, UK officials were determined to protect the domestic community of Britishness from the perceived harm of racial mixing.[67]

This process was taken further again in subsequent decades. The 1971 Immigration Act reclassified all former British subjects as either patrial (subjects who themselves, or whose father or paternal grandfather had been born in the UK) or non-patrial (those without such family

[195]

connections). By giving rights of entry and residency only to the former, who were overwhelming white, and excluding the latter, who were over-whelmingly black, the Act gave public face to the long-existent competing communities of Britishness. Ironically, however, although designed to pre-serve the rights of the children of the Empire – those whose fathers and grandfathers had migrated to the Dominions – by associating rights of entry, and therefore the status of Britishness, with a recent personal famil-ial connection with the territory of the United Kingdom, the Act simulta-neously emphasised the importance of geography over race. Thus, although still racial in design, the new family of Britons was more clearly linked to the current or at least recent population of the United Kingdom rather than to the larger and extensive family of imperial subjects. As a result, the Act produced a yet more exclusive definition of Britishness, devoid now of both subjects of colour and imperial subjects of ancient connections. In terms of nationality legislation, and concepts of citizen-ship and belonging, it appeared as though the Empire was getting smaller all the time.

By 1981, and the introduction of yet more legislation, it seemed as though the Empire had shrunk to the point of disappearing. The 1981 Nationality Act withdrew all remaining commitments to residents of former colonies or dominions and redefined the formal definition of citi-zenship to include only former UKC citizens who had themselves or whose parents or grandparents had been born in the United Kingdom. Conservative Home Secretary William Whitelaw justified the Act on the basis that it was time 'to dispose of the lingering notion that Britain is somehow a haven for all those countries we used to rule'. His parliamen-tary colleagues apparently agreed, arguing, for example, that Britain had no 'duty – moral or legal – to the inhabitants of those countries that were formally in the British Empire'.[68] With these sentiments, UK policy-makers dismissed the importance and myth of empire, and the broader political community it entailed, in favour of a much more narrowly conceived domestic community of Britishness based firmly in the geographical territory of the United Kingdom.

Although not formally announced until 1981, the divisions within Brit-ish nationality had, as this chapter has shown, been present since at least 1948. At that time, however, policy-makers had been confident that they could continue to paper over the divisions for the sake of the international power and prestige which would result from a continuing proclamation of imperial vision. Over the subsequent decades, but particularly during the 1950s and 1960s, these efforts came under attack as members of the peripheral Empire began to migrate independently to the core, and as con-stituent parts of the Empire began ever more firmly to break away. As this process occurred, the political advantages of maintaining a universal nationality began to be outweighed by the potential damage to the domestic geographical community of Britishness. Thus, in successive legislative acts, UK policy-makers felt able to reveal gradually their narrow understanding of what constituted 'true' Britishness, and in so doing conveyed an implicit recognition of the end of empire.

Notes

1   See, for example, the *Guardian*, 18 April 1999; 12 January 2000; *Daily Telegraph*, 22 April 2000.
2   *Guardian*, 16 July 1999; 29 March 2000.
3   *Guardian*, 28 March 2000.
4   The British had been compelled to introduce the Act in the first place because the Canadians, anxious to assert their status as a separate country, albeit within the Commonwealth, wanted to introduce a nationality act which would make Canadian citizenship the primary nationality for Canadian citizens. Unable to prevent the Canadian bill, Britain responded by introducing a bill of its own, a bill which though designed to overcome the problems raised by the Canadian bill, still had to follow the format of creating a new national area of citizenship. PREM8/851, CP(45)28.7, 16 November 1945, Canadian Citizenship Bill. (Unless otherwise cited all archival references refer to the Public Record Office, London.) This argument is elaborated in greater detail in my book *Whitewashing Britain: Race and Citizenship in the Post-War Era* (Ithaca, NY, Cornell University Press, 1997).
5   HO213/202, Cabinet, Changes in British Nationality Law, Part III, Dowson to Sir Alexander Maxwell, 13 July 1946; HO213/200, 3rd Meeting of the Interdepartmental Working Party on British Nationality, 17 May 1946.
6   Parliamentary Debates (Lords), 5th ser., {1948}, vol. 155, col. 784.
7   Parliamentary Debates (Commons), 5th ser., {1948}, vol. 453, col. 410.
8   Parliamentary Debates (Lords), 5th ser., {1948}, vol. 155, cols 788, 784; Parliamentary Debates (Commons), 5th ser., {1948}, vol. 453, col. 482.
9   Parliamentary Debates (Lords), 5th ser., {1948}, vol. 155, cols 757, 794.
10   Parliamentary Debates (Lords), 5th ser., {1948}, vol. 155, col. 785.
11   HO213/202, Colonial Office Memorandum, British Nationality Proposals for Change in the Law, 5 July 1946.
12   PREM8/851, CP(45)287, 16 November 1945, Canadian Citizenship Bill.
13   Parliamentary Debates (Commons), 5th ser., {1948}, vol 454, col 4849; vol 453, col. 495.
14   In this context, the term 'racialised' refers to the belief that humanity is divided into distinct breeding populations based on perceived immutable genetic characteristics. For a more complete analysis of the process of racialisation see Robert Miles, *Racism* (London, Routledge, 1989).
15   CAB129/107, C(61)201, British Emigration Policy: Memorandum by the Secretary of State for Commonwealth Relations, 1 December 1961.
16   LAB13/281, Ministry of Labour speech written for Dame Mary Smieton to be delivered to the Society for the Overseas Settlement of Women, 1950.
17   DO35/4881, Report of the Interdepartmental Committee on Migration Policy, 1956.
18   DO35/4877, Draft Report of the Interdepartmental Committee on Migration Expenditure, 1954; Parliamentary Debates (Commons), 5th ser., {1958}, vol. 583, col. 155.
19   Parliamentary Debates (Commons), 5th ser., {1952}, vol. 499, cols 71, 1217.
20   LAB13/277, Emigration to New Zealand, Note of a Meeting, 15 May 1947.
21   LAB13/199, A. J. S. James, Note, 24, 29 October 1945.
22   LAB13/204, Southern Rhodesia Legislative Assembly Debates, 25 May 1950; DO35/

6361, Canada: Immigration into Canada, UK High Commissioner in Canada to Secretary of State for Commonwealth Relations, 5 February 1955.

23 Kathleen Paul, 'Changing Childhoods: Child Migration and British Society', in Pat Starkey (ed.), *Child Welfare and Social Action* (Liverpool, Liverpool University Press, forthcoming).

24 CAB129/6, CP(46)32, 30 January 1946; CP(46)35, 1 February 1946; CAB134/301, Foreign Labour Committee, 14 March 1946.

25 LAB13/257, Third Progress Report, 8 May 1947.

26 LAB12/513, Publicity for the Education of Popular Opinion on Foreign Workers, 14 October 1947.

27 Parliamentary Debates (Commons), 5th ser., {1947}, vol. 433, cols 387, 749–766.

28 LAB13/42, Sir Harold Wiles to M. A. Bevan, 8 March 1948.

29 Parliamentary Debates (Commons), 5th ser., {1947}, vol. 433, col. 757.

30 LAB13/1005, Statistics Relating to Persons Arriving from Overseas Applying for National Insurance Cards during 1960 compared with 1959, February 1961.

31 CAB129/30, CP(48)262, Aide-Memoire from Eire Government, 20 October 1948; Parliamentary Debates (Commons), 5th ser., {1948}, vol. 458, col. 1414; FO371/76369, Minute by G. W. Furlonge, 21 January 1949.

32 CAB128/13, CM74(48), 18 November 1948.

33 *Windrush* passengers later described their surprise and disappointment at their reception, pointing out that many colonials had considered themselves to be coming home. See, for example, the interview cited in Onyekachi Wambu's Introduction to *Empire Windrush: Fifty Years of Writing about Black Britain* (London, Phoenix, 1999), pp. 20–1.

34 CAB129/28, CP(48)154, Arrival in the UK of Jamaican Unemployed, June 1948.

35 Parliamentary Debates (Commons) 15th ser., {1948}, vol. 451, cols 422, 1851.

36 LAB13/42, Sir Harold Wiles to M. A. Bevan, 8 March 1948.

37 CAB134/1469, CCM(61)2, Progress Report by the Interdepartmental Committee on the Social and Economic Problems Arising from the Growing Influx into the United Kingdom of Coloured Workers from other Commonwealth Counties, 1 February 1961; CAB134/1465, CCI(63)4, Commonwealth Immigrants Committee, Rate of Issue of Vouchers, 1 November 1963.

38 Andrew Roberts, *Eminent Churchillians* (London, Phoenix, 1995), p. 225.

39 CO1032/119, Swinton note.

40 CO1032/119, Report of the Working Party on Coloured People Seeking Employment in the United Kingdom, 17 December 1953.

41 CO1032/121, Commonwealth Relations Office Re-Draft of Social and Economic Report, August 1955.

42 CAB128/30, CM39(55), 3 November 1955.

43 CO1032/119, Report of the Working Party on Coloured People Seeking Employment in the United Kingdom, 17 December 1953.

44 CAB128/16, CM49(49), 27 July 1949.

45 PREM11/824, Report of the Committee on the Social and Economic Problems arising from the Growing Influx into the United Kingdom of Coloured Workers from Other Commonwealth Countries, 3 August 1955; CO1032/121, Commonwealth Relations Office Re-Draft of Social and Economic Report, August 1955.

46 CAB134/1210, CI(56)3, 17 May 1956, Cabinet Committee on Colonial Immigrants, Revised Draft Report to the Cabinet.

47 *The Economist*, 6 June 1953; 13 November 1954; *Daily Sketch*, 3 November 1954; 8 December 1954.

48 CAB128/28, CM3(55), 13 January 1955; CM15(55), 17 February 1955; PREM11/824, Brook to Churchill, 17 February 1955.

49 PREM11/824, C(54)379, 6 December 1954; CAB128/27, CM(78)54, 24 November 1954.

50 PREM11/824, Brook's memo to Prime Minister, 14 June 1955; CAB128/30, CM14(55), 14 June 1955.

51 See, for example, Peter Fryer, *Staying Power* (New Jersey, Humanities Press, 1984),

which claims that successive British governments failed to formulate any policy initiatives to deal with the new migrants and that 'between 1958 and 1968 black settlers
in Britain watched the racist tail wag the parliamentary dog'. Kenneth O. Morgan, *The
People's Peace* (Oxford, Oxford University Press, 1990), pp. 202–4, suggests that the
Cabinet attitude towards 'coloured immigration' was one of 'extraordinary complacency' and that it was only in 1962 that Macmillan 'felt compelled' to take action.
Dilip Hiro, *Black British White British* (London, Paladin, 1992), p. 207, writes that the
Conservative Government followed 'a laissez-faire policy ... regarding coloured immi-
gration until popular anxiety forced its hand in 1961'.

52 See, for example, E. R. Braithwaite's moving description of his experiences as a welfare
officer in the 1950s where he experienced the racial prejudice of white colleagues first
hand. E. R. Braithwaite, 'Paid Servant', in Wambu (ed.), *Empire Windrush*, pp. 107–11.
See also the testimonies included in Ben Bousquet and Colin Douglas (eds), *West
Indian Women at War* (London, Lawrence & Wishart, 1991).

53 CAB134/1469, Working Party to Report on the Social and Economic Problems Arising
from the Growing Influx into the United Kingdom of Coloured Workers from Other
Colonial Countries, 25 July 1961.

54 CAB128/35, CC(61)29, 30 May 1961; CAB129/107, C(61)153, 6 October 1961.

55 CAB134/1469, CCM(61), 2nd Meeting, 17 May 1961.

56 CAB129/103, C(60)65, 15 November 1960.

57 CAB134/1469, CCM(61) 3rd Meeting, 31 July 1961.

58 CAB128/35, CC(61)55, 10 October 1961.

59 CAB129/107, C(61)153, 6 October 1961.

60 FCO50/123, Brief for Mr Foley's Meeting with Brian Harrison, January 1967.

61 FCO50/123, L. E. T. Storar to Blair, 27 January 1967.

62 FCO50/123, A. H. Bruce to Douglas Jay, 10 February 1967.

63 CAB129/135, C(68)34, 12 February 1968, Memorandum by the Secretary of State for
the Home Department.

64 CAB128/43, CC13(68), 15 February 1968.

65 CAB128/43, CC13(68), 15 February 1968; CAB128/43, CC(14)68, 22 February 1968.

66 CAB129/35, C(68)36, Memorandum by the Attorney-General, 14 February 1968.

67 FCO50/97, Kampala to the Commonwealth Relations Office, 25 February 1968; New
Delhi to the Commonwealth Relations Office, 26 February 1968.

68 Parliamentary Debates (Commons), 5th ser., {1981} vol. 997, cols 997, 983.

CHAPTER ELEVEN

South Asians in post-imperial Britain: decolonisation and imperial legacy

Shompa Lahiri

While empire in India formally ended in 1947, the migration of South Asians to Britain in the decades that followed continues to be an enduring reminder of Britain's imperial past. This chapter explores how the legacies of empire became manifest in British attitudes and policies towards South Asians in their midst, as well as South Asian responses to the British and Britain during the era of decolonisation, within the realms of politics, migration, employment, social attitudes and cultural forms. The nationalist struggle to mobilise support for Indian self-rule united disparate groups of Indians in Britain, divided by class, religion and language. However, after the Second World War, the community split along sectarian lines, replicating politics in India. These divisions were themselves a result of Britain's imperial policy of 'divide and rule'.

A more direct physical by-product of the end of empire in South Asia concerns migration. Why did increasing numbers of South Asians choose to migrate to Britain to reclaim the rights and privileges of colonial subjecthood at a time of imperial retreat? What attracted South Asians to Britain, and how did British governments respond to the influx of immigrants? And did the period from the 1960s onwards represent a clear break with empire or simply a reformulation of emphasis? These questions will be examined within the framework of the dual imperial legacy of benevolence and exclusion. The conservative aspect of the imperial inheritance, expressed in nostalgia for the imperial past, which surfaced in both popular British culture and in the everyday experiences of South Asian residents, can also be seen, more tangibly, in the perpetuation of racially discriminatory attitudes and policies of British employers and trade unions, as well as corrupt work practices. The persistence of British imperial attitudes was accompanied by a reluctance to relinquish colonial mentalities completely, evident in the lingering appeal of Britain for western-educated Indians, particularly writers. But this aspect of the imperial legacy, like the others, was subject to ambivalence and conflict.

Indian attitudes to decolonisation: unity and division

Despite disagreements about the process of decolonisation and the partition of India that followed, the evidence available suggests that few Indians in Britain favoured prolonging British rule. Travelling to Britain in the era before independence had politicised Indians from a variety of backgrounds and encouraged them to view the end of British rule in India as an issue of great urgency.[1] Both middle-class and working-class Indians in Britain contributed towards the nationalist struggle. One of the key organisations which brought diverse groups of seamen, students and professionals together was the influential India League, under the charismatic leadership of Vengalil Krishan Krishna Menon,[2] who rallied many to the cause of Indian self-rule in the 1930s and 1940s. Through its various local branches it attracted men and women, brown and white. Between 1930 and 1949 it had a membership of approximately 180, over half of whom were Indian. Despite its clear ideological associations with the Indian National Congress, it was in fact an independent organisation founded in 1912. But it only became a serious political force in Britain after Krishna Menon became secretary.[3] Menon also managed to muster the support of working-class Indians in Britain. Sylhetti seamen who settled in London during the 1930s, such as Sheikh Abdul Majid Qureshi, attended and co-chaired League meetings.[4] The League adopted a twin-pronged approach to acquiring support in Parliament and from the public at large. Tactics included lobbying MPs and key figures in the Labour movement including Harold Laski, Bertrand Russell and Fenner Brockway, as well as raising political consciousness and support in Britain with information campaigns about India and organising public meetings.

Although the nationalist movement's message of unity appealed to most groups of Indians in Britain, it was also potentially divisive. Oral testimony from Bangladeshi seamen shows that while there was considerable support for the end of British rule in India, religious divisions, which had remained largely hidden prior to the Second World War, began to emerge after 1945, when support for the Muslim League among Muslim seamen escalated. Sylhetti sailors such as Nawab Ali and his friends had regularly attended India League meetings organised by Krishna Menon at Hyde Park Corner in the 1930s and were staunch supporters of the Indian National Congress. But as support for a separate Muslim state, Pakistan, grew in India, Indian Muslims in Britain started to question their allegiance to a united India. Eventually the leader of the Muslim League, Mohammed Ali Jinnah, was invited to London, where Muslim seamen held a party in his honour and pledged their support for Pakistan, resulting in the establishment of the UK branch of the Muslim League. Sheikh Abdul Majid Qureshi described his conversion to the Muslim League in

1944–45, when a League representative from India approached him. At the time Qureshi owned a restaurant in Charlotte Street, London, known as the 'India Centre', where Congress meetings were held. Following an altercation with some Hindu students who denounced Jinnah, he retaliated by whole-heartedly embracing Islam and later became the General Secretary of the London Muslim League.[5] Hindu/Muslim rivalry shows how colonial relations in India had a direct impact on diaspora communities. These divisions were a product of the unequal allocation of power and resources by British rulers, a legacy of British rule not apparent in pre-colonial India.

Another group which was pivotal in influencing attitudes towards decolonisation, particularly among Punjabis, was the Indian Workers' Association (IWA). Confusion surrounds the origins of this group. According to one source the IWA was formed in the 1930s by a group of businessmen, students and professionals residing in the London area.[6] Others claim it was founded in Coventry in 1938 by Punjabi peddlers. One of the original founders, Anant Ram, believed that the IWA was instrumental in inculcating Indian labourers, who had little knowledge of Indian politics or nationalism prior to arrival in Britain, with ideas about national liberation. He told an interviewer how he had joined the Association at the beginning of the Second World War: 'I think since we were all from small villages in the Punjab and had no idea what freedom and slavery was, we came as labourers and had very poor knowledge of the world ... IWA meetings were about telling those who attended about such matters ... Our aim was to voice a concern for Indian freedom.'[7] He recalled nostalgically his memories of the day India achieved Independence: 'No one called us "Blackie" even if children said something to this effect, the parents would forbid them, so it was a great day for all of us'.[8] Although there is very little evidence that treatment of South Asians by working-class neighbours improved drastically after independence, for South Asians in Britain unable to benefit directly from post-coloniality in South Asia, Independence Day had great symbolic and mythic value. While Indians in Britain during the colonial period were relatively vocal in their opposition to British rule in India, Commonwealth immigrants who settled in the decades after independence were more reluctant to criticise British rule of India openly in front of English workmates. The reasons for this silence can only be speculated upon, but reluctance to antagonise work colleagues for fear of reprisals and the painful memories associated with partition are likely.[9]

Migration and social policies: benevolence and exclusion

For specific sections of the South Asian population the dislocation resulting from decolonisation, especially partition of the subcontinent into two successor states, acted as powerful motors for migration to Britain. But even if partition had not taken place, traditions of emigrating from India were well established for specific groups of Indians such as Tamils, Suratis and Punjabis, who had travelled to the West Indies, Africa and South-East Asia as indentured labour. The demise of British hegemony in India and the creation of Pakistan triggered the transfer of approximately eight million Muslims and equivalent numbers of Sikhs and Hindus across the Indo-Pakistan borders in the north-west and north-east of the subcontinent. Pressure on land was most intense in the Punjab with the arrival of four million refugees from Pakistan. The absence of primogeniture and density of population led to the fragmentation of land and a huge growth in uneconomic landholdings. Jullundar, the area from which most migrants to Britain originated, had the largest number of uneconomic holdings in the Punjab. In particular the economic security of the middle-ranking Sikh peasantry was thrown into turmoil.[10]

It was not just rural poverty and competition for land in post-partition India which provoked migration from the Punjab; for Indian villagers, who formed three-quarters of those emigrating, the quest for *izzat* (personal honour) was also crucial. Land was the most visible symbol of *izzat*, and thus loss of land and the prospect of becoming a landless labourer was doubly symbolic.[11] Even for post-war immigrants who had some experience of Britain, it was the catalyst of partition, resulting in the loss of family property and land, which triggered the decision to leave India and Pakistan and seek out opportunities in Great Britain.[12] Farmers were not the only group to be adversely affected by partition. Muslim seamen from West and East Pakistan no longer had access to the key Indian ports of Calcutta and Bombay, as employment opportunities were restricted to Indian nationals. Both groups looked to old imperial masters in Britain to improve their prospects. The instability that accompanied the process of partition also impacted on the urban middle classes. Dilip Hiro, an Indian intellectual, who settled in post-imperial Britain, wrote of how partition had caused his family to leave behind property in Sind (Pakistan) and migrate to the outer suburbs of Bombay, experiencing impoverishment for the first time. Hiro was obliged to take up the burden of supporting a family of six while attending university.[13] Participation in the independence movement and the trauma of partition caused disruption to traditional career development. For the sons of rich peasants and landowners who found themselves unable to carve out careers in India and fulfil the expectations of their families, 'migration to England was a form of escape from unfortunate circumstances'.[14]

While the economic and social disruption associated with the end of empire in India was important in stimulating interest in new opportunities for improvement of prospects abroad, equally post-war Britain offered numerous attractions for would-be migrants. As the ex-imperial power in the region, sentimental attachment and familiarity made Britain the natural choice of destination for South Asians wishing to leave the subcontinent. It is significant that the group which constituted the largest number of migrants, North Indians, had historically been highly regarded by the British as part of their preference for 'martial races'. Sikhs in particular were favoured, characterised as good fighters (hence recruitment into the Indian army), physically attractive by virtue of pale skin, height and strength, and valued for their loyalty, established during the 1857 Indian 'Mutiny'. Indeed, the imperial connection could prove useful for some Sikh immigrants searching for employment in post-war Britain. The personnel manager of one factory explained that he had employed Indians because he had made friends with members of a Sikh regiment in the Middle East during the Second World War.[15] However, although the imperial legacy proved remarkably resilient in many respects, British preference for North Indians appeared to wane when increasing numbers of South Asians took up permanent residence in Britain.

Most immigrants who came to Britain from the 1950s onwards were motivated by the desire for economic advancement. The prosperity of those who returned from Britain in the 1950s and 1960s encouraged others to follow suit. Anant Ram was first drawn to Britain when he read the letters sent by his Muslim neighbour's relatives from England. Ram and the other villagers were also impressed by the large remittances frequently received from abroad. One observer wrote: 'humble and commonfolk all over the sub-continent of India are coming more and more to believe that they will no longer remain poor if only they can make their way to England. Who brings this story to them? Indian workmen and tradesmen who have been to England, of course.'[16] The end of empire coincided with an economic boom in Britain, which provided employment opportunities for South Asians at the bottom rung of the employment structure. Decline in status for South Asians was partially alleviated by improved financial rewards, as unskilled jobs in Britain paid better than skilled employment in the subcontinent.

South Asian immigrants settling in post-war Britain established themselves mainly in London, the midlands and the industrial conurbations of the north, taking up employment in factories and foundries. Much of the character of post-war migration from India, Pakistan and Bangladesh was a product of chain migration, based on individual men who, having established themselves, sponsored other men, usually from the same kinship group or village. From the late 1960s, women and children arrived to supplement the population. How did British policy-makers respond to the post-war arrivals from South Asia? Indian independence in 1947 and the introduction of citizenship laws in India, Pakistan and Ceylon forced

Britain to define citizenship explicitly for the first time. The 1948 Nationality Act reaffirmed the right to British citizenship to all members of the Commonwealth, without restriction. Thus Britain confirmed its commitment to the Empire/Commonwealth by refusing to draw a distinction between citizen and subject and conferred a common set of rights and privileges which entitled every subject in the Empire to enter Britain, serve in the armed forces, stand for Parliament and vote. Throughout the 1950s, the Empire/Commonwealth was instrumental in British attitudes and policies towards the growing number of South Asian newcomers. Just as empire had been seen as crucial to Britain's world status during the high tide of imperialism, in the 1950s its inheritor, the Commonwealth, was also regarded as vital if Britain was to stave off decline and sustain world power and influence. India was viewed as a particularly valuable trading partner, as well as a bulwark against Soviet encroachment in Asia. Thus, in the light of the importance assigned to South Asia and the Commonwealth in general, any measures to restrict the entry of Indians and Pakistanis would have been highly controversial.[17]

The legacy of imperial benevolence, which characterised the immediate post-war years, can be seen in the paternalistic tone accompanying public discussions of Commonwealth immigration. Colonial subjects were still viewed as children in need of protection and guidance. Britain's role as the 'mother country' was a cornerstone of the 1948 Nationality Act, which was based on the view that as a former imperial ruler, Britain was obliged to take some responsibility for her subjects. But paternalism was not new; it had been a feature of British policy towards Indians at the beginning of the twentieth century. Officials were concerned to shield students from what they viewed as negative influences in Britain. Aspects of this thinking can also be seen in policy towards princes, seamen and soldiers.[18] South Asians who experienced paternalism in person expressed resentment. One opined: 'my earlier gratefulness to the British for their kind behaviour towards me personally, in spite of our bitter memories of the past, has gone and I seem to discover a "paternal" attitude towards me and my country, which I find distasteful'.[19] African students also complained of the 'let's have a colonial for tea' mentality of some Britons they met.[20] Dilip Hiro was infuriated by the imperial smugness and condescension which accompanied discussions on India. He wrote: 'With very few exceptions they all shared a notion that the British ... gave the "natives" railways, hospitals, schools and roads and what is more taught them how to administer their countries, an altruistic mission that the British had willingly and honourably accomplished'.[21]

The liberal tradition of empire is also discernible in the rhetoric of racial partnership within the Commonwealth, which permeated political discourse in the period up to the 1960s. However, in the succeeding

decades, another aspect of the multi-faceted imperial legacy – racial differentiation and exclusion – began to prevail. The underlying motive behind
the strategy of restriction for Commonwealth immigrants and colonial
subjects was obsession with the size of the South Asian community in
Britain. This was considered important for two reasons. Indian students
and Commonwealth immigrants were identified as problems when their
numbers increased. Secondly British officials, both past and present,
claimed that good race relations were dependent on keeping numbers
down and maintaining the position of the established Asian community.
Thus, the reasons for restriction, whatever the new situation, were ostensibly based on the need to protect those on whom the restrictions were
imposed. Concern about numbers stemmed from the increased visibility
of a 'black' presence in mainland Britain. Fear of the consequences of black
settlement was most graphically expressed in Enoch Powell's infamous
'rivers of blood' speech, in which he prophesied violent racial war. This
speech is significant for what it shows about how the imagery of the
decolonisation process, especially partition, re-emerged to inform the
rhetoric of post-imperial politicians like Powell.[22]

One of the most interesting features of immigration control is the extent to which the Governments of India and Pakistan colluded with the
British Government to control the type of South Asians settling in Britain.
In 1955 the Indian Ministry of External Affairs issued a directive to stop
the migration from India of the poorly qualified and financed. Proof of
entry to educational institutions was required. The Pakistani Government
went to even greater efforts to prevent illiterate migrants from travelling to
Britain. Applicants had to show working knowledge of English and evidence of a job offer or college place. Despite these measures, those deemed
unsuitable were still able to thwart controls by entering on forged passports.[23] Similarly, the British Government determined to limit access to
South Asians of 'good type'.[24] Apart from turning away the unskilled and
illiterate and those without sponsors, other devices were used to discour-
age potential working-class economic migrants. The Pakistani Government increased passport fees. Vernacular newspapers were utilised, as
they had been in the past, to warn potential migrants of the difficulties
that they would face in Britain.[25] The motivation behind these actions can
be assigned, in part, to the ingrained class prejudice of all governments
involved, as well as concerns of the fledgling republics of India and Pakistan that working-class migrants entering Britain would diminish their
status in the eyes of ex-imperial masters.[26] This is yet another example of
how imperial and colonial preoccupations continued to resonate.

Indian experiences of Britain: nostalgia and discrimination

Even though decolonisation in the colonies may have suggested de-imperialisation in the imperial centre, Asian immigrants arriving in the decades following British withdrawal from India faced many of the same responses and difficulties experienced by earlier sojourners. The end of empire in India gave rise to periods of Raj nostalgia in post-war Britain, most notably in the late 1970s and 1980s, both in popular culture and in government.[27] A more general sense of imperial hangover is detectable in post-war British cinema and children's literature.[28] Attempts to relive the imperial past had special appeal for 'old colonials' who had worked for the British administration in India. A Sylhetti restaurateur, Abdul Mannam, recalled how British administrators who had lived in India would frequently visit his restaurant and request that waiters call them 'sir' and in return they would revert back to the familiar master/servant relationship enjoyed in India and call the waiter 'bearer'.[29] Bangladeshi waiters were prepared to act out the fantasy of imperial domination in return for remuneration. The ghosts of the imperial past also haunted Indian students arriving in the 1950s and 1960s. Rajagopal Parthasarathy, who came to Britain as a British Council scholar in 1963, told an American audience: 'The Americans unlike their English cousins are innocent of the nostalgia of Empire ... whereas in England history caught up with me'.[30] While it is clear that Hollywood was involved in the production of empire films with British imperial heroes during the mid-twentieth century such as *Kim* and *Gunga Din*, Parthasarathy's speech to an American audience many decades after he had left Britain to take up residence in America illustrates how disillusionment with post-war Britain, as a student, still rankled long after he had left the post-imperial centre.[31]

Racial stereotyping continued to taint post-imperial mindsets. For example, the biological determinism which conditioned how and where Indian seamen were employed prior to 1914 was also used to justify their employment in low status and physically demanding jobs from the 1950s onwards. Throughout the colonial period Indian sailors were confined to working in tropical climates. This was based on the spurious and false argument that lascars were, as a result of their biological make-up, peculiarly intolerant of low temperatures, but conversely better able to endure extremes of heat than European seamen. Pseudo-science was used to confine lascars to the hottest part of the ship, the engine-room.[32] This erroneous belief in the South Asian's enhanced resilience to heat proved to be such a powerful myth that it was used to sanction the employment of Commonwealth immigrants in the boiler rooms of big hotels in London. British employers claimed 'the Asiatic does not find the humid atmosphere quite so unbearable as others might and is more likely to stick to the job for a longer period than most'.[33] In reality, the suffocating atmosphere caused by temperatures in excess of 120 degrees was no less debilitating for South Asians than for Europeans. However, for newly arrived unskilled (and in some cases educated) South Asian immigrants, necessity and the lack of alternative job prospects led to the acceptance of unpopular jobs. Improved economic conditions in Britain enabled members of the indigenous population who would have traditionally taken up such jobs, to set their sights higher.

Racial discrimination, a prominent feature of the colonial experience, proved to be equally problematic for Commonwealth students and settlers. The greatest difficulty was in finding accommodation; students were particularly disadvantaged in the early 1950s when community support networks were still in their infancy. Once Asian settlements began to develop, peasant farmer migrants, mainly from the extreme north-west and east, could arrive and take up residence in Asian-owned houses. Some fortunate students were not burdened by the additional problem of finding work, but for most immigrants obtaining employment was essential. One Indian who tried to obtain a job in the car industry was told that employment was only open to union members, but when he attempted to obtain a union card he was refused. He faced similar discrimination when applying for jobs in Coventry transport services.[34] Even those who did find employment were often unable to retain their positions. One example was 25-year-old Sohan Lal, who was forced out of a job at a foundry in Derbyshire when 200 of his white colleagues went on strike in protest at his appointment. The workers complained that an agreement with the management of the foundry, whereby no more Asians would be employed if white labour were available, had been breached when Lal, the sixth Asian, was employed. Lal's press interview demonstrates the betrayal felt by many Asians when pledges of racial equality proclaimed in the 1948 Nationality Act were not redeemed: 'I am a British citizen and I thought when I came here it would count for something, but apparently it is not so'.[35] Other remnants of colonial work practices accompanied the migration of South Asians to Britain. There is some evidence that British foremen and personnel managers used Asian go-betweens to extort bribes from fellow Asians to obtain employment in factories. This replicates the corruption which Indian seamen were subjected to in the colonial era.[36]

Colonial mentalities: attraction and alienation

Despite the break-up of the British Empire in India, Britain continued to attract large numbers of students and intellectuals. One study suggests that by the end of the 1950s, nearly 5,000 students from India (excluding

Pakistanis) were studying in Britain.[37] Thus, in the decade after independence the student population had grown by 3,000 to over twice its previous size. Clearly for those who could afford it, the attraction of studying at the heart of the former empire had not diminished, nor had the value and kudos of being an 'England-returned'. Although the post-imperial generation of students preferred to study science, technology, engineering and medicine rather than law, which had been popular with their predecessors, the motivation of students and intellectuals remained similar. Of a random sample of 400 students in the late 1950s, nearly half cited social advancement when questioned about their reasons for studying in Britain.[38] In the era of decolonisation, British qualifications still had great market value. In the past, employment in government service was dependent on qualifications obtainable in Britain. Similarly, studying for the Bar in Britain had many advantages. Although the obligation to travel to Britain was no longer present after independence, nevertheless the belief persisted that studying in Britain would enhance career prospects – an illustration of how colonial mentalities were perpetuated irrespective of new circumstances. Practical incentives such as increased facilities and scholarships also helped to boost the number of students. Just as students in the heyday of empire attributed their decision to study in Britain to a complex cocktail of variables, assigning equal importance to intellectual and material considerations, middle-class South Asians who travelled to Britain in the era of decolonisation also identified a host of similar influences, including 'economic deprivation, desire to improve professional status, intellectual curiosity about the West and a spirit of adventure'.[39]

Echoes of the imperial past feature prominently in the work of writers of Indian origin in post-war Britain. The South Indian author Kamala Markandaya explored Indo-British relations at the end of empire in both India and Britain.[40] She had worked in a solicitor's office in London and married an Englishman in 1948, before settling in Britain permanently. In her novel *Nowhere Man* she deals directly with the life of an Indian family in Britain, before and after independence. The chief protagonist, Srinivas, is traced from his beginnings in India after the First World War to his death forty years later at the hands of a racist thug, who sets fire to his home. Srinivas and his wife settle in South London and bring up two sons. One dies during the Second World War and a rift is created when the second marries an Englishwoman. Srinivas literally and metaphorically becomes an outcast when he contracts leprosy. Empire is represented in the novel as liberalism and benevolence, as well as an expression of brutal violence. In the early part of the book 'Imperial London' of the 1930s provides a safe haven for Srinivas, who is being hunted by the British police in India in connection with his nationalist activities. In contrast, the post-imperial London of the 1960s, which is the setting for the rest of the novel, is an inhospitable and violent place. Despite Britain's retreat from empire in India, for the racist villain of the novel, Fred Fletcher (Srinivas's neighbour), racial antagonism is fuelled by violent fantasies of imperial conquest and colonial subordination. In his daydreams Fletcher imagines he is the Viceroy, 'in cockaded hat, erect on a dais one arm over which gold braid fell in thick loops, raised stiffly in salute acknowledg[ing] the homage of dark millions'.[41] Through such powerful imagery Markandaya shows how the oppressive vision of imperial domination continued to fester in the minds of the post-imperial generation. It also demonstrates her concern that the violent brutality of imperialism was continuing to cast a long dark shadow over the lives of Indian immigrants. *Nowhere Man* was written in the early 1970s in the wake of Powellism, which may have influenced the novel.[42] Reactions to the novel have been divided. Many critics have viewed the novel as a pessimistic view of race relations, characterised by alienation and rejection.[43] However, the literary critic Fawzla Azal-Khan prefers to see the relationship between Srinivas and Mrs Pickering, the English divorcee who nurses him through leprosy, as providing a message of hope and reconciliation.[44]

A more contemporary writer, Hanif Kureishi, also explores the reality of racial violence in the lives of South Asians. But as a much younger writer, born in Britain after imperial rule ended in South Asia, he resists the temptation to draw so heavily on colonial imagery. However, like Markandaya, he does refer to the contrasting treatment of Asians in imperial (1930s) and post-imperial Britain (1960s) in his novel *Borderline*, by alluding to the ways in which the welcome extended in the colonial period grew into hostility in the 1960s and 1970s. The degree to which racial animosity is a specific legacy of Britain's involvement in empire building or a modern manifestation of race relations is a moot point. It is possible to argue that racial discord also exists in societies with no imperial associations. Nevertheless the unequal power relations which characterised British imperialism in India, leading to the subjugation of the population, added a crucial dimension to the traditional xenophobia shown to outsiders and served to sharpen intolerance to Asian/Commonwealth immigrants in post-imperial Britain.

For western-educated Indians brought up on English literature and steeped in high culture, Britain had an irresistible allure. Krishnan Kumar, a Trinidadian Indian, observed middle-class Indians in Britain at first hand. He wrote: 'England was for them the source of all things, the originating and total reality'.[45] But this ignores the ambivalence present in the work of writers such as V. S. Naipaul. The burden of empire weighs heavily in his autobiographical book *The Enigma of Arrival*. Naipaul is extremely conscious that the Wiltshire cottage he is renting is both a product of imperial acquisition and an expression of imperial self-confidence and prosperity. He wrote: 'My landlord's Indian romance ... was rooted in Eng-land, wealth, empire, the idea of glory, a material satiety, a very great secu-rity'.[46] While for Markandaya, dualism revolves around the plural legacy of empire – oppressive and redemptive – Naipaul's relation to post-imperial Britain is also multi-dimensional, fractured on the one hand by adolescent imperial fantasy in the periphery (Trinidad), and on the other hand by alienation when the reality of the centre fell short of his expectations. This in turn provokes a search for authenticity and purity, a theme central to Naipaul's work. As the above quote illustrates, hankering after an imperial cultural fantasy of the metropolitan centre is offset by a simultaneous exclusion from a shared past, provoking both envy and desire.

The post-colonial migrant's fantasy of England, born out of colonial education,[47] and the rude awakening that came from confronting the real-ity of the post-imperial centre, was a theme examined not just by Naipaul, but by other post-colonial writers and poets such as Sam Selvon, George Lamming, Rajagopal Parsatharathy and G. V. Desani. Parsatharathy, for example, reflected in the early 1970s: 'I found myself crushed under two hundred years of British rule in India. My encounter with England only reproduced ... disenchantment. Here was an England I was unable to come to terms with. The England I had known and loved existed nowhere, ex-cept in my mind ... I felt betrayed.' [48] These authors wrote about the lives of early waves of immigrants recruited to work in factories, the National Health Service and the transport system, to build up Britain's post-war economic base and welfare state. They also reflected the views of students who came at the height of empire. But whereas most colonial students returned to India, some Commonwealth intellectuals decided to settle in Britain, occupying the niche of professional outsider. V. S. Naipaul's penetrating prose captures the alienation and loneliness felt by many particularly well:

> I came to London. It had become the centre of my world and I had worked hard to come to it. And I was lost. London was not the centre of my world ... Here I became no more than an inhabitant of a big city, robbed of loyalties, time passing, taking me away from what I was, thrown more and more into myself, fighting to keep my balance ... in the big city I was confined to a smaller world than I had ever known. I became my flat, my desk, my name.[49]

Yet the process of deconstructing the myth of the imperial centre, which required both self-examination and psychological readjustment, was cru-cial to the ongoing process of decolonisation and continues in the writing of contemporary writers such as Salman Rushdie. Whereas for Naipaul exposure to empire, resulting in transplantation from India to Trinidad, created a continuous longing for origins, Rushdie, by contrast, uses the displacement arising out of the colonial encounter as a positive opportunity for reinvention and freedom to break free from the constraints imposed by a unitary identity.

The cycle of heightened expectation and eventual disillusionment which characterised the published accounts of educated South Asians who wrote about their experiences of post-imperial Britain[50] contrasts sharply with working-class colonial subjects and Commonwealth immigrants who came to Britain with few cultural expectations. Limited contact with the host community diminished the possibility of disappointment for these groups.[51] This relates to the main colonial legacy influencing the way South Asians experienced Britain in the era of decolonisation: differential access to western education. Working-class immigrants had extremely limited access to western education and the linguistic inheritance of the Raj. Consequently they were unfamiliar with British language, history and literature. This is reflected by the fact that in 1947 less than 2 per cent of the Indian population were familiar with the English language. In contrast, educated urban migrants and sojourners had already acquired elements of the host culture. None more so than renowned anglophile writer Nirad Chaudhuri. He, like Naipaul, was championed in the West and received a hostile critical reception in India, rebuked for identifying himself with the culture and mindset of the imperial ruling class. Chaudhuri dedicated the second volume of his autobiography to the memory of the British Empire in India. He wrote: 'all that was living within us was made shape and quickened by British rule'. Despite its shortcomings he regarded British rule of the subcontinent as 'the best political regime which had ever been seen in India'.[52] For Chaudhuri, the decline and fall of the British Empire was synonymous with the immeasurable decline of Indian civilisation. The British had abdicated their role prematurely. In his chapter entitled 'Faith in Empire' he elucidated his theory of the moral benefits of imperial rule. According to Chaudhuri, both Mountbatten and Congress capitulated to Jinnah, resulting, as he saw it, in the mutilation of India and the betrayal of the Indian people. His criticism of the nationalist movement and the British transfer of power in India distanced him from the mainstream of Indian opinion from the 1920s onwards.[53] Chaudhuri's divergence from post-imperial diaspora writers and intellectuals can also be illustrated by his positive experience of post-war Britain documented in his book *Passage to Britain*. He wrote: 'never before except in the intimacy of my family had I been so happy as I was during my short stay in England'.[54] However, when he returned to Britain in 1970 to settle permanently, he was dismayed to find the country in decline. Chaudhuri attributed this decline to a lack of allegiance to imperial values. He yearned for a return to the glories of the past. It is in his continued commitment to British rule in India, long after British withdrawal, that Chaudhuri's representativeness is most open to question. The ability to imbibe western literature, art, history and philosophy without forsaking indigenous culture is a characteristic Chaudhuri shared with many of his class. But his persistent devotion to British rule singles him out for exceptional status among his peers.

The economic and cultural appeal of Britain, together with the dislocation produced by decolonisation in India, operated to produce a realignment in Indo-British relations transposed to the site of imperial power, just when, paradoxically, Britain was abandoning its imperial role in India. Although most groups of South Asians seem to have been in favour of colonial liberation and worked towards achieving it, cleavages did emerge along class and religious lines, testimony to the enduring effects of divisive imperial policies. Individuals such as Nirad Chaudhuri, who exhibited regret at the passing of the imperial era, appear to have been rare, if not unique. Nevertheless, while western-educated Indians were steadfast in their opposition to imperial domination, they proved less censorious in their attitudes to British culture. Thus, rejection of political mastery did not necessarily correspond with a total disengagement from the culture of the ex-imperial power, which continued to exercise a lasting appeal. Similarly, the British approach towards South Asians showed a marked reluctance to adapt to the new post-imperial order, particularly in the period prior to the 1960s. Does this indicate a sea-change in attitudes and policies towards empire from the 1960s? On the surface Britain's greater involvement with Europe, at the expense of the Commonwealth, and the introduction of harsh immigration legislation would appear to suggest the end of benevolent neo-imperialism and a break with the imperial past. But such an interpretation ignores the multiplicity of the imperial legacy. In reality, the increasing racial differentiation and exclusion which has characterised the 1960s onwards can be traced back to the imperial period, and is just another facet of Britain's complex imperial heritage, highlighting continuity rather than change. One Indian student, Adil Jussawalla, describing his experiences of Britain in the 1960s, was in little doubt about the tenacity of the imperial outlook when he wrote:

> In short, the mentality that produced the two-faced Hastings, outwardly so kind to Indians, privately so vicious; the mentality that produced a Cornwallis or a General Dyer ... the mentality of the professional civiliser and the 'civilised' professional carrying the cross of his faith to the less-fortunate races he would like to make his burden, is still the predominant one here and has not changed appreciably sixteen years after the Empire lost its first hunk, India.[55]

Mrs Thatcher's neo-imperial vision is another example of the resurrection of the imperial ideal in recent times.[56] It has also been argued that the British establishment's reaction to the Rushdie affair carried strong imperial overtones.[57] At the beginning of the twenty-first century the imperial drama continues to be played out on the streets of Britain, often with violent consequences. Evidently, Britain is still struggling to come to terms with its imperial past and confront the challenges and opportunities presented by a post-imperial multi-racial society.

Notes

I am deeply indebted to Stuart Ward and particularly Hsu-Ming Teo for their constructive and stimulating comments on an earlier draft of this chapter. I, of course, take full responsibility for all remaining deficiencies.

1   See S. Lahiri, *Indians in Britain: Anglo-Indian Encounters, Race and Identity, 1880–1930* (London, Frank Cass, 1999). Many of the references to Indians in the colonial period in this study can be found in this book.
2   Although Menon was vehemently opposed to British rule in India, he was reluctant to curtail all relations with Britain. As a leading champion of the Commonwealth ideal, he hoped to ensure good relations in the post-independence era. He became High Commissioner for India and continued his prolonged exile, witnessing the arrival of new immigrants.
3   K. C. Aurora, *The Indian Nationalist Movement in Britain, 1930–1949* (Delhi, Inter-India Publications, 1991).
4   C. Adams, *Across Seven Seas and Thirteen Rivers: Life Stories of Pioneer Sylhetti Settlers in Britain* (London, THAP Books, 1987). In 1943 Qureshi and his friend Ayub Ali formed the Indian Seamen's Workers League, the first Bangladeshi organisation in Britain.
5   Ibid., pp. 78–9, 163–4.
6   S. Josephides, 'Principles, Strategies and Anti-Racist Campaigns: The Case of the Indian Workers Association', in H. Goulbourne (ed.), *Black Politics in Britain* (Aldershot, Avebury, 1990), pp. 115–29.
7   D. S. Tatla, 'This is Our Home Now: Reminiscences of a Punjabi Migrant in Coventry. An Interview with Anant Ram', *Oral History*, 21:1 (1993), pp. 68–74.
8   Ibid., p. 71.
9   However, there were exceptions. For example, one university-educated Gujarati argued with his English factory colleagues during the Suez crisis and accused the British of infamous behaviour in their rule of India. Unfortunately the response to the Gujarati's accusation has not been recorded. R. Desai, *Indian Immigrants in Britain* (Oxford, Oxford University Press, 1963), p. 131.
10 'The marginal landholder, who in mortal fear of becoming a menial servant, gambles his last and comes to Britain after selling his land, cattle and other family valuables.' G. S. Aurora, *New Frontiersmen: A Sociological Study of Indian Immigrants in the United Kingdom* (Bombay, Popular Prakashan, 1967), pp. 25–6.
11 R. Ballard and C. Ballard, 'The Development of South Asian Settlement in Britain', in James L. Watson (ed.), *Between Two Cultures: Migrants and Minorities in Britain* (Oxford, Blackwell, 1977), p. 27.
12 See Pnina Werber, 'Rich Man, Poor Man – A Community of Suffering: Heroic Motifs in Manchester Pakistani Life Histories', *Oral History*, 8:1 (Spring 1980), p. 47.
13 Dilip Hiro, 'Another Kind of Minority', in B. Parekh (ed.), *Colour, Culture and Consciousness in Britain: Immigrant Intellectuals in Britain* (London, Allen and Unwin, 1974), p. 17.
14 Aurora, *New Frontiersmen*, p. 137.
15 Ibid., p. 35.
16 N. C. Chaudhuri, *Passage to Britain* (London, Macmillan, 1959), p. 205. On two separate occasions Chaudhuri came across England-returned businessmen who, on

hearing of his impending departure for England, praised its high standard of living, abundant cheap housing and hospitality.

17 See Kathleen Paul, *Whitewashing Britain: Race and Citizenship in the Post-War Era* (Ithaca, Cornell University Press, 1997). See also Kathleen Paul's contribution to this volume.

18 See Lahiri, *Indians in Britain*.

19 A. M. Singh, *Indian Students in Britain: A Survey of their Amusements and Attitudes* (New York, Asia Publishing House, 1963), pp. 63–4.

20 J. Ayodelo Langley, 'Through a Glass Darkly', in Parekh (ed.), *Colour, Culture and Consciousness*, pp. 31–40.

21 Hiro, 'Another Kind of Minority', p. 19. The Sri Lankan student S. Weeraperuma was exposed to similar views when he was told by an English acquaintance: 'We civilised you Indians'. H. Tajfel and J. L. Dawson (eds), *Disappointed Guests: Essays by African, Asian and West Indian Students* (London, Oxford University Press, 1965), p. 127.

22 H. Goulbourne, *Race Relations in Britain* (London, Macmillan, 1998), p. 58. 'It was as if Powell saw such savagery reversed in a visitation by ex-colonial peoples or as if he had a nightmare of the kind ... envisaged by Franz Fanon.'

23 Ian R. G. Spencer, *British Immigration Policy Since 1939: The Making of Multi-Racial Britain* (London, Routledge, 1997), pp. 104–5.

24 A. Dummett and A. Nicol, *Subjects, Citizens, Aliens and Others* (London, Weidenfield & Nicolson, 1990), p. 180.

25 Paul, *Whitewashing Britain*, p. 152.

26 Public Record Office, Kew, CAB134/1466, Committee on Colonial Immigrants, June 1957.

27 See Salman Rushdie's criticism of Raj nostalgia in *Imaginary Homelands: Essays and Criticism, 1981–1991* (London, Granta Books, 1991), pp. 92, 101.

28 See John M. MacKenzie, *Propaganda and Empire: The Manipulation of British Public Opinion, 1880–1960* (Manchester, Manchester University Press, 1984) as well as relevant chapters in this volume.

29 Adams, *Across Seven Seas*, pp. 50, 155.

30 E. S. Nelson, *Writers of the Indian Diaspora* (London, Greenwood Press, 1983), p. 314. See also V. S. Naipaul, *Enigma of Return* (London, Viking, 1987).

31 Disillusionment with Britain is a theme in Parthasarathy's major collection of poems entitled *Rough Passage* (Delhi, Oxford University Press, 1977).

32 See S. Lahiri, 'Patterns of Resistance: Indian Seamen in Imperial Britain', in A. J. Kershen (ed.), *Language Labour and Migration* (London, Ashgate, 2000), pp. 156–79.

33 K. Hunter, *History of Pakistanis in Britain* (London, Pakistan House, 1962), p. 63.

34 Josephides, 'Principles, Strategics', pp. 115–29.

35 *Guardian*, 27 October 1959.

36 G. Balachandran, 'Recruitment and Control of Indian Seamen: Calcutta, 1880–1935', *International Journal of Maritime History*, 9:1 (1997), pp. 1–18.

37 Singh, *Indian Students*, p. xiii.

38 Ibid.

39 Hiro, 'Another Kind of Minority', p. 18.

40 In Markandaya's other novels set in India, such as *The Coffer Dams*, the conflict in Indo-British relations stems from the inability of English characters to abandon old imperial attitudes.

41 K. Markandaya, *Nowhere Man* (New York, John Day & Co., 1972), p. 245.

42 Markandaya's interest in South Asians in Britain was not shared by many other diaspora writers of her generation. For example, the writer Zulfikar Ghose's residence in Britain between 1952 and 1969 remains conspicuously absent from his fiction.

43 See Suresht Renjen Bald, 'Images of South Asian Migrants in Literature: Differing Perspectives', *New Community*, 17:3 (1991), pp. 413–31.

44 F. Azal-Khan, *Cultural Imperialism and the Indo-English Novel: Genre and Ideology in R. K. Narayan, Anita Desai, Kamala Markandaya and Salman Rushdie* (Pennsylvania, Pennsylvania State University Press, 1993).

45 Krishnan Kumar, 'A Child and a Stranger, or Growing Out of English Culture', in

Parekh (ed.), *Colour, Culture and Consciousness*, p. 87.

46 Naipaul, *The Enigma of Arrival*, pp. 192–3.
47 Ibid., p. 41. Naipaul wrote: 'The London I know or imaginatively possessed was the London I had got from Dickens'.
48 R. Parsatharathy, 'Whoring after English Gods', in S. Bhagwat (ed.), *Perspectives* (Bombay, Popular Prakashan, 1970), pp. 45–6.
49 V. S. Naipaul, *An Area of Darkness* (London, André Deutsch, 1968), p. 42.
50 This view, represented in both prose and poetry (see above), is also articulated in the essay of an unnamed Indian student: 'I came over believing in my gifts, my ability to absorb, build, be assimilated by society here. At 23 I found most British attempts at friendship dangerous, think most jokes involving Negroes, darkies and wogs are tasteless, regard most failures to get a room as a deliberate slight and whenever there is talk of British justice, law and order pretend I'm not listening.' Tajfel and Dawson, *Disappointed Guests*, p. 155.
51 It is important to stress that while cultural expectations of peasant migrants were limited, nevertheless young men who came in the 1950s did harbour unrealistic visions of Britain's wealth and prosperity, which inevitably led to some level of disappointment, although not on a par with those who had been exposed to western education. See I. Imran, T. Smith and D. Hyslop (eds), *Here to Stay – Bradford's South Asian Communities* (Bradford, City of Bradford Metropolitan Council of Arts, Museums and Libraries, 1994).
52 N. C. Chaudhuri, *Thy Hand Great Anarch! India 1921–1952* (London, Chatto & Windus, 1987), p. 27.
53 Naipaul also showed little sympathy with anti-imperial struggles.
54 Chaudhuri, *Passage*, p. 227.
55 Tajfel and Dawson, *Disappointed Guests*, p. 131. Jussawalla later became a critic and poet.
56 See Rushdie, *Imaginary Homelands*.
57 See T. Asad, 'Multiculturalism and British Identity in the Wake of the Rushdie Affair', *Politics and Society*, 18:4 (1990), pp. 455–80.

CHAPTER TWELVE

India, Inc.? Nostalgia, memory and the empire of things

Antoinette Burton

Will the British Empire ever be over, or are we destined to witness its eternal return in the form of nostalgia masquerading as history, of drama pretending to rehearse its relentless end? The transfer of Hong Kong to China, the devolution of Scotland and, on the very eve of the new millennium, the precarious shift of power from London to Belfast – if these, taken either separately or together, do not signify the final, halting end of the British Empire, it is hard to imagine what would. And yet, as Ackbar Abbas has suggested, we must be suspicious of the 'cultures of disappearance' which have emerged in the context of post-colonial history – in part because disappearance rarely means erasure, and indeed often entails a 'pathology of presence' which permits that which is 'gone' to be reincarnated in new historical or cultural forms. Our scepticism is also warranted, Abbas argues, because 'It is as if the possibility of ... [certain] social and cultural space[s] disappearing ... has led to our seeing ... [them] in all ... [their] complexity and contradiction for the first time, an instance, as Benjamin would have said, of love at last sight'.[1]

In the case of empire, the danger is not that it will disappear as a subject, but rather that the staging of its end will produce heroes and heroines in new, and newly seductive, romances of empire. In the case of Raj nostalgia, the challenge is to understand the ways in which the loss of India offers an apparently endless opportunity to see empire – the *déjà disparu* – one last time, as well as to experience (if not enjoy) its peculiar forms of commodification in the present.

Tom Stoppard's *Indian Ink*, first performed in London at the Aldwych Theatre in 1995, stages just such a paradoxical disappearing act: for what does 'india ink' offer if not the promise of indelibility in the face of erasure, disappearance, history? As with that performance, the earlier BBC Radio 3 version (entitled *In the Native State*, 1991) centres around a painting of uncertain provenance which holds the key to the mysteries of the imperial past as set against the background of early 1930s India. Although the pun evoked by the original title is lost in the stage version, 'Indian Ink' has its own significance. It doubles first as the title of a book of poems being written by Flora Crewe, a London poet with socialist connections and modern ideas about sex who comes to India in 1930 to give a lecture tour while recuperating from an undiagnosed pulmonary condition, and second as a symbol of the lingering imprint, the permanent stain, the indelible inscription of India on the British imperial imagination. While on her tour, Flora meets an Indian painter named Nirad Das. What begins as a rather innocent flirtation ends up as a rather more complex, if unelaborated, tryst,[2] the only evidence of which is a watercolour by him of her in the nude. Flora's bohemianism is reflected in the fact that she has been painted in the nude before – by Modigliani, in Paris – and that she is fairly insouciant about being a subject in 'her native state'. More importantly, the life of the painting after the death of its subject is a major theme in the play, as the voice of Flora reading her poetry sounds a stirring contrapuntal note.

Simultaneous with these events in 1930 India is the quest by two men to discover 'the truth' about Nirad Das and Flora Crewe in the mid-1980s: Eldon Pike, an American professor of literature whose research speciality is Flora Crewe, half a century on; and Anish Das, Nirad's son. Having travelled across the globe to find the lost canvas, Pike is a veritable torrent of words in footnote form. Because he can only manage to perorate, however, he ends up not just as a caricature of an American academic, but as an emblem of the failure of Americans to understand history *tout court*. Das's son is a stark contrast. Like the protagonist of Hanif Kureishi's novel *The Buddha of Suburbia*, Anish is 'a funny kind of Englishman, a new breed, as it were, having emerged from two old histories'.[3] The nexus of past and present in both versions of Stoppard's play is Eleanor Swann, also known as Nell, who is Flora's sister and the keeper of her effects, including the oil painting. In each of the two acts of the play, the story moves virtually seamlessly between India and Nell's home in Shepperton – i.e. suburban London and environs. Laurie Kaplan has parsed the radio play against the stage play and I do not want to repeat her work here.[4] What I do want to emphasise is that the staging at the Aldwych by Peter Wood (Stoppard's long-time collaborator/director) effectively dramatised the imaginative coincidence of time and place by juxtaposing 1930s India with post-imperial Britain physically, as in side by side.[5] Though not intended as a 'blueprint' for all productions, the published version of the text endorses overlapping furniture, shared floor space and even common characters like the Maharajah of Jummapur, head of the fictitious princely state in which the action in India is set.[6] One effect of this collapse of time and space is that certain objects – Flora's suitcase, a variety of teapots as well as the controversial canvasses themselves – take on a heightened significance: they are the visual reference points which allow the audience to follow the action across time and space and back again. We become invested in their travels, in part because we quickly realise that they will end up telling the story of Flora and Nirad's encounter. Whether as ethnographic artefacts or works of art, these 'things' serve as witnesses to history, and their material presence testifies to the persistence, durability and commodification of empire in the contemporary present.

In order to understand the purchase of things in *Indian Ink*, some background on Stoppard is necessary. Born in Czechoslovakia in 1937, Stoppard was living with his family in Singapore when the Japanese invaded in 1942. Women and children were evacuated and young Tom and his mother went to India, where she eventually became the manager of a Bata (shoe) store in Darjeeling. His father was killed during the Japanese occupation, and his widowed mother later married an English army man, Kenneth Stoppard. Stoppard admitted rather sheepishly to an interviewer in 1974 that her marriage had placed them squarely in the 'lower sahib' class.[7] Or, as he told another critic, 'we weren't really Raj people' – perhaps in part because, as Stoppard recently announced, they were not only exiles but Jewish exiles as well.[8] They moved to England in 1946, where he went to school, began as a journalist, worked as a theatre critic, and wrote *Rosencrantz and Guildenstern are Dead*, his first hit, in 1964. When *In the Native State* aired on Radio 3 in the spring of 1991, theatre critics were eager to match Stoppard's latest success with his story of childhood displacement in and experience of India, but he resisted their efforts to overdetermine his work in that way. He made a point of saying that he did not return to India until after writing the radio script, and only then in connection with the making of *Rosencrantz and Guildenstern are Dead* into a film.[9] 'The visit back actually was in the nature of an experiment with memory', Stoppard told Paul Allen in an interview for the radio programme *Third Ear*. 'I had quite a few images in my head which really were as nebulous as dreams.'[10] He had earlier confided to an American journalist who interviewed him in California (where a production of *Hapgood* was being mounted) that writing the play was something of a struggle for him. This was not necessarily a break with his usual pattern of writing, but apparently the idea of India, and the fact of his childhood relationship to it, was having some effect. 'I was eight when I left India for England', he is quoted as saying in 1989. 'I felt I should be able to use my own experience of India to write about the ethos of empire. But right now [the idea] isn't really going. I've never really abandoned a play. In the end I've always found something I wanted to do, and I hope that happens with this one, too.'[11]

One of the ways that this 'ethos of empire' manifests itself in *Indian Ink* is through the subtle but powerful seduction of things which move across the stage throughout the play. Stoppard has long been open to the criticism that he is not as interested in characters as he is in ideas. In this case, the repertoire of household objects familiar to life under the Raj cre ates an authenticity that Stoppard feared his Indian characters especially did not have.[12] His investment in reproducing the material culture of daily life in colonial India – part of 'that recreation of the English Eden',[13] as he referred to it – is clear from the first few lines of the play, in which Flora details her train journey from Bombay to Jummapur:

> Darling Nell, I arrived here on Saturday from Bombay after a day and a night in a Ladies Only, stopping now and again to be revictualled through the window with pots of tea and proper meals on matinee trays, which, remark- ably, you hand back through the window at the next station down the line, where they do the washing up; and from the last stop I had the compartment to myself, with the lights coming on for me to make my entrance on the platform at Jummapur.[14]

Here, as throughout *Indian Ink*, we are drawn into the story through images of objects like teapots and tea-trays, which stand in for, and in this case anticipate, the process of cultural encounter and exchange between Britons and Indians, even as they evoke the unequal power relations char- acteristic of the Raj.[15]

But as Arjun Appadurai has argued, 'things' are rarely mere passive objects: they have social, cultural and political lives of their own.[16] In *Indian Ink*, they give the narrative precisely the momentum it needs to negotiate the relationship between past and present, Britain and India, home and 'away'. Flora's suitcase is a particularly compelling visual prop, since we see her arrive with it in Jummapur; we watch it being spirited away by an Indian servant; we look on as Eldon Pike arrives at Nell's Shepperton house to ask for it because he feels sure it contains the oil painting he's been searching for; and in the last scene, we see her carry it on the train with her as she heads out of Jummapur.[17] Things like the suitcase do more than simply carry the plot across time and space: they act as souvenirs, evoking and commemorating a past cultural experience and an equally distant historical moment by keeping it alive, and in sight, in the present.[18] Eleanor's tea-tray is instructive as well: for the one she uses in Shepperton comes from India, from the days when her husband was a district officer there, and reveals to us that she is no mere disinter- ested observer of the Raj, but is in fact an old India hand. It is Anish, Das's son, who recognises the tray as Nepalese, prompting Eleanor to comment on the movement of people and goods from home to away and back again across the twentieth century: 'In India we had pictures of coaching inns and foxhunting, and now I've landed in Shepperton I've got elephants and prayer wheels cluttering up the window ledges, and the tea-tray is Nepalese brass'.[19] Eleanor's remark suggests the equivalence of aristocratic foxhunting scenes and Buddhist prayer wheels. It also underscores the portability of imperial commodities and their interchangeability with common metropolitan household items – as well as the visible presence of the old Raj in contemporary domestic space. Eleanor is written as a stiff-upper-lip character with a soft spot for India. Her identification with the objects stranded in her living room leads her momentarily into a recollection of how good the tea was in India and how hard it is to approximate in England: 'I expect it's the water. A reservoir in Staines won't have the makings of a good cup of tea compared to the water we got in the Hills.'[20] Although brief, her nostalgia for better days – and better cups of tea – erupts into the text and even manages to conjure the Himalayas just beyond the audience's horizon.

If the staging of various objects helps to carry the past into the present, it is the two paintings which dominate the scene in *Indian Ink*. Through these canvasses, the past becomes accessible to those who desire it; and through their elusive presence Flora and Das's love affair is brought to our sightline.[21] Fear about the fragile state and possible loss of the paintings is shared by all the characters in the play. At the same time, however, and true to Stoppard's inimitable passion for dialogue, it is words which compete with characters and things and above all with art as the enduring legacy of the Raj in *Indian Ink*.[22] Reflecting upon the BBC radio script on which *Indian Ink* was based, Tom Stoppard remarked that 'I thought I was going to write a play simply about the portrait of a woman writing a poem and her poem is about being painted. Then I found the idea of her poetry so perversely enjoyable I went on writing her poetry for far longer than you'd believe.'[23] In this off-handed comment to Gillian Reynolds of the *Daily Telegraph* in an interview in 1991, Stoppard captures the dialectic between words and images, between language and things, which structures the play and makes the final disappearance of empire a matter of form rather than a matter of fact. The debate at the heart of the play revolves around the relative merits of words versus image, art versus logos. For Stoppard, it would seem, the fate of colonial empires seems to hang in the balance – as the following scene between Das and Flora suggests.

Das has given Flora a copy of Emily Eden's 1866 book *Up the Country*, which details Eden's tour of India. The gift prompts Flora's complaint that he is too 'English', too enamoured of Dickens and Holman Hunt and Chelsea and Bloomsbury, despite the fact that he has never been to Britain. She even has the temerity to suggest that she is more nationalist than he, since she is willing to say, however obliquely, that the English should get out of India. Her criticism provokes him, and he cries out ('passionately', according to the stage directions), 'the bloody Empire finished off Indian painting!'[24] What ensues is a lively discussion in which they debate the merits of the British Empire (it brought roads and schools, but all the saris are still made in Lancashire) with Das ending the riff by prophesying the end of empire: 'the Empire will one day be gone like the Mughal Empire before it, and only their monuments remain – the visions of Shah Jahan! – or Sir Edwin Lutyens!' Flora responds with a line from Shelley, 'look on my works, ye mighty, and despair!' The script continues:

> Das: (Delighted) Oh yes! Finally like the Empire of Ozymandias! Entirely forgotten except in a poem by an English poet. You see how privileged we are, Miss Crewe. Only in art can empires cheat oblivion, because only the artist can say, 'Look on my works, ye mighty, and despair!' There are Mughal paintings in London, in the Victoria and Albert Museum.[25]

The watercolour he is working on while they converse turns out to be Das's attempt to imitate a Mughal miniature, and it survives both of their deaths to keep the debate about art alive into the present, as Anish and Nell engage in a similarly spirited discussion when he brings it to her in Shepperton fifty years on. The nude itself ends up being a kind of hybrid aesthetic form: the mosquito netting in Flora's bungalow serves as the house-within-the-house (read, mock harem) and Flora herself as a modern-day Radha in Das's own recreation of the Krishna story from the *Gita Govinda*.

The contest over what forms of art can survive the fall of empires is a major arc in the play, and debates about the relationship of politics to aesthetics under colonial rule are clearly implicated in the sexual encounter between Das and Flora. Their dialogue – the *Hobson-Jobson*[26] words they play on, the jibes and clever retorts – is artistry itself and frankly competes for our attention with both image and poetry as the drama unfolds. Poetry, painting, love and empires past and present intertwine, in other words, as Das's canvas and Flora's book of poems take shape. The contest between word and image is ever-present, as when Das tells Flora that he is Rajasthani, and 'all our art is narrative art, stories from the legends and the romances'.[27] Among these stories, the favourite of Rajput painters was from the *Chaurapanchasika*, which, Das tells her, is 'poems of love written by the poet of the court on his way to execution for falling in love with the king's daughter, and the king liked the poems so very much he pardoned the poet and allowed the lovers to marry'.[28]

Das's own arrest and imprisonment for participating in an anti-government riot is foreshadowed in this account, an experience which leads to his untimely death as well. The survival of his nude of Flora, not to mention the preservation of Mughal art in London museums and elsewhere, may well signify that in the competition for immortality, painting and literature are equally enduring. Flora herself suggests a similar interpretation, when she hopes that 'perhaps my soul will stay behind as a smudge of paint on paper, as if I'd always been here, like Radha who was the most beautiful of herdswomen, undressed for love in an empty house'.[29]

And yet there is much in Stoppard's play to suggest that, as Das remarked above, empires are entirely forgotten 'except in the poetry of English poets' like Flora and, by extension, in the English language itself – of which Stoppard is so famously enamoured and which he calls his 'first tongue', despite his Czechoslovakian birth.[30] For one thing, we scarcely see the famous canvasses around which the whole play revolves; they are either rolled up, shrouded from view or turned away from the audience, as they often are from Flora as well. Pike's stentorian footnote-readings take up more space than they do on stage.[31] In typical Stoppard mode, words predominate in general, so much so that he has confessed to feeling that all his plays, for radio and the stage equally, are overwritten, and that *Indian Ink* is no exception.[32] More specifically, it is Flora's poetry which is a major presence in the play: she is constantly writing drafts, reading portions aloud and working it out word by word. As we know from Pike's researches, Flora's volume of poems called *Indian Ink* not only endures, it makes a comeback in the 1980s through the efforts of Pike and the market for 'exotic' writing by white women of the Empire created by western feminism *and* the craze for Raj nostalgia of that decade – twin phenomena to which Stoppard gives a nod in the stage script. In fact, the role of western feminism in excavating, re-presenting and thereby helping to guarantee the 'eternal return' of empire in the West has been crucial to the Raj's survival in the *fin de siècle* – in part because western feminists have been slow to recognise the costs of recovering the memsahib as a long lost heroine, in part because white liberal feminism is no less subject to the seductive fantasies which lie at the heart of the historically imperial romance between English women and India.[33]

Stoppard had never even heard of Emily Eden until he came across her book in a London bookshop. One cannot help but wonder if the copy he found was the Virago reprint, made directly possible by the feminist publishing that was one very visible outgrowth of the women's movement in Britain in the 1980s.[34] That feminist publishing houses like Virago – which re-issued Eden's *Up the Country* in 1983 as part of its effort to rescue women from the invisibility of traditional history – should have participated in Raj nostalgia in such a direct and unselfconscious way is telling evidence of the ways in which traditions of imperial feminism in Britain (from the anti-slavery campaigns to the campaign for women's suffrage) have made their way into twentieth-century popular culture through the logic of late capitalism.[35] Stoppard's romance with India may thus be said to be derivative of (if not reliant on) a certain version of postcolonial feminist imperialism, especially where the character of Flora is concerned. Eden, significantly, is not merely Flora's foil. Stoppard makes

[223]

Eden an unmistakably Victorian antecedent to Flora's modern version of 'English womanhood', offering a progressive, evolutionary model of that identity. Equally powerfully, it is Emily Eden and her text who have the last word. The play ends with Flora boarding the train to Jaipur with her copy of *Up the Country* in hand. As the train 'clatters loudly' and the light fades on stage, Flora is heard reading aloud from a passage of the book dated 1839, which gives an account of the Queen's Ball in Simla.

> It was a most beautiful evening; such a moon, and the mountains looked so soft and *grave*, after all the fireworks and glare. Twenty years ago no European had ever been here, and there we were with a band playing, and observing that St. Cloup's Potage à la Julienne was perhaps better than his other soups, and that some of the ladies' sleeves were too tight according to overland fashions for March, and so on, and all this in the face of those high hills, and we are one hundred and five Europeans being surrounded by at least three thousand mountaineers, who, wrapped up in their hill blankets, looked on at what we call our polite amusements, and bowed to the ground if a European came near them. I sometimes wonder they do not cut all our heads off and say nothing about it.[36]

Things can, and do, get lost. Suitcases, teapots, paintings are all perishable, as is, of course, the Empire itself. But words – especially English words – live on, as the survival of Flora's poems and the text of her historical double testify.

In an important sense, then, gender is more than incidental to the script. This is not just because women are the heart of the play, or even because the encounter between Flora and Nirad Das is a source of mystery and intrigue. White women are, rather, the keepers of imperial memory, and in the end, like many memsahibs before 1947, they remain guarantors of empire's reproduction for future generations. And yet, if Flora and Eden are intended as evidence of the liberalism of empire, they succeed in revealing the limitations of political critique in the heroic mode, even and especially when women get to be the heroes.[37] For to imagine that Eden wished the end of British rule is nothing short of fantasy. Not only was her brother then Governor-General of India, but *Up the Country* is in many ways a classically orientalist text – not least because of its 'sympathetic' view of 'the natives'. That someone like Flora, even with her Bloomsbury and socialist connections as alluded to in the play, would have welcomed the end of British India is less dubious but still unlikely. It is a possibility that is not in any case borne out by the rest of the narrative, where we see her exhibiting a number of fairly conventional orientalist behaviours, including her suspicion that it is Das who has gossiped about her health problems and spread misinformation about the purposes of her visit. Orientalism is not, of course, equivalent to anti-nationalism. But in the end Flora is a basically apolitical person, as careless about politics as she is about posing nude. To read her as a 'mutinous free-spirit', as one London critic did (and as Stoppard surely intended her), is to overestimate her commitment to the end of the Empire in Britain – though it does suggest the enduring purchase of the modern liberal imperialist fantasy that white women were typically predisposed to anti-imperial sympathies.[38] Indian women, meanwhile, make no appearance at all – a vacuum characteristic of most if not all imperialist narratives about decolonisation in India, and one which perpetuates the myth that British India and its fate rested solely in the hands of Anglo-Indians, colonial officers, native servants and a few Indian men.[39]

Indeed, despite the play's representations of the anti-colonial resistance which helped to determine the last days of the Raj, *Indian Ink* is not subversive of imperial histories or ideologies; it is, rather, one of empire's contemporary residual effects. Nowhere is this clearer than in the character of Nirad Das. Stoppard writes Das's public protest against colonial rule as a sad, pathetic and finally futile attempt to attack the British government in India. As Peter Kemp put it in his review of the 1995 Aldwych production (in a piece called 'Flinging Mangos at the Resident's Daimler'):

> that the missile is nothing more than a menacing fruit typifies this play's softening of political antagonisms. In other ways, too, Stoppard seems insouciantly content not to probe too deeply into the situation he re-stages; he remains, for instance, apparently heedless of his play's curious suggestion that, in order to liberate himself from colonial promptings, an Indian needs an erotic nudge from an Englishwoman.[40]

Stoppard is not interested either in staging a full-scale critique of empire or in moving beyond a kind of friendly caricature of its foibles. As he remarked to Mel Gussow in 1995, he thought the play was 'worryingly cosy', but that he 'really enjoy[ed] its lack of radical fierceness. It has its checks and balances. There's no ranting or storming around; there are no long monologues.'[41] Nor is he careless where the sexual politics of the play is concerned. The relationship between Flora and Das is quite carefully and deliberately crafted so that it replaces or at least distracts from the political action of nationalists and nationalism on the ground – against which the lovers are made to seem far more sophisticated and Flora quite 'radical'. The fact that all the turmoil of 1930 happens off stage, and that news of unrest and riots and violence is carried onto the set by various Indians who have encountered it, further distances the audience from it and makes it easier and indeed more pleasurable to read decolonisation as a highly individual, personal process. By moving political questions into the bedroom, *Indian Ink* effectively domesticates the end of empire and arguably depoliticises the whole 'affair'. More accurately, the play re-politicises the last days of the Raj as a comfortable, consumable tale which does little to disrupt dominant narratives of empire's end in India as the 'granting' of autonomy, rather than as the concession of independence in the face of a popular anti-imperialist movement that was, by 1947, several decades old.

How audiences would have responded to the play in the spring and summer of 1995 is, of course, notoriously difficult to evaluate. But it is possible to speculate about what the total theatre experience would have been like for them by looking at the playbill – which, it must be said, is a monument to a bygone imperial era. The programme was oversized compared with the usual 'Playbill' variety, and that alone may have caused ticket-holders to take a closer look than they otherwise might have. It featured a map of India, sketches of various 'native scenes', and quotes from Charles Allen's *Plain Tales from the Raj*, a coffee-table book which originated as a BBC production. A reprint of an image of Emily Eden, complete with a short biography, also appears, just underneath two photos: one, a 1930s vintage photo of 'native' crowds in India being beaten back with *lathis*, the other of a Modigliani nude. Theatre-goers were obviously being encouraged to admire the facticity of the play, to embrace not just its historical accuracy but its aesthetic verisimilitude as well. The playbill also contains excerpts from *Hobson-Jobson* with definitions for various words used in the play, including 'punkah', 'dawk' and 'verandah'.[42] In addition to being an orientalist production, the Aldwych version of *Indian Ink* was clearly an exercise in feeding what was left of the Raj nostalgia machine in the 1990s. And for the price of a pound sterling, theatre-goers could come away with a souvenir programme as well as the memory of the play itself. The commodification of *Indian Ink* in this form suggests the ways in which Stoppard's play participated in a larger economy of 'India Inc.' in the 1980s and 1990s – a phenomenon manifest in this case as a species of 'tourist art' which continued the ideological work of the play beyond the confines of the Aldwych by moving public history into private hands.[43]

Critics writing about the play rushed to pigeon-hole it as a Stoppardesque equivalent of *The Jewel in the Crown*, and so to reiterate what were, by the time the BBC aired *In the Native State* in 1991, the familiar lineaments of the Raj nostalgia syndrome. Stoppard was as aware of the appetite the British public displayed for rehearsals of the Raj's glory days as he was of the fact that the subject was in danger of exhausting its appeal. 'I mean the whole Anglo-Indian world has been so raked over and presented and re-presented by quite a small company of actors who appear in all of them', he told Paul Allen almost apologetically when interviewed in 1991 about the radio play. By 1995 the genre was presumably even more hackneyed, though this did not prevent the producers of the stage version from continuing to capitalise on what was left of Raj nostalgia. Art

Malik, who had played Hari Kumar to such critical acclaim in the British television production of *The Jewel in the Crown*, was cast as Nirad Das. Even if viewers didn't know his name, they may well have recognised the face. And if they read reviews of the show, they could not help but notice Malik – 'that old Raj drama hand', as Peter Kemp dubbed him – to whom critics invariably drew attention. Stoppard professed not to have known that Malik was in *The Jewel in the Crown* – he claimed in 1995, in fact, that he had never seen the television production nor read *The Raj Quartet* – but he did admit to knowing that Malik had appeared as the Arab terrorist in Arnold Schwarzenegger's blockbuster film *True Lies*.[44] Given the fact that many London theatre-goers, especially in summer, are white middle-class Americans, the role of *Indian Ink* in sustaining Raj nostalgia is even more interesting – stoking what seems like an inexhaustible market for the exotic allure of British imperialism. All this in the wake of a historical moment when the 'special' Anglo-American relationship had undergone a highly publicised revival, with Margaret Thatcher and Ronald Reagan cavorting about the international stage like transatlantic cousins. Unlike *Arcadia* (1993), however, which was a huge hit in London and New York, *Indian Ink* did not make it to Broadway, though it did debut in Washington DC in the autumn of 1999 to rave reviews ('the jewel in the Crown of the season').[45] Nor has it yet been made into a film – despite Stoppard's position as 'a leading playwright on either side of the Atlantic' and despite his express desire for a movie version.[46]

Stoppard's images of India in the 1930s are wistfully inaccurate at best, regrettably unrepresentative at worst. His representations of Britain in the 1980s are perhaps more unsettling, not so much for the ideological work they actively do as for the absences they enshrine at the heart of the narrative. It bears emphasising that the 'contemporary' portion of the play is meant to be the mid-1980s and *not* the early 1990s, as some reviewers of the radio play seemed to assume. The difference of five years is not to be dismissed as negligible, for the 1980s was a decade of tremendous racial contention, when Britain's post-imperial status was vigorously debated and images of black–white–brown violence in London and elsewhere in the British Isles circulated widely on television and in film.[47] This is crucial for understanding the politics of *Indian Ink* and its critical reception, if only because one could come away from the play with no knowledge of such volatile events, despite their prominence in the headlines during the very years the contemporary action is supposed to be occurring – i.e. during the latter part of Margaret Thatcher's premiership, for which race and the legacy of empire were such defining questions.[48] Nor did these debates only express themselves through violence: they occurred in city and county council elections, in television drama, and in the pages of national newspapers virtually daily, as Thatcher's quest for 'enterprise culture' alternatively scorned black Britons and wooed Asians for capitalist ventures.[49] Britain was, in other words, a veritable racial battleground in which contests over national-identity-as-racial-identity were continually played out. In Stoppard's play in contrast, mid-1980s Britain 'takes place' in suburban London, in the living room of the ex-memsahib Nell, whose world is intruded by a brash American scholar and a softer-spoken England-resident 'Indian' man but never by even a hint of the tumult that was going on in the streets of UK cities over the racial make-up of *fin-de-siècle* Britain. This occlusion, and the blind eye it turns toward the impact of empire at home in economic and political terms, is in many respects far more revealing than the imperial sexual politics of the play. The complete lack of reference to the kind of racial strife evident in Hanif Kureishi's *My Beautiful Laundrette* (1985) and *Sammy and Rosie Get Laid* (1987) on the one hand, and the enclosure of Nell in her house in Shepperton on the other, are, of course, intimately related. They are the effects of the same de-politicising strategy, one which re-politicises the end of empire as a kind of domestic quarrel, easily consumable from the comfort of one's armchair – or theatre seat.

In a plot evidently determined to merge home and empire, or at the very least to suggest the ways in which they overlapped imaginatively and in terms of the traffic of goods and people, the omission of any allusion to the racial violence and contestation of the 1980s is surely a remarkable one. Not a single critic has asked Stoppard about this in print. Not surprisingly, given the stranglehold that the culture of celebrity has exercised on public intellectual life and political debate in both Britain and America in the post-war period, the British press at the time was more interested in the fact that Stoppard and the actress who played Flora Crewe in the Aldwych production, Felicity Kendal, were lovers. Though Kendal had been the leading woman in several other of his plays, news of their relationship broke just before the Radio 3 broadcast, prompting the *Radio Times* to speculate on Kendal's 'love affair' 'with India'.[50] Once again, and in ways that echo the work of the play itself, *Indian Ink* was touted as a love affair, with its sins of commission and omission cast to the side in favour of 'sexual scandal' of the most prurient, and hence marketable, kind.

The re-domestication of the end of the British Raj in and around the production of *Indian Ink* has, moreover, an intimately familial history. For as Stoppard explained to Mel Gussow as the Aldwych production was about to open, the stage play is dedicated to Laura Kendal, Felicity's mother.[51] She and her husband Geoffrey had a company of actors who toured South and South-East Asia – a story which was made into the 1965 film *Shakespeare Wallah* by Ismail Merchant and James Ivory.[52] *Shakespeare Wallah* was also Felicity Kendal's movie debut; and, as many theatre-goers might have known, Felicity's sister Jennifer also appeared in that film, and was herself married into the Hindi film family of Shashi Kapoor, who in turn had a role in *Shakespeare Wallah*.[53] Thus the transnational film and celebrity culture of the late twentieth century gave Stoppard an insider's view that his own, somewhat marginalised, childhood relationship to British India could not begin to approximate. In an echo of the historical experience of many lower-class Britons who emigrated to India, Stoppard's return to Britain and his rise in the British theatre gave him the kind of cultural capital, as well as the class status, which his family could not achieve during the final days of the Raj.

As Yasmin Ali has observed, the British Empire has had many echoes at century's end.[54] The productions of *Indian Ink* and the brief traces they left on the *fin-de-siècle* cultural scene prompt one to ponder, among other things, the relationship of BBC radio plays to films like Kureishi's; of the Strand to Brixton and South Shields; of television to Hollywood and 'Bollywood'; of tea-trays and Mughal painting and the Victoria and Albert Museum to Pakistani groceries and Indian take-outs and other targets of violence and racial hatred in contemporary Britain. Surely the stories that each of these 'opposites' tells compete in the contemporary imagination not just for the ground of memory and history, but for commodification in a global capitalist marketplace as well. Perhaps the story about British citizens and subjects of colour who 'have borne the brunt of elite and popular anger that the Britain of 1995 is not the Britain of 1945' simply will not sell in a West End patronised mostly by middle- and upper-class white Britons and Americans.[55] This may be especially true of the white American clientele, who prefer their Britain PBS-style, where they can avoid the images of racial tension and violence which crowd network television in the United States and can escape into Georgian, Victorian and Edwardian worlds where bourgeois existence is uninterrupted by such things. And when race does intrude, it is packaged, like *The Jewel in the Crown*, as nostalgia with just the appropriate tinge of regret and self-censure about 'what we did over there'.

Like the past and the present, however, the 'Orient' and the West End are not merely opposites, but work dialectically in culture *and* through the cultural imagination, sometimes to unmask hegemonies, more often to reconsolidate them in new historical forms. Is *Indian Ink* simply another form of colonial knowledge, to be ranged against a long history of other such knowledges?[56] How different it is in this respect from its Irish contemporary, Brian Friel's *Dancing at Lughnasa*, which was published in 1990 and is also set in both the 1930s and 1980s. As Declan Kiberd has observed, 'by exploring the parallels between African and Celtic harvest festivals', Friel's play 'brought to the fore the post-colonial elements of Irish culture after a decade of chronic emigration and unemployment had led many to ask whether Ireland might not itself be a third world country'.[57] Irish cultural workers have long been willing to admit to 'universal boundaries' compared with the resolute embrace of 'splendid isolation' that is England's trademark. And Brian Friel was willing to see his stage-scapes – his Irelands – in colonial terms long before arguments about post-colonialism were fashionable, no doubt because of his critical appreciation for Ireland's historically colonial relationship to England. This is a comparison worth dwelling on, if only because of the appeal of Celtic nostalgia in the transatlantic public sphere, among middle-class white Americans rapturous about the Raj but unwilling or perhaps unable to embrace Ireland and India as part of a similar, if historically distinctive, world-historical colonial phenomenon. Such a disjuncture is, arguably, merely characteristic of the persistent disaggregation of India from the rest of Britain's colonial possessions and experiences – a disaggregation which means that India returns as the 'jewel' in the post-colonial crown.

As with all nostalgia, Stoppard's text longs for a 'future-past' made possible by the intrusion of the 1930s into the 1980s. As if the rhetorics of nostalgia and mourning, memory and loss, which the play stages are not enough, the death of Flora allows us to experience 'elegiac processes of leave-taking' from the past which makes the imperialist nostalgia of both the script and the 1995 production impossible to escape.[58] As a narrative of desire for an empire destined to be history, *Indian Ink* represents a return to and ultimately a disavowal of the end of empire, rehearsing for us the role that imperialist nostalgia continues to play in the late twentieth-century British cultural imagination.[59] Meanwhile, the popularity of Raj productions like *Indian Ink* in the context of a multi-racial, post-imperial culture leads one to wonder at the relentless re-staging of empire's end and, more productively, to inquire about what aesthetic forms post-colonial memory takes when empire is apparently gone, but continues to 'vanish' again and again before our very eyes.

Notes

This essay is dedicated to the memory of Doreen Hantzis, whose courage was quiet and inspirational. My thanks go to Paul Arroyo, Gary Daily, Lara Kriegel, Laura Mayhall, Barbara Ramusack, Maura O'Connor, George Robb, Mrinalini Sinha and Hsu-Ming Teo – all of whom offered comments and lively engagement which have undoubtedly improved the final outcome. Heidi Holder gave me crucial references, for which I thank her. Members of the Social History Workshop at the University of Illinois also provided valuable feedback and suggestions for further reading. Without Stuart Ward, this piece might have had quite a different incarnation, I appreciated his encouragement and persistence. I am especially grateful to Darlene Hantziz, who alone knows how much of it belongs to her.

1 Ackbar Abbas, *Hong Kong: Culture and the Politics of Disappearance* (Minneapolis, University of Minnesota Press, 1997), p. 23.
2 As Stoppard himself admits, both the radio and the stage plays remain unclear about whether a relationship was literally consummated between Das and Flora. See [Tom

Stoppard], 'I Retain Quite a Nostalgia for the Heat and the Smells and the Sounds of India', interview with Mel Gussow in February 1995 in Mel Gussow (ed.), *Conversations with Stoppard* (New York, Grove Press, 1995), pp. 121–2. But I would maintain that it is both a 'love affair' and a 'sexual encounter', if only in the metaphorical senses of those terms.

3   Quoted in Onyekachi Wambu (ed.), *Empire Windrush: Fifty Years of Writing About Black Britain* (London, Victor Gollancz, 1998), p. 397.

4   See Laurie Kaplan, '*In the Native State/Indian Ink*: Footnoting the Footnotes on Empire', *Modern Drama*, 41:3 (Fall 1998), pp. 337–46.

5   For a contrast to some other Raj fictions, see Tana Wollen, 'Over Our Shoulders: Nostalgic Screen Fictions for the 1980s', in John Corner and Sylvia Harvey (eds), *Enterprise and Heritage: Crosscurrents of National Culture* (London, Routledge, 1991), p. 187.

6   Tom Stoppard, *Indian Ink* (London, Faber and Faber, 1995).

7   Roger Hudson, Catherine Itzin and Simon Trussler, 'Ambushes for the Audience: Towards a High Comedy of Ideas', *Theatre Quarterly*, 4:14 (May 1974); reprinted in Paul Delaney (ed.), *Tom Stoppard in Conversation* (Ann Arbor, University of Michigan Press, 1994), p. 52.

8   Gussow, *Conversations with Stoppard*, p. 131; Tom Stoppard, 'On Turning Out to Be Jewish', *Talk* (September 1999).

9   Paul Allen, *Third Ear*, BBC Radio 3, 16 April 1991, in Delaney (ed.), *Tom Stoppard*, pp. 239–47.

10 Ibid., p. 241; see also Stoppard, 'On Turning Out to Be Jewish', p. 241.

11 Thomas O'Connor, 'Welcome to the World of Tom Stoppard', *Orange County Register*, 2 April 1989; reprinted in Delaney (ed.), *Tom Stoppard*, p. 229.

12 See Allen, *Third Ear*, p. 242; Gussow, *Conversations with Stoppard*, pp. 123–34.

13 Allen, *Third Ear*, p. 241.

14 Stoppard, *Indian Ink*, p. 1.

15 Tim Barringer and Tom Flynn (eds), *Colonialism and the Object: Empire, Material Culture and the Museum* (London, Routledge, 1998).

16 Arjun Appadurai (ed.), *The Social Life of Things: Commodities in Cultural Perspective* (Cambridge: Cambridge University Press, 1986).

17 The placement of the scene where Nell shows Anish the painting rolled up in the suitcase varied from the text of the play to the performance on stage; see Gussow, *Conversations with Stoppard*, p. 137

18 Ibid., p. 122.

19 Stoppard, *Indian Ink*, p. 24.

20 Ibid., p. 25.

21 See note 2, above.

22 Allen, *Third Ear*, pp. 239–47.

23 Gillian Reynolds, 'Tom's Sound Effects', *Daily Telegraph*, 20 April 1991; reprinted in Delaney (ed.), *Tom Stoppard*, p. 249.

24 Stoppard, *Indian Ink*, p. 43.

25 Ibid., p. 44.

26 *Hobson-Jobson* was a glossary of colloquial Anglo-Indian words and phrases indispensable to India-Wallahs in the twentieth century.

27 Stoppard, *Indian Ink*, pp. 44–5.

28 Ibid., p. 45.

29 Ibid., p. 82.

30 Quoted in Gussow, *Conversations with Stoppard*, p. 132; John Taylor, 'Our Changing Theatre, no. 3: Changes in Writing', in Delaney (ed.), *Tom Stoppard*, p. 26.

31 Pike's role was amplified in the transition from radio to stage; see Gussow, *Conversations with Stoppard*, p. 118.

32 Hudson *et al.*, 'Ambushes', p. 61.

33 See Vron Ware, *Beyond the Pale: White Women, Racism and History* (London, Verso, 1992); Antoinette Burton, *Burdens of History: British Feminists, Indian Women and Imperial Culture, 1865–1915* (Chapel Hill, University of North Carolina Press, 1994).

34   See Gussow, *Conversations with Stoppard*, pp. 128–9.
35   See Clare Midgley, *Women Against Slavery: The British Campaign, 1780–1870* (London, Routledge, 1992); Ware, *Beyond the Pale*; Burton, *Burdens of History*.
36   Stoppard, *Indian Ink*, p. 83.
37   See Annette B. Weiner, *Inalienable Possessions: The Paradox of Keeping-while-Giving* (Berkeley, University of California Press, 1992), p. 48.
38   Michael Billington, 'No Stoppard Fireworks, Just Meditations on Love and Empire', *Guardian*, 28 February 1995, p. 28.
39   For evidence of Indian women's contributions to nationalism see Vinay Lal, 'The Incident of the Crawling Lane: Women in the Punjab Disturbances of 1919', *Genders*, 16 (Spring 1993), pp. 80–120; Kamala Visweswaran, 'Small Speeches, Subaltern Gender: Nationalist Ideology and its Historiography', in Shahid Amin and Dipesh Chakrabarty (eds), *Subaltern Studies IX* (Delhi, Oxford University Press, 1996).
40   Peter Kemp, 'Flinging Mangos at the Resident's Daimler', *Guardian Weekly*, 17 March 1995.
41   Gussow, *Conversations with Stoppard*, pp. 124–5.
42   *Indian Ink* playbill, Aldwych Theatre, summer 1995.
43   See Susan Stewart, *On Longing: Narratives of the Miniature, the Gigantic, the Souvenir, the Collection* (Baltimore, Johns Hopkins University Press, 1984), p. 138.
44   Gussow, *Conversations with Stoppard*, p. 126. Stoppard's Anglo-American prestige has no doubted increased since the movie for which he co-wrote the screenplay, *Shakespeare in Love*, won several Oscars in 1999.
45   Jyotirmoy Datta, 'Unprecedented Extension for "Indian Ink" is Announced', *India Today*, 3 December 1999, p. 46. The opening of his play about A. E. Housman, *The Invention of Love*, in February 2000 brought *Indian Ink* back into public discourse; see Bernard Weintraub, 'When Stoppard Sends His "Love", San Francisco Reciprocates', *New York Times*, 2 February 2000; Carlin Romano, 'High-flying Love Story', *Philadelphia Inquirer*, 8 February 2000.
46   Gussow, *Conversations with Stoppard*, p. 141. Russell Twisk opined that if the play were ever made into a movie, 'at least a third of the dialogue will be lost'. Russell Twisk, 'Stoppard Basks in a Late Indian Summer', *Observer*, 21 April 1991; reprinted in Delaney (ed.), *Tom Stoppard*, p. 254.
47   The 1980s was of course by no means the first decade in which people of colour appeared in British films or television; see Stephen Bourne, *Black in the British Frame: Black People in British Film and Television, 1896–1996* (London, Cassell, 1998).
48   See Anna Marie Smith, *New Right Discourse on Race and Sexuality: Britain, 1968–1990* (Cambridge, Cambridge University Press, 1993).
49   See Yasmin Ali, 'Echoes of Empire: Towards a Politics of Representation', in Corner and Harvey (eds), *Enterprise and Heritage*, pp. 194–211.
50   Quoted in Paul Delaney's introduction to Gillian Reynolds's article, Delaney (ed.), *Tom Stoppard*, p. 248.
51   As Laurie Kaplan has noted, the radio play was dedicated to Felicity; see Kaplan, 'Footnoting the Footnotes', p. 346, fn. 14.
52   Gussow, *Conversations with Tom Stoppard*, p. 119.
53   For details and photos see Felicity Kendal's autobiography, *White Cargo* (London, Michael Joseph, 1998).
54   Ali, 'Echoes of Empire', p. 194.
55   The quote is from Kathleen Paul, *Whitewashing Britain: Race and Citizenship in the Postwar Era* (Ithaca, Cornell University Press, 1997), p. 190.
56   See Bernard S. Cohn, *Colonialism and its Forms of Knowledge*, edited with an introduction by Nicholas B. Dirks (Princeton, Princeton University Press, 1996).
57   Declan Kiberd, 'The Universal Borders of Brian Friel's Ireland', *New York Times*, 14 July 1999, p. 14.
58   See Eric Santner, *Stranded Objects: Mourning, Memory and Film in Postwar Germany* (Ithaca, Cornell University Press, 1991).
59   See Stewart, *On Longing*; Renato Rosaldo, 'Imperialist Nostalgia', *Representations*, 26 (Spring 1989).

INDEX

Note: 'n.' after a page reference indicates a note number on that page